Facing D

Epicurus and his Critics

JAMES WARREN

CLARENDON PRESS · OXFORD

This book has been printed digitally and produced in a standard specification in order to ensure its continuing availability

OXFORD
UNIVERSITY PRESS

Great Clarendon Street, Oxford OX2 6DP

Oxford University Press is a department of the University of Oxford.
It furthers the University's objective of excellence in research, scholarship,
and education by publishing worldwide in

Oxford New York

Auckland Cape Town Dar es Salaam Hong Kong Karachi
Kuala Lumpur Madrid Melbourne Mexico City Nairobi
New Delhi Shanghai Taipei Toronto
With offices in
Argentina Austria Brazil Chile Czech Republic France Greece
Guatemala Hungary Italy Japan South Korea Poland Portugal
Singapore Switzerland Thailand Turkey Ukraine Vietnam

Oxford is a registered trade mark of Oxford University Press
in the UK and in certain other countries

Published in the United States
by Oxford University Press Inc., New York

ISBN 978-0-19-929769-6

For Sara

ACKNOWLEDGEMENTS

'molestum est', inquis, 'mortem ante oculos habere'.
primum ista tam seni ante oculos debet esse quam iuveni.
'It is uncomfortable', you say, 'to have death before one's
eyes.' But young and old equally ought to fix their eyes on it.

Sen. *Ep. Mor.* 12.6

I have been thinking about death for some time. Perhaps that
alone does not make me unusual, since surely most people think
about death, even if not in a sustained and systematic way. But
I chose to think a lot about death, and that perhaps deserves some
explanation. It seems to me that the philosophical consideration
of the nature and value of death leads naturally and rapidly to the
consideration of a number of central and significant philosophical
questions in ethics and metaphysics. Considering death involves
considering what it is to live a life, and considering whether death
can be a harm involves considering how to live a good life. If any
questions are worth pursuing, these are.

I also discovered that many of these questions could be
considered in the company of Epicurus, an ancient Greek
philosopher who offered a number of deceptively simple arguments in an attempt to show that death is not to be feared since
it is not a harm. Thinking through the issues involved in these
discussions using Epicurus as a guide will, I hope, not only
illuminate Epicurus' own theory but also offer some assistance in
our own engagement with the same questions. I offer this study,
therefore, as a contribution both to the study of Epicureanism and
also to the philosophy of death.

My thoughts on these topics have been aided and corrected by
a number of people. I first tackled this subject in a 1996 Cambridge
M.Phil. thesis, supervised by David Sedley and examined by
Robert Wardy and Dominic Scott. Since then David, Robert, and
Dominic have offered generous and useful comments on the work
as it progressed. David kindly read a draft of the entire book and
provided, as usual, helpful comments and corrections. For two

years, I taught with Dominic a course for third-year philosophy students in the University of Cambridge on 'Epicurus on death and nature'. The comments offered by participants in those seminars have also aided me a great deal. Various cohorts of Cambridge classics students who attended my lectures on Lucretius and my supervisions on Hellenistic philosophy also allowed me to try out some of these thoughts and often provided helpful reactions. The two readers for the Press also offered useful suggestions and helpful corrections.

I owe thanks to David Armstrong for showing me a draft of his translation of Philodemus *On Death* book four, and also for showing me his forthcoming work on the text, and to Izzy Holby, whose own work on these Epicurean arguments helped me to see more clearly some of the problems they raise. Peter Aronoff kindly sent me some of his unpublished work, particularly on the 'Symmetry argument'.

I began work on this book while a Henry Lumley Research Fellow at Magdalene College and continued to work on it at Corpus Christi College. The Master and Fellows of both colleges provided me with wonderful places in which to work and I thank them all. As ever, the Faculty of Classics in Cambridge and the B Caucus in particular have provided inspiration and instruction.

I could not have produced this book without the constant support of my family. Sara Owen already knows, I hope, how much I owe to her.

Some portions of the material presented here have appeared previously in the following publications.

Parts of Chapter 3 originally appeared in 'Lucretius, symmetry arguments, and fearing death'. *Phronesis* 46, 2001, 466–91. I thank Brill Academic Publishers for permission to reprint this material.

Parts of Chapter 5 originally appeared in 'Epicurus' dying wishes', *PCPS* 47, 2001, 23–46.

Other parts of Chapter 5 originally appeared in 'Democritus, the Epicureans, death and dying', *CQ* 52, 2002, 193–206. I thank Oxford University Press and the Classical Association for permission to reprint this material.

JIW

Cambridge, September 2003

CONTENTS

ABBREVIATIONS

CErc	*Cronache Ercolanesi*
DK	H. Diels and W. Kranz (1952) *Fragmente der Vorsokratiker* (6th edition) Berlin
D.L.	Diogenes Laërtius
DRN	T. Lucretius Carus, *De Rerum Natura*
Ep. Men.	Epicurus, *Letter to Menoeceus*
KΔ	Epicurus, *Kyriai Doxai*
LSJ	H. G. Liddell and R. Scott, rev. S. Jones (1925–40) *Greek–English Lexicon* (9th edition) Oxford
NH	Pliny, *Natural History*
PHerc.	Herculaneum papyri: see *Catologo dei papiri ercolanesi* (1979) Naples
S.E. *M*	Sextus Empiricus, *Adversus Mathematicos*
Sent. Vat.	Epicurus, *Sententiae Vaticanae*
Us.	H. Usener (1887) *Epicurea* Leipzig

I

Fears of Death

You know, it's really very peculiar. To be mortal is the most
basic human experience and yet man has never been able to
accept it, grasp it, and behave accordingly. Man doesn't
know how to be mortal.

Milan Kundera, *Immortality*

To be immortal is commonplace; except for man, all creatures
are immortal for they are ignorant of death; what is divine,
terrible, incomprehensible, is to know that one is mortal.

J. L. Borges, 'The immortal'

It is possible that people have always been interested, if not
concerned, by the question of the nature and significance of
death. Mortality, after all, is something which all humans share
and is something which has important consequences for how we
live and how we think about our lives. In addition to this general
interest, there is a long tradition of philosophical interest in
the question of death. One long and influential tradition of
thought looks to answer these questions by showing that, despite
appearances to the contrary, humans are in fact not mortal. We,
or at least some part or parts of us, are immortal. There is, in
other words, 'life after death'. My interest here is in the treatment
of the question of the significance of death by an alternative
tradition of thought which is convinced that there is no such life
after death. Death, for this line of thought, is the end. It is the
annihilation of the person. Whatever survives death is merely a
corpse. If that is in fact the case, then how should we think of
death and of our own mortality? Should we be concerned, even
alarmed, at this prospect of our coming to a final and total
end? There has recently been a great deal of interest in the
philosophical question of whether death is something to be
feared from philosophers who share the assumption that there is

no *post mortem* survival of any significant sort. Put another way, the question is whether death is or can be a harm. For if death can be a harm, and it can be shown that it is such, then it surely becomes reasonable to fear it. (Avoiding death entirely is not an option for us mortals.) It is usually further specified in such discussions that they are predominantly interested in the more specific question of whether death is a harm to the person who dies, as distinct from the question of whether the death of someone else may harm one's own life. Of course these two are not unrelated. Some people feel grief at another's death principally out of a belief that the deceased has suffered some harm.[1] If it turns out that we should not think of death in that way then perhaps some of the pain of grief can be lifted. But even if it is agreed that death is not bad for the person who dies then it is still possible that someone else's death may be bad for the lives of friends, relatives, and so on who survive, since they surely had some emotional and personal ties with the now deceased and their lives may well be adversely altered by this new absence. My attention here will for the most part be on the more usual philosophical question: 'Is someone harmed by dying?' or 'Is death bad for the person who dies?' My attention is focused as it is not merely by the conviction that this is the more interesting question philosophically, but also because I want to ground my discussion of this question in the evaluation of a particular set of arguments produced by the Hellenistic philosopher Epicurus (341–270 BC). His prime aim was to persuade his audience that death is not bad for the person who dies although death is inevitable and is the total annihilation of that person.[2] Often, modern

---

[1] Cic. *Tusc.* 1.30: M. asserts that this is indeed the cause of grief in order to argue that there is a natural tendency for men to believe that there is some sort of *post mortem* survival. We grieve for the deceased who has been deprived of the goods of life. For the 'deprivation' account of the harm of death see p. 28ft.; for the most part this is expressed counterfactually in order to avoid what M. wishes to show here, namely some sort of *post mortem* existence. For the Epicureans' own account of the correct attitude to take on the death of a friend, see below pp. 39–41.

[2] In the arresting metaphor of *Sent. Vat.* 31, all humans lived in an 'unwalled city'. There is no defence against death: πρὸς μὲν τἆλλα δυνατὸν ἀσφάλειαν πορίσασθαι, χάριν δὲ θανάτου πάντες ἄνθρωποι πόλιν ἀτείχιστον οἰκοῦμεν ('We can put up a defence against other things, but in the case of death all we humans live in an unwalled city'). Philodemus reuses the metaphor at *De Morte* XXXVII.27–9. See Gigante 1983b, 194–9 and cf. Clay 1983, 186–91.

philosophical discussions use Epicurus and Epicurean arguments as a touchstone and inspiration for their own analyses of these questions. However, often these writers brand an argument as Epicurean or characterize a stance as Epicurean based upon one brief stretch of text without due regard for other relevant ancient texts or the context and detailed structure of the particular argument in question. I do not wish to deny that a lot of sophisticated and intelligent work has been produced on these topics, and my debt to these writers will become very clear as I proceed. However, it seems to me to be worth asking just what the Epicureans' position was and, once it has been properly elaborated, only then can it most profitably be placed in conversation with more recent treatments of this topic.

Before proceeding any further it is important to notice that in asking 'Is death bad for the person who dies?' I might be asking one of a number of questions. It is important to keep these different possibilities distinct. By asking whether death is bad for the person who dies, or whether someone is harmed by dying, I might be asking if someone is harmed by the *process* of passing from life to death. Or I might be asking whether someone is harmed by being dead—the state which results after the process of dying. Or I might be asking if someone is harmed by being mortal, by being an organism which will die. Or I might be asking if someone is harmed by dying at this particular point in his or her life rather than another. Let me try to disentangle these different threads by articulating four major questions.

1. Is being dead bad for the deceased?
2. Is it bad for someone that he or she is going to die?
3. Is it bad for someone if he or she dies sooner rather than later?
4. Is it bad for someone to undergo the process of passing from being alive to being dead?

Concentrating on these four questions, we can begin to disentangle four related fears. Epicurus addressed himself to the eradication of the fear of death rather than to the examination of whether death is a harm, but this is merely a matter of emphasis. If we understand fear to be an emotion felt in the face of some future harm,[3] then it is clear that there will be a fear

---

[3] This is a standard ancient definition of fear. See Arist. *NE* 1115ª9.

corresponding to each of the four questions above. If any of the questions is answered in the affirmative then a fear will be generated. Those fears will be:

1*. The fear of being dead.
2*. The fear that one will die, that one's life is going to end.[4]
3*. The fear of premature death.
4*. The fear of the process of dying.

It should be clear, therefore, that when we speak of '*the* fear of death' then we are at best guilty of a simplification or of shorthand. There are at least these four distinct fears. Nevertheless, these fears are not unrelated. It is possible that someone is assailed by the fear of mortality principally because they fear the state of being dead which awaits them. Also, if one fears mortality then one will perhaps fear premature death because *any* death will count as premature. All the same, these fears are not necessarily compresent. It is possible for someone not to fear the state of being dead but to fear the fact that he or she is going to die.[5] It is also possible for someone not to fear being dead but to fear the process of dying which precedes that state. Similarly, it is possible that someone feels no distress at the bare fact that his life is going to end but nevertheless is afraid that he might die before he has lived a satisfying life. And it is possible both to feel none of fears 1*, 2*, and 3* but be afraid of the process of dying (4*) and also to feel a combination of some or all of 1*, 2*, and 3* in addition to this fear.

I shall attempt to show that Epicurus and the Epicureans addressed themselves to each of these distinct fears. Therefore, there is no single Epicurean 'argument against the fear of death'. Rather, they had an armoury of arguments which could be deployed against the various different kinds of fear of death. This too is not necessarily recognized by those modern philosophers who have looked at such questions.

There is good evidence of ancient recognition of distinct ways in which one might fear death. Sextus Empiricus, a Pyrrhonist

---

[4] True, it is perhaps a stretch to call this a 'fear', if fears take future events as their objects, since that a human's life will end is true throughout life. If calling this a fear is thought too strained, we can instead talk of distress at the thought that one's life will end. Nagel 1986, 225, dubs this the 'expectation of nothingness'.   [5] See, for example, Ewin 2002, 10.

writer of the second century AD, offers a number of reasons for denying the Epicureans any innovations in philosophy, including their claim to have shown that 'death is nothing to us'. Rather, Sextus claims that this thesis, along with other central Epicurean concerns, was stolen from earlier Greek poets. His prime exhibit for the thought that the Epicureans were not the first to claim that death is nothing to us is a verse of Epicharmus, a Sicilian comic poet of the fifth century BC:

ἀποθανεῖν ἢ τεθνάναι οὔ μοι διαφέρει.

Neither dying nor being dead makes any difference to me.

Epicharmus *ap*. S.E. *M*. 1.273

There is some doubt whether this was in fact Epicharmus' own formulation, and in the subsequent Epicurean rebuttal of this accusation of plagiarism the purported source is said to be Sophron, not Epicharmus (*M*. 1.284).[6] However, Sextus' version of the Epicharman verse does clearly offer a distinction between two possible causes of concern. Depending on how we interpret the aorist infinitive 'to die' (ἀποθανεῖν), the contrast is between on the one hand either the fact that one is dying or that one is mortal and, on the other, the eventual state of being dead. Neither, so far as Sextus' Epicharmus is concerned, causes any worry. Similarly, early in Cicero's first *Tusculan Disputation*, the same distinction is made. Having been made to concede that the dead are not in fact wretched, A. offers a further challenge:

age iam concedo non esse miseros qui mortui sint, quoniam extorsisti ut faterer, qui omnino non essent, eos ne miseros quidem esse posse. quid? qui vivimus, cum moriendum sit, nonne miseri sumus? quae enim potest in vita esse iucunditas, cum dies et noctes cogitandum sit iam iamque esse moriendum?

All right, I concede that those who are dead are not wretched, since you have forced me to admit that those who do not exist at all cannot even be wretched. But what of it? We who are alive, surely we are wretched since we have to die? What joy can there be in life when we have to contemplate day and night the fact that inevitable death is imminent?

Cic. *Tusc.* 1.14

---

[6] The text of Epicharmus DK B11 reads: ἀποθανεῖν <μὴ εἴ>η, τεθνάκειν δ' οὐκ ἐμίν <γα> διαφέρει. Diels offered this formulation on the basis of M.'s

It is likely, therefore, that Epicurus was similarly aware of the distinct fears of being dead and of being mortal, my 1* and 2*. These two will require importantly different treatments, as will the other two fears, of premature death and of the process of dying. Indeed, there is good evidence that the Epicureans were quite aware not only of the complex nature of 'the' fear of death but also the complex roles that its various species play in human behaviour and psychology. Two texts to which I will return constantly, the latter half of the third book of Lucretius' *De Rerum Natura* (*DRN*) and the fragmentary remains of the fourth book of Philodemus' *On Death* (*De Morte*), are designed to persuade the reader that there is no reason to fear death by using a variety of tactics and by addressing a number of different concerns and anxieties which stem from the central anxiety about death itself.[7]

Epicurus and fearing death

The Epicureans placed the eradication of the fears of death at the very heart of their ethical project.[8] They identified the goal of a good life as the removal of mental and physical pain. Mental pain they further characterized as anxieties and fears. The two major sources of such fear, they thought, were religious

---

quotation from Epicharmus at Cic. *Tusc.* 1.15: *emori nolo, sed me esse mortuum nihili aestimo* ('I do not want to die but think nothing of being dead'). Cf. Blank 1998, 291 and 308. The Epicurean rebuttal replies that although Epicharmus/ Sophron may have *said* this first, Epicurus was the first to demonstrate it.

[7] On the Philodemus text see Tsouna 2001a, esp. 237, 256–8, 258 n. 50: 'In the Epicurean view (which is shared by many of us), the fear of death is *the* fundamental emotion of human pathology, singularly powerful and deeply implanted in us. Therefore, therapy cannot be limited to fragmentary expressions of it, but should aim to transform radically the patient's frame of mind. For only then will death stop being the focus of our thoughts and, instead, will yield its place to the concept of living the good life. In order to achieve such a shift, the therapeutic process should overlap considerably, I submit, with the further education of the patient. In that sense, Philodemus' therapeutic strategies treating the fear of death are also part of his pedagogical project.'

[8] There is evidence from the titles of works by other philosophers that the topic was not unusual, but the Epicureans certainly made it central to their ethical project. For example, Xenocrates wrote a work *On death* (D.L. 4.12) and Antisthenes wrote an *On dying, On life and death*, and *On things in Hades* (D.L. 6.15–18).

beliefs and the fear of death. Epicurus distilled the major theses of his ethical teaching into a simple fourfold remedy, the *tetrapharmakos*.[9]

> God should not concern to us.
> Death is not to be feared.
> What is good is easy to obtain.
> What is bad is easily avoided.

By internalizing these four views and by altering our view of the world accordingly, Epicurus assures us that we can attain the goal (*telos*) of a human life. Removing the fear of death, therefore, is an essential step towards that goal. Indeed, for the Epicureans learning to think about death *correctly* is an integral part of living a good life (see *Ep. Men.* 126). Our conceptions of the value of life and the nature of death are inseparable. In that case, we learn not to stop focusing on death, but to stop thinking about it in the wrong way. If we think about death correctly, we think about living a good life correctly, and vice versa. This places a great deal of pressure on the strength of the various Epicurean arguments marshalled against fearing death. If they turn out to be weak or if they turn out to leave an important sense of fearing death intact then Epicurus' ethical project stands fatally wounded. The goal of human life, as Epicurus himself has characterized it, becomes unattainable. In other words, the stakes are high—not just for us who are contemplating death and how we should feel towards it, but also for Epicureanism and its claim to offer a viable and attractive recipe for living a happy life.

It is important to recognize at the outset a crucial Epicurean assumption. Epicurus is convinced that the fear of death stems—like all other damaging attitudes—from false opinions and, specifically, false value judgements. It may well be difficult to uncover those opinions and judgements within an individual's general psychological make-up but, nevertheless, the enterprise of moral inquiry and improvement is an intellectual one.[10] This intellectualist assumption is crucial because it justifies the

---

[9] For a version of the *tetrapharmakos* see Philodemus *Adv. Soph.* (*PHerc.* 1005) 5.9–13 Angeli.

[10] For accounts of Epicurean therapeutic practice see Nussbaum 1994, 102–39, and Tsouna 2001a, who catalogues Philodemus' 'symptomatology' of the fear of death, which in various ways contributes to mental suffering. Tsouna

Epicurean conviction that the fear of death, since it is based on false value judgements, can be exposed and eradicated by means of rational argument. It is possible to stop fearing death as the result of thinking clearly and correctly.

For Epicurus, therefore, the fear of death is 'irrational' only in the sense of that word which is synonymous with 'misguided' or 'incorrect'. The fear of death is a rational fear in the sense that it is founded on, albeit misdirected, reason and opinion.[11] This assumption is certainly questionable, since it might be argued that the fear of death is a basic and ineradicable part of human psychology which is not susceptible to rational inspection or alteration on the basis of rational argument.[12] It might even be argued that it would be wrong even to attempt to remove the fear of death because—even granted it may have occasional drawbacks and on occasion lead to the odd sleepless night—we simply could not function properly without it. For example, it is possible to claim that the fear of death is a crucial evolutionary product, 'hard-wired', as it were, into our minds in order to allow us to survive. Were we to rid ourselves of this fear (were it possible to do so) we would leave ourselves unable to avoid possibly fatal situations. Another related form of this kind of objection can even grant the truth of the Epicurean dictum that 'death is nothing to us' but nevertheless accept that it is justifiable to fear death on the grounds of utility. While it might certainly be the case that the state of being dead involves nothing which should be feared even in prospect, nevertheless we could claim that it is best for us to try to avoid that state for as long as possible. It is best for each individual to live for as long as possible—perhaps in order to procreate as often and successfully

2001a, 237: 'As superstition, the fear of death is worrying on account of the hereafter (*De Elect.* VII.15–18, IX.13–20, X.16–18, XVIII.4–19). As financial insecurity and greed, it occupies the mind night and day (*De Elect.* XIX.12–16, XX.6–8, 11–13; *De Morte* XXXVIII.36–7): as anxiety concerning the perpetuation of the self. it fills us with grief, regrets. frustration, and repulsion (*De Morte* XXII.9–XXXVI.37).'

[11] Cf. Murphy 1976.

[12] e.g. Ewin 2002, 11: 'Persuading people that grasshoppers are not dangerous might well remove a fear of grasshoppers if anyone had such a fear, but the role of the fear of death in our lives means that, were philosophers successful in their attempts to persuade people that fear of death is irrational, people would still fear death.'

as possible—and one way in which this aim might be achieved is
through an innate aversion to death. This kind of objection could
be made in two ways. Either it can be offered as a reason to
suspect the entire Epicurean project from the outset as something
impossible (and undesirable) to complete. Alternatively, it could
be offered as an objection once the Epicurean theory has been
pursued to its conclusion by contemplating what it would be like
to live without a fear of death and arguing that it then becomes
clear that an Epicurean could not, in fact, 'live his Epicureanism'
or, if he could, that such a life would be radically unlike a normal
human existence. I shall be considering this kind of objection in
Chapter 5 below.

Epicurus himself, as is the custom in much ancient biography
designed to make the subject a moral exemplar, is prominently
depicted displaying the correct attitude towards death.[13] The
account of his final hours, no doubt composed and circulated by
those eager to offer it in support of Epicureanism's claims, shows
the great philosopher accepting his demise with absolute
equanimity. In the process it also demonstrates how the
Epicurean ought to think about one of the various possible
fears of death, namely the fear of dying.[14]

τελευτῆσαι δ' αὐτὸν λίθῳ τῶν οὔρων ἐπισχεθέντων, ὥς φησι καὶ Ἕρμαρχος ἐν
ἐπιστολαῖς, ἡμέρας νοσήσαντα τετταρεσκαίδεκα. ὅτε καί φησιν Ἕρμιππος
ἐμβάντα αὐτὸν εἰς πύελον χαλκῆν κεκραμένην ὕδατι θερμῷ καὶ αἰτήσαντα
ἄκρατον ῥοφῆσαι· τοῖς τε φίλοις παραγγείλαντα τῶν δογμάτων μεμνῆσθαι,
οὕτω τελευτῆσαι.

He died from a stone which prevented him urinating—so Hermarchus
says in his letters—having been ill for fourteen days. Hermippus too
says that he climbed into a bronze bath filled with hot water, asked for
a cup of unmixed wine and gulped it down. Telling his friends to
remember his doctrines, this is how he died.

D.L. 10.15–16

---

[13] On Diogenes Laërtius in particular and ancient philosophical biography in
general see Gigante 1986. Decleva Caizzi 1993, and Warren, forthcoming. Such
biographical anecdotes also offered a fertile ground for critics of a particular
philosophical stance. We shall see Cicero using Epicurus' last words to
demonstrate a contradiction between Epicurean theory and Epicurus' own
practice: below pp. 165–6.

[14] Philodemus *De Elect.* (*PHerc.* 1251) XVI notes that only when death is
imminent and its time predictable do most people focus their minds on it and
begin to think about it seriously.

The story of Epicurus' death is designed to demonstrate Epicurus' calm in the face of a fatal and long-lasting illness which no doubt caused a great deal of physical pain. (This physical pain was counteracted, so Epicurus tells us himself, by his recollecting past pleasant philosophical conversations.)[15] His supposed resolution in the face of death is a characteristic shared by many stories of ancient philosophers' deaths, certainly from Socrates' death in Plato's *Phaedo* onwards.[16] In any case, the overall impression is one of a philosopher with no anxieties about meeting his final demise and therefore offers some support for the power and persuasiveness of those Epicurean doctrines which Epicurus recommends to his friends just as he passes away.

By considering the example of Epicurus' own death we can construct an immediate and preliminary reply to some of the worries already raised about the very possibility, let alone desirability, of removing entirely the fear of death. The fear of death in question throughout these Epicurean arguments must always be kept distinct from the fear of pain, which might of itself be said to make us avoid certain potentially fatal situations. The fear in question is not the fear of dying in some particular way; it is the very general and basic aversion to ceasing to be. Epicurus, of course, as a good hedonist would wholeheartedly endorse any mechanism which allows us to avoid pain. But still he insists that life would be better, indeed more pleasant, if we were to stop fearing death. The question here is whether specifically fearing death can be seen to serve some function such that if it were not present our lives would be rendered unliveable or, less drastically, less pleasant overall. It is clear enough that Epicureans, once they have removed the fear of death, are not supposed to become suicidal dare-devils.[17] Presumably enough of the functional aversions to risk and pain remain, once the

[15] This information comes from the letter to Idomeneus, retained at D.L. 10.22 and Cic. *Fin.* 2.96, where it is called the letter to Hermarchus. Cicero is unsurprisingly unimpressed by Epicurus' claim to have warded off this pain (2.98). See also *Tusc.* 5.74–5 and Plut. *Non Posse* 1099D–E for further expressions of disbelief and ridicule.

[16] Laks 1976, 78–9 notes that, for example, a number of Hermippus' accounts of deaths of philosophers include their drinking unmixed wine: 'la description montre Épicure maître de sa mort'.

[17] Rorty 1983 has a good discussion of the 'functional fears' of death, and concludes that there is an irreconcilable dilemma between the irrationality of

debilitating fear of being dead is abolished, to allow an Epicurean to navigate safely through the world.[18] It seems to me therefore that the fear of pain can carry most of the weight supposed by these objections to be borne by the instrumental fear of death and that therefore there is no reason to believe that it is impossible to live a recognizably human life without fearing death.

The second-century AD Epicurean Diogenes of Oinoanda offers the following observations about the relationship between the fear of death and the fear of pain:

ν[ῦν δὲ] | οὗτος ὁ φόβος τ[οτὲ] | μέν ἐστιν τετρα[νωμέ]|νος, τοτὲ δ' ἀτρα[νής]· τετρανωμένος [μὲν] | ὅταν ἐκ φανεροῦ [κακόν] τι φεύγωμεν ὥσ[περ] | τὸ πῦρ φοβούμε[νοι δι'] | αὐτοῦ τῷ θανάτῳ [περι]|πεσεῖσθαι, ν ἀτραγ[νής] | δὲ ὅταν, πρὸς ἄλλ[ῳ τι]|νὶ τῆς διανοίας ὑ[παρ]|χούσης, ἐνδεδυμ[ένος τῇ] | φύσει καὶ ὑποφω[λεύων]

But as it is, this fear is sometimes manifest and sometimes not. It is manifest when we clearly avoid some evil, for example fire, fearing that we might meet our deaths as a result of it. It is not manifest when while we are thinking of some other thing fear has crept into out nature and lurks...

Diogenes of Oinoanda fr. 35 II Smith

It is not immediately clear whether by 'we' in this passage Diogenes is referring to 'us Epicureans'. If he is, then it is difficult to see how, without contradicting his professed agreement with the thesis that death is nothing to us, he can here talk as if death is something which 'we Epicureans' fear. More likely, since this appears to occur at a point in Diogenes' text where he is talking about disturbing emotions in general and the fear of the gods in particular (fr. 34 Smith),[19] Diogenes is trying to make clear

the metaphysical fear of death, and the inevitable functional fear of death. She concludes, however, that this dilemma is not debilitating. Cf. Oaklander 1994, 349. Haji 1991, 177, points out that this 'sociobiological conjecture' 'may provide the beginnings of an explanation about why, from moments *within* their lives, people care more about life's goods of which death could deprive them, than about life's goods they could have enjoyed had they not been conceived so late'. This asymmetrical attitude will de discussed further below, p. 76ft.

[18] Of course, it is perfectly acceptable—and surely plausible—for an Epicurean to argue that we do and should if at all possible avoid dying painfully. Cf. Luper-Foy 1987, 241: 'It is not necessary to want to *avoid* dying in order to want to do things that tend to make dying unlikely.'

[19] See Smith 1993, 486. *KΔ* 13 seems to have been inscribed in the margin running beneath this fragment.

that it is not always an easy matter to identify just what the object of fear might be, nor sometimes whether someone's actions are primarily motivated by fear. The fear in question may be 'hidden' even from the agent himself. Diogenes is making a claim in support of the familiar Epicurean thesis that the fear of death, the gods, and of punishment in the afterlife is the root of a number of human pathologies, including the desire for fame, power, and a constant series of pleasures (see Lucr. *DRN* 3.31–93). In that case, he need not be allowing that an Epicurean will avoid fire because he fears the death which may result from it. Rather, that is intended as a clear example of a 'manifest fear' to contrast with the hidden fears which particularly interest Diogenes at this point. His references to what 'we' do, therefore, are references to what 'we humans' do. Further, given that an Epicurean ought to have rooted out even a hidden fear of death, he is here using the first person to refer to what non-Epicureans, the readers he is attempting to convert, in fact do.[20] It remains open, therefore for the Epicureans to claim that a good Epicurean will fear pain but not death, and that this fear of pain will suffice to ensure that the Epicurean can function in day-to-day situations without needlessly endangering himself.

The fear of pain, which the Epicureans recognize as a legitimate concern since pain is indeed bad on their account, can also be used by them to explain and attempt to clarify one of the fears of death, namely 4*: the fear of the process of dying. In so far as the process of passing from being alive to being death is painful, it is appropriate to fear it. But, importantly, it ought to be clear that it is the pain of this process which qualifies it as an appropriate object of fear, not the fact that the process will result in death. *Qua* painful event, therefore, dying is something to be concerned about. *Qua* loss of life, it is not at all to be feared. Epicurus' own death, as we have seen, exemplifies the correct attitude. Epicurus is neither afraid of dying, nor is he experiencing any pain during this process since he is able—so he claims— to counterbalance physical pain by recalling past pleasures. The message is that while dying can be painful, it need not be.

---

[20] Fr. 34 Smith, which was probably close to this fragment in the original inscription, also uses first-person verbs (see e.g. VII.9–12). I take this inclusive and cooperative tone to be part of Diogenes' rhetorical and persuasive strategy. Cf. Warren 2000a.

In fact, given the amount of time they spend discussing death, the Epicureans have surprisingly little to say about the ethical significance of the process of dying and what they do say is often rather implausible and relies heavily on the Epicurean physical theory of the particular atomic nature of the soul.[21] Philodemus (*De morte* VIII) insists that dying is a very swift event. It must be, he argues, since the atoms which make up the soul are incredibly small and mobile and therefore rapidly dissipate at the moment of death. If any sensation is experienced this is soon curtailed by the onset of *anaisthēsia* once the soul has been destroyed. This is offered in answer to some unnamed opponents who insist that the separation of body and soul must *always* be accompanied by great pain. Philodemus also surprisingly claims that the dissipation of the soul can even on occasion be a pleasurable experience.[22] It is hard to think that there was much evidence to support this contention, besides perhaps the story of Epicurus' own death.

Lucretius, for example, tends like Philodemus to stress the fragility of the soul's position in the body, implying that dying will be a momentary process as the fragile soul dissipates.[23] He certainly does include in his poem pictures of violent and savage pain and mutilation. He describes horrific fatal injuries sustained during war (see for example 5.994-8). But while he agrees that life *can* be painful and full of injury, he equally insists that it need not be. Rather than exemplifying the inevitable horror of death, these examples serve to turn the reader towards Epicureanism and its promise of constant pleasure and a death which causes no anxiety or pain. The overall message is that life can be lived in pleasure and dying need not be painful or lingering. Indeed,

---

[21] I offer some suggestions why this might be the case, and contrast the Epicureans with Democritus' apparent interest in the process of dying, in Warren 2002a.

[22] Philod. *De Morte* VIII.20-24, VIII.30-34 Gigante. Cf. Sen. *De Prov.* 6.9, where he stresses the speed of the dying process, and *Ep. Mor.* 77.9, where he confirms the thought that dying can sometimes be a pleasant experience; Cic. *Tusc.* 1.82 similarly rejects the thought that dying is necessarily painful and maintains that, in any case, the process takes merely an instant so is rapidly all over. At *DRN* 3.172-3, Lucretius describes a wounded warrior's fall to the ground as pleasant (*suavis*). Some editors thought this so absurd as to be a textual corruption. See Bailey ad loc. for arguments for its retention.

[23] Lucr. *DRN* 3.208-30. Cf. Segal 1990, 46-73.

death might even come as a relief from pain and dying might be a pleasant, even exhilarating process. In any case, dying is neither intrinsically painful nor intrinsically pleasant.

Notoriously in such discussions, the Epicureans often offer a weak argument in an attempt to show that dying is not to be feared. Any intense pain, they try to reassure us, will be short-lived. Any prolonged pain is not so intense as to be distressing.[24] If this is based merely on empirical argument it is at best questionable. Is it not at least imaginable that someone might undergo protracted excruciating pain? The Epicureans appear to have thought that intolerable pain is supposed to be short-lived simply because it is *literally* intolerable; it rapidly results in death which, as the Epicureans will attempt to show us, is the absence of any possibility of further harm. Other ancient texts offer what looks like an argument for this position. Seneca offers the following:

[dolor], levis es si ferre possum; brevis es si ferre non possum.

'If you are light, pain, I can bear you; if I cannot bear you, you are short.'

Seneca Ep. Mor. 24.14

If this is intended as an argument at all, it is a sophism, which turns on an equivocation on the notion of pain's being 'tolerable'.[25] Protracted pain is tolerable in sense 1: it can be endured without too much discomfort. But the pain which is curtailed by death is intolerable in sense 2: it literally cannot be endured; it results in death. There is clearly room for protracted pain which, while not so terrible that it causes death (so 'tolerable' in sense 2), is nevertheless not so slight that it can be ignored and merely 'tolerated' (so 'intolerable' in sense 1). In that case, we might charitably say that Seneca is offering here a rhetorical flourish rather than a serious argument. As a Stoic he must think, in any case, that physical pain—and life itself—is morally indifferent. If, however, the hedonist Epicureans used any

---

[24] For versions of the claim that intense pain does not last see: Epic. *Ep. Men.* 133; *KΔ* 4; *Sent. Vat.* 4; Diog. Oin. 42 Smith (lower margin), 105 Smith (where it is made clear that such pain is curtailed by death); Cic. *Tusc.* 2.44; Plut. *De Poet. Aud.* 36B. See Us. 446–7.

[25] Cf. Sen. *Ep. Mor.* 78.7: *sic nos amantissima nostri natura disposuit ut dolorem aut tolerabilem aut brevem faceret* ('So nature, being so loving to us, has decided to make us so that pain is either endurable or brief').

such argument seriously, thinking that it is a piece of effective therapy, then they were very mistaken. They would do better to try harder to persuade us of the soul's ability to counterbalance physical pains by recollecting or anticipating past or future pleasures.

In this way, the Epicureans attempt to reduce the fear of dying to the legitimate fear of pain. If dying will not be painful then it is not to be feared, but the legitimate fear of pain is allowed to do the work of dissuading us from various damaging and possibly fatal causes of action. The fear of pain, according to the Epicurean, is natural, just as the pursuit of pleasure is natural, and is present in all animals from birth without the prompting of reason (*Ep. Men.* 129, D.L. 10.137).[26] The fear of pain is intended to do much of the work which is sometimes assigned by critics of the Epicurean view to the fear of death itself. For these critics, the fear of death is natural and 'hard-wired', an indelible psychological trait produced by evolution and natural selection and necessary to the continued functioning of both individuals and the species. From this point of view the entire Epicurean assault on the fear of death is beside the point. Whether or not it is conceivable that we could live without fearing death, it is not a practical possibility. This objection can also rely on a competing notion of the nature of fear, or at least of some fears of which the fear of death is one example. On this view, the fear of death simply cannot be addressed through the powers of rational persuasion. In a more extreme version, the fear of death cannot be addressed at all through rational persuasion, habituation, or whatever other techniques of psychological change may be available. Fearing death is simply part of what it is to be human, like the feelings of hunger or thirst.[27]

Epicurus, clearly, disagrees. The disagreement will have to be resolved in a number of ways. By outlining and contemplating the Epicurean arguments we can ourselves begin to assess their effectiveness. If they turn out to be sound and persuasive

---

[26] Cf. Brunschwig 1986.

[27] Cf. Ewin 2002, 19: 'The attitude of regarding death as a natural evil is … natural to people by and large, though there are exceptional people who do not share it. That attitude is important to the life of the species. It underlies, though it does not give justification for, our values. It is something that is presupposed by our reasoning, not something arrived at by reasoning from other premises.'

arguments but still not effective at ridding us of fear, then perhaps there is something to be said for this objector's view. Second, by seeing what would be the consequences of an Epicurean view we can approach the question of whether humans naturally and necessarily fear death. If it is possible to live a human life without fearing death then fearing death is not essential to being human. It is important also to recognize that the Epicureans do not expect a life free from the fear of death to be indistinguishable from a life lived with that fear. Ridding ourselves of the fear of death is part of attaining a better life. Better life or not, if the Epicurean life is a human life at all, then humans need not live with the fear of death. In short, the full answer to this kind of objection can be given only after the Epicurean arguments have been given a full inspection.

From these introductory remarks two important items emerge to be tracked through the more detailed examination of the Epicurean arguments and the criticisms they have provoked. First, there is no single 'fear of death'. Rather, there is a set of related fears about non-existence itself, the fact that we are mortal and therefore will at some time cease to exist, and the uncertainty of when death will come. It will be important to keep these distinct fears in mind and see how effectively Epicurean therapy can deal with any or all of them. Second, the fear of death is intimately connected with the way in which we lead our lives. Importantly, we will need to ask whether it is at all possible to lead a life without fearing death and, if it is, whether a life free from fearing death is a recognizable and attractive human life.

2

Death and Deprivation

non fui. fui. non sum. non curo.

I was not. I was. I am not. I care not.

Roman epitaph

Epicurus produced a number of 'Key Doctrines' (in Greek: *Kyriai Doxai*, or *KΔ*) which offered the main tenets of his teaching in the most condensed form. These maxims were intended to be memorized and internalized by the Epicurean in order to form a readily available source which could be consulted to give advice on any particular topic. They could also be memorized and contemplated as concise expressions of what a fully fledged Epicurean must believe. The prominence which Epicurus gave to dispelling what he saw as irrational concerns about death is evident from the fact that the second of these *Kyriai Doxai* concerns that topic. It is this brief saying which presents the bare essentials of the first of the Epicureans' arguments.

ὁ θάνατος οὐδὲν πρὸς ἡμᾶς· τὸ γὰρ διαλυθὲν ἀναισθητεῖ· τὸ δὲ ἀναισθητοῦν οὐδὲν πρὸς ἡμᾶς.

Death is nothing to us; for what is dispersed does not perceive, and what does not perceive is nothing to us.

KΔ 2

The conclusion of this argument, that 'death is nothing to us', may need some clarification. For the Epicureans it is simply true as a matter of fact that death does not constitute a harm for anyone. They are adamant that the only way a person may be harmed is by suffering pain—mental or physical. A pain-free state, which they controversially identify as the highest pleasure, is the goal of life (the *telos*). The dead cannot perceive, so they cannot feel pleasure or pain. Therefore they cannot be harmed. In that sense, it does not matter whether or not anyone believes that death is not a harm; death will not harm anyone whatever they believe. Similarly, it is true as a matter of fact that pleasure is what humans naturally ought to pursue, whether or not anyone believes that it is. This hedonist position therefore asserts that there are objective standards for assessing whether a person is living a good life, but since the criteria for judging the goodness of a person's life involve assessing what the person is perceiving—specifically what pleasure or pain that person is feeling—there is an important element of subjectivity involved. What counts as a good life is not open to question, but whether a given person is living a good life depends crucially on that person's experiential state, whether they are feeling pleasure or pain. It is still necessary to bring people to accept and live with the true belief that death is nothing to them. The Epicureans are also concerned to point out that false beliefs can be damaging to people's lives since these misapprehensions can themselves be a source of mental pain and distress. Actions taken on the basis of such false opinions, together with desires formed on the basis of such false opinions, can all lead to further mental and physical pain, preventing the agent from living a good life. Therefore, the belief that 'death *is* something to us' is potentially harmful. It must be removed and the contradictory belief put in its place. Once we come to believe what is in fact the case, that death is not a harm, then we can be free of any damaging effects of our former misapprehension.

It is also important to note that this brief argument offers only one part of the position advanced in the more extended summary of Epicurus' ethical teachings, the *Letter to Menoeceus*. Certainly, the *Letter* does begin its discussion of death with a reference to the absence of perception, but this time it omits the claim that death is the dissolution of something necessary for perception to occur. Rather, death is here simply stated as the absence of perception, and perception is a necessary condition of benefit or harm.

συνέθιζε δὲ ἐν τῷ νομίζειν μηδὲν πρὸς ἡμᾶς εἶναι τὸν θάνατον· ἐπεὶ πᾶν ἀγαθὸν καὶ κακὸν ἐν αἰσθήσει· στέρησις δέ ἐστιν αἰσθήσεως ὁ θάνατος.

Make yourself accustomed to the thought that death is nothing to us, since every good or bad resides in perception and death is the absence of perception.

Ep. Men. 124

However, in what follows Epicurus offers a supplementary argument which does not rely on the premise that all goods and evils reside in perception.

τὸ φρικωδέστατον οὖν τῶν κακῶν ὁ θάνατος οὐθὲν πρὸς ἡμᾶς, ἐπειδήπερ ὅταν μὲν ἡμεῖς ὦμεν, ὁ θάνατος οὐ πάρεστιν· ὅταν δὲ ὁ θάνατος παρῇ, τόθ' ἡμεῖς οὐκ ἐσμέν. οὔτε οὖν πρὸς τοὺς ζῶντάς ἐστιν οὔτε πρὸς τοὺς τετελευτηκότας, ἐπειδήπερ περὶ οὓς μὲν οὐκ ἔστιν, οἱ δ' οὐκέτι εἰσίν.

Therefore death, the most terrifying of evils, is nothing to us, since for the time when we are, death is not present; and for the time when death is present, we are not. Therefore it is nothing either to the living or the dead since it is not present for the former, and the latter are no longer.

Ep. Men. 125

Of course, these arguments are not incompatible (and fortunately so, for Epicurus' sake). In particular, the unexpressed intermediate premise in *KΔ* 2—that death is some kind of dissolution—is just that relied upon at *Ep. Men.* 125 for the assertion that no relevant subject persists after the point of death and at *Ep. Men.* 124 for the assertion that after death there is no perception. As such, *KΔ* 2 should probably be viewed as a concise amalgamation of the two independent arguments in the *Letter*. When Lucretius comes to express what he presumably took to be the force of this general form of argument, however, he offers a further variant on the general theme.

> nil igitur mors est ad nos neque pertinet hilum,
> quandoquidem natura animi mortalis habetur.

Therefore death is nothing to us, nor does it matter to us at all, since the nature of the soul is understood to be mortal.

DRN 3.830–31

It is not clear whether Lucretius intends us to understand here that the mortality of the soul is relevant to this question because if the soul 'dies' then it no longer perceives and therefore no longer perceives pleasure or pain, or whether his point is that since the soul is mortal and the survival of the soul is a necessary condition of personal survival, then when the soul passes away we too pass away—in which case, there is no subject remaining for death to harm.[1] It is therefore unclear which of the arguments

---

[1] The Epicurean account of personal identity is perhaps best summarized at Lucr. *DRN* 3.845–6: a person is a union of a (material) soul and body. Cf.

from the *Letter to Menoeceus* he intends to recall. True, Lucretius passes on in the immediately subsequent lines (where he produces the first of his 'Symmetry Arguments' which I shall discuss in Chapter 3) to assert that before birth we felt no pain, and this suggests that he has the former alternative in mind. Nevertheless, 3.830–1 as it stands is not a 'translation' of *KΔ* 2. Only the first few words, the conclusion that 'death is nothing to us', could be counted as a translation of any sort, but in that case it could just as well be a translation of the same phrase which occurs in the *Letter*.[2] Presumably at this point of the poem Lucretius stresses the importance of the soul's mortality in order to effect a smooth transition from this very topic, which has been the focus of much of the third book so far, to his next topic of the fear of death.

   That Lucretius could try to capture the force of this line of argument in a manner intermediate between the formulations in *KΔ* 2 and those in the *Letter* demonstrates the large extent to which they are similar—and related—arguments. But these arguments differ markedly in their emphasis. Whereas *KΔ* 2 and *Ep. Men.* 124 rely upon the idea that harms must be perceived (and therefore in turn rely upon the truth of Epicurean hedonism, although one need not be a hedonist to subscribe to *KΔ* 2 as it stands), the argument from *Ep. Men.* 125 relies on the notion that death is the absolute annihilation of the subject. For death to be a harm, on this view, it ought to be *contemporaneous* with some appropriate subject of harm. But, says Epicurus, death never is contemporaneous with the subject since death is by definition the absence of that subject.

   Lucretius also combines these two considerations in another famous passage. He imagines someone who claims to accept the Epicurean thesis that 'death is nothing to us' but nevertheless reveals the weakness of his wholehearted commitment to that assertion and its consequences.

Warren 2001a. As Annas 1992, 155, points out, the survival of the soul is not a sufficient condition of personal survival.

   [2] See Wallach 1976, 12–13 who notes that Quintilian 5.14.12 includes a Latin translation of *KΔ* 2: *mors nihil ad nos, nam quod est dissolutum | sensu caret; quod autem sensu caret, nihil ad nos*. Cf. Bailey and Kenney ad loc. and Clay 1983, 176–9.

proinde ubi se videas hominem indignarier ipsum,
post mortem fore ut aut putescat corpore posto
aut flammis interfiat malisve ferarum,
scire licet non sincerum sonere atque subesse
caecum aliquem cordi stimulum, quamvis neget ipse
credere se quemquam sibi sensum in morte futurum;
non, ut opinor, enim dat quod promittit et unde,
nec radicitus e vita se tollit et eicit,
sed facit esse sui quiddam super inscius ipse.
vivus enim sibi cum proponit quisque futurum,
corpus uti volucres lacerent in morte feraeque,
ipse sui miseret; neque enim se dividit illim
nec removet satis a proiecto corpore, et illum
se fingit sensuque suo contaminat astans.

So whenever you see a man complaining to himself, that it will turn out
after death that when his body is laid out he will either rot, or be
destroyed by fire and the jaws of wild animals, then it is clear to see that
he does not ring true and that some hidden spur lies in his heart however much he himself denies that he thinks he will retain any perception
when dead. He does not, I think, grant what he professes, nor the
premise from which it is derived. Nor does he remove and expel himself
from life roots and all, but allows that there is a certain part of himself
surviving (though he himself does not realise this).[3] For when someone
alive conjures the picture of birds and wild animals harming his dead
body at some time in the future, then he pities himself; for he does
not keep himself sufficiently distinct from the body laid out, and he
imagines it to be himself, and, as an onlooker, infects it with his own
perception.

DRN 3.870–83

Armed now with the essential Epicurean doctrines about death,
Lucretius asks Memmius to contemplate an example of what is
implied to be a common failing. The man Lucretius describes
professes to accept the Epicureans' conclusion that death is not

---

[3] Perhaps it is this comment above all which has led some commentators to
see in this passage a sign of an early identification of the 'unconscious'.
Although this individual professes to adhere to Epicurean ideas something else
prevents him from doing so. See Segal 1990, 23–5; Nussbaum 1994, 196–201.
However, what he is unaware of, specifically, is an inconsistency between his
beliefs: that 'death is nothing to us' and that he, as a corpse, may experience
harm. And these beliefs may both be held quite consciously but the inconsistency not realized. See Gladman and Mitsis 1997. Cf. ps. Pl. *Axioch.* 370a7–b1.

an evil, but nevertheless in his fear of what will happen to his
corpse after death he not only negates that assertion but also
shows that he does not in fact hold firm to the premise from
which that assertion derives (876). Just what Lucretius has in mind
as this premise is not immediately made clear. In the subsequent
text two problems are noted. First the man imagines that he will,
as a corpse, be able to perceive the pain caused by the predation
of his body by birds and wild beasts or the fire which is lit under
the burial pyre. In that case, we can assume that the premise of
which he has a shaky grasp is that 'after death there is no
perception, and *a fortiori* no perception of pleasure or pain'.
Second, he mistakenly identifies himself with the corpse, pitying
himself when he considers what the corpse will undergo.[4] This
poor person 'imagines the corpse to be himself, and, as an
onlooker, infects it with his own perception'. So another premise
of which this person has a shaky grasp at best is that 'death is
annihilation; when death is we are not'.[5] Were he to be consistent
and hold firm to either one of these Epicurean tenets then he
would not be affected by the fear which currently grips him.
Death is not so fearful, one might think, if one is convinced either
that while a corpse nothing will be perceived or that although a
corpse may perceive what is done to it, the corpse is not identical
with the person whose body this was. It would, of course, be better
still for the person concerned if he were properly convinced of
both these tenets since then his conviction that death cannot
harm him would be strongly supported by two independent
arguments. This unfortunate person, however, although he professes allegiance to these theses either does not in fact believe
them at all, but merely mouths the words, or does believe them
but fails to see that he also possesses some other beliefs which
lead him to fear death nevertheless. In the second case, he fails

---

[4] See McMahan 2002, 29–31 and 53, who points out that the view that a
person is numerically identical with a human organism has the consequence
either that a person persists after death as a corpse or that there is, strictly
speaking, no such thing as a dead organism. Cf. Olson 1997, 136, 150–2.

[5] Philodemus similarly combines the claims that death is annihilation and
that death will not be perceived at *De Morte* XIX 30–33: λυπήσετ[αι] δ' οὐδαμ[ῶς
ἐξαι|ρ]ούμενος ἐκ τῶν ὄ[ν]των ὡς εἰ μηδε|μίαν ἴσχεν τῆ[ς] ἐλλείψεω[ς ἐπαί]σθη|σιν
('He will in no way feel pain in being removed from existence as he has no
awareness of the loss').

properly to integrate the relevant Epicurean theses into his whole outlook. If this failure to accept Epicurean conclusions fully and wholeheartedly is the failing we are intended to diagnose, then Lucretius is also pointing out here that merely nodding acceptance of Epicurean theses is not enough. They must be held properly, understood, and made the core of one's other beliefs about oneself and one's relation with the world.

Unperceived harms

There are two possible theses whose absence would lead to the fear of death. Let me therefore address the Epicurean arguments for each of these in turn, beginning with the second *Kyria Doxa*. Since it is intended to be a memorable gnomic statement of the Epicurean position, the *Kyria Doxa* is not a complete argumentative unit. It must be supplemented. The full argument must be as follows:

	1. Death is nothing to us.
since	2. Death is the dissolution of the soul.
and	3. What is dissolved does not perceive.
therefore (by 2 and 3)	4. Death is the absence of perception.
	5. What is not perceived is nothing to us.
and (by 4 and 5)	6. Death is nothing to us. QED

There is a possible ambiguity in this formulation. In 2, 'Death' might refer to the point or moment of death, at which the soul dissolves. But Epicurus wants not merely to conclude that the point or moment of death is nothing to us, rather that the whole of time including and subsequent to that moment is nothing to us. This possibility can be avoided by rewording 2 as something like 2*: 'When the person is dead, the soul is dissolved'.[6]

---

[6] The Epicureans do not identify the person with his or her soul but do maintain that the soul is the locus of perception and thought.

We can immediately see the two important premises, 2 and 5. (One can deny premise 2 but agree with 3.) There are therefore two ways to attack Epicurus. The first tactic is to argue that the soul survives death (i.e. deny 2); the second is to argue that not all harms need to be perceived (i.e. deny 5). However, these two tactics are related in an important way. It is generally thought, especially among modern commentators on this argument, that even if 5 can be denied then 2 nevertheless remains a difficulty. The denial of 5 opens the possibility for non-perceived harms and so removes one obstacle to the analysis of death as a harm. However, for death to be a harm in any sense there must surely be some subject for that harm. Here the anti-Epicurean must tackle head-on the assertion of 2, and the argument which Epicurus gives in the *Letter to Menoeceus*. Even if death need not be perceived to be a harm, what is the subject of the harm which it is supposed to constitute? Surely not the deceased person, since that person is no longer—he has ceased to exist. In other words, even if Epicurus loses the battle over 5 and is forced to concede the possibility of unperceived harms, he can retreat to the assertion in 2 and the more sophisticated form of this assertion given in the argument of *Ep. Men.* 125. Let us therefore try to follow this order of discussion: first, the question of whether harms must be perceived; second, the hunt for the subject of the harm of death. We shall see, however, that these two questions are not so easily separated.

Consider the following three scenarios.

1. Mr A thinks his life is going well. He enjoys his job and his family life. However, he does not know that his close friend has betrayed him and all his colleagues ridicule him mercilessly every time he leaves the room. In fact, although he thinks he is loved and respected he is neither. He never discovers this.

2. Mr B is a keen motorcyclist. On his way home one night he is involved in an accident and badly injured. His brain is damaged and he is reduced to the mental capacity of an infant. He retains none of the beliefs, ambitions, or memories of his life before the accident. His new life is nevertheless content. He is cared for and his needs fulfilled.

3. Mr C lives a reasonably happy and successful life and then dies. He dies before his children get married and have children

of their own. He is not there to see his family grow and prosper.

Are any of these people harmed? Perhaps we are inclined to say yes. That is certainly the reaction which the first two examples are intended to elicit. They are versions of examples to be found in Thomas Nagel's classic paper, which has now become the standard point of departure for this kind of discussion.[7] Examples 1 and 2 are supposed to draw the response that Mr A and Mr B are indeed harmed by the situation they find themselves in regardless of whether they themselves are aware of this harm. These in turn are intended to be relevantly analogous situations to that in case 3, which is an example of the sort of case we are interested in when asking whether death itself is a harm. There is clearly a degree of persuasion being exerted by the progressive examples. The three cases offer gradually increasing degrees of *anaisthēsia*—from simple lack of awareness, to brain damage, to total loss of life. A similar increase in the harm of the situation is implied. (It is worse to suffer brain damage than ridicule. Is death, in that case, worse than suffering brain damage?) The force of the tricolon implies, although Nagel makes no such claim explicitly and would perhaps wish to resist this implication, that Mr A is harmed, but not as much as Mr B, and that harm itself is not so bad as the harm to Mr C.[8]

If we agree that Mr A is harmed, then we must agree that Mr A's own subjective experiential state is in this instance at least not pertinent to the question whether he is the subject of some harm. Similarly, if we agree that Mr B, although now in a contented state, has suffered harm in comparison with the life he led before the accident despite his not realizing that loss or remembering that period, again we must agree that Mr B has been harmed. If that is so, the train of thought runs, why can we not agree that although perceiving no harm when dead Mr C is harmed nevertheless?

[7] Nagel 1979. Cf. Fischer 1999.

[8] Nagel 1979, 2, does grant at least that simply being conscious is a great good: 'Therefore life is worth living even when the bad experiences are plentiful, and the good ones too meagre to outweigh the bad ones on their own. The additional positive weight is added by experience itself, rather than by any of its contents.' Note that this does not amount to the claim that simply being alive is a great good. It is not clear from this what value, if any, Nagel would find in a life of permanent unconsciousness, but cf. Nagel 1986, 226.

The argument relies on maintaining as closely as possible a degree of analogy between the three cases. If either case 1 or case 2 is considered relevantly similar to case 3 and we agree it is indeed an example of unperceived harm, then case 3 can be a case of unperceived harm, and we can reject the Epicurean argument. However, it is not difficult to see problems in maintaining the desired analogies.

First, in case one it can be argued that the harm is discernible only because at any minute Mr A could discover the truth about his life. He is harmed only because of the constant possibility of this realization. As it happens, Mr A never does discover the truth. If we know and maintain this guaranteed ignorance in advance, as it were, does this alter our judgement of the case? Critics of this particular argument have wondered whether it is equally tempting to identify a case of harm in the following situation:

4. Mr D lives a happy life. He is a writer. One of his books is bought in a shop thousands of miles from where he lives. The purchaser reads the book, hates it, and criticizes it vocally to his friends. He even goes on to ridicule the portrait of the author on the back. His friends laugh and share the joke. Mr D never discovers any of this.

Is Mr D harmed by this? I doubt many would think he is. But how is this relevantly different from case 1? If it is merely because Mr D is so much more unlikely to hear about his being ridiculed than Mr A is of finding he is betrayed by his friend, then this would identify what is in fact intuitively harmful about Mr A's situation. We think Mr A is harmed because of the proximity to him of the harm and because of the danger of his discovering it. Perhaps instead Mr A is harmed because in his case the betrayal has various damaging effects on his life (for example, he may miss a promotion because of his poor reputation at work). Even though he does not perceive the cause of this loss and may not notice that there is something he has lost, he nevertheless does experience the life which is affected by the betrayal. So the consequences of the betrayal are harmful to him although he does not recognize them as consequences of a betrayal. The betrayal itself, which remains undiscovered, is only harmful in so far as it produces these perceived effects. No such effects are at work in Mr D's case. But if we are tempted to say that Mr A is harmed but Mr D is not, then perhaps these effects of the betrayal are the source of the harm rather than the betrayal itself.[9] It is difficult to secure the conclusion that the unperceived betrayal itself harms Mr A.

Let us leave Mr A in his blissful—or not—ignorance. Mr B is harmed, we might think, even though he does not perceive that he has been harmed, because of his being reduced to a particular state. His situation is different from that of Mr A because he cannot ever come to recognize that he has been so harmed. If Mr B is a relevant analogue for the harm of death, therefore, then the case of Mr D can be evaded. That Mr B is harmed is sufficient on its own to counter the subjectivist assumption of the Epicurean argument. But what shall we say about Mr B? Epicurus can offer two defences. First, he can claim that contrary to our initial intuitions Mr B has not in fact been harmed. His life after the accident is contented and his needs are cared for. In the absence of any further explanation and justification of the exact harm supposed to have been sustained by Mr B, Epicurus is perhaps entitled simply to make this contrary assertion. The debate will now move on to the examination of various candidates for the supposed harm. Remember that in his original argument Epicurus maintained that harms must be perceived by their subject. Clearly, Mr B is not able to recognize the fact of his condition and we might further specify that he is left psychologically unable to conceive of what has happened to him if informed by someone else. In that case, Epicurus argues, Mr B is in a state of blissful ignorance—just like that of Mr A or Mr D.

Second, Epicurus could take the option of arguing that in fact the person before the accident and the person after the accident are not identical. Sufficient psychological differences obtain to make it true that in fact Mr B was destroyed in the accident. Whoever is sitting in the hospital bed is not him.[10] This would mean that, in effect, Mr B died in the accident. If that is the case, Nagel cannot claim that Mr B has been harmed without begging the question of whether death can be a harm. Epicurus can simply maintain that since Mr B is no longer, he cannot be harmed.

---

[9] Cf. Kamm 1993, 16–17; Kaufman 1999, 2. Nagel 1979, 5, insists that discovering such a state is bad because the state is bad independently of whether it is in fact discovered. [10] Cf. Kaufman 1999, 3.

Those who wish to counter the Epicurean position must express a sense in which someone may be harmed but not recognize that they are being harmed or, since it is possible to recognize that one is experiencing something without necessarily recognizing that one is thereby being harmed, at least not recognize the harm taking place. One such account, which I will call the 'comparative account', trades on a distinction between an 'intrinsic' and 'extrinsic' harm. Intrinsic harms are those which are directly experienced by the subject. In Epicurean terms, of course, pain is the only intrinsic harm. Indeed, premise 5 of my reconstruction of the overall Epicurean argument denies that there can be any harms other than intrinsic harms. If there can be extrinsic harms, then premise 5 is false and the Epicurean argument fails.

Feldman, who introduces this distinction in order to erode the Epicurean stance, argues that when Epicurus claims that death is not bad, he must mean that death is not intrinsically bad. It cannot be directly experienced. But, Feldman argues, the Epicureans do agree that various things are extrinsically bad—for example, over-indulgence, acting unjustly, being cripplingly poor. (Feldman specifies that he is trying to object to Epicurus' argument on hedonist grounds.)[11] These are not bads *per se* but they overwhelmingly tend to produce pain and can therefore be said to be extrinsically bad.

> To maintain the validity of the argument, we would have to take the conclusion to be that being death is not *intrinsically* bad for the one who is dead. But this is no news. Most of us who think that death is bad for the one who is dead do not think that death is bad in itself. We think that death is bad for a person because of what it does to him or her; death is bad somehow indirectly because of what it does to us.
>
> Feldman 1992, 134

Feldman also recognizes that such an objection is not immediately fatal to the Epicurean account since they can argue that what Feldman calls extrinsic harms are only harms at all in so far as

---

[11] See Feldman 1992, 157: 'I have attempted to provide my answers within a fundamentally Epicurean framework'. This is a dialectically responsible principle but it is not so clear to me that Feldman takes this to mean much more than that he must assume hedonism and that there is no *post mortem* survival. 'Hedonism', however, is not a simple and unitary position—it has may variants and species. In Ch. 4 I discuss how Epicurean hedonism may be used to counter the counterfactual account of the harm of premature death.

they produce intrinsic harm—pain. Recall the contrast between Mr A and Mr D. We might say that Mr A is harmed in any sense only when he comes to know that he is being slandered or—if he never comes to recognize that he is being slandered—only in so far as the slander produces effects in his life which he can experience (such as his being passed over for promotion). It is possible to construct scenarios which either reduce any putative extrinsic harm to an intrinsic one or simply deny that the putative harm is in fact a harm at all; indeed any hedonist ethical theory will seek to do just that. Anything classified as an extrinsic evil, such as illness or poverty, is in fact an evil only because and in so far as its presence causes a loss of intrinsic good or an increase in intrinsic bad. If any so-called extrinsic evil causes neither a loss in intrinsic good nor an increase in intrinsic bad, then it should not be classified as an evil at all. In fact, this is what the Epicureans say about something like over-indulgence, which Feldman adduced as something which the Epicureans would count as an extrinsic harm. Over-indulgence is bad, on the Epicurean account, because of the pain which it tends to produce. It is only derivatively bad. Were it the case that over-indulgence did not lead to these later pains, then there would be nothing wrong in over-indulgence.[12] At least, this seems to be the conclusion suggested by considering Mr D's position, as outlined above. Something which has no effect whatsoever on the life Mr D lives is not easily seen as a harm at all. Indeed, it becomes difficult to conceive of any sort of evil which is, so to speak, 'purely extrinsic'—an evil which has no effect whatsoever on the subject's state—without it becoming question-begging whether such a thing ought to be thought of as an evil at all. If this line of argument is successful, then it seems possible to reduce all extrinsic evils to intrinsic evils. Extrinsic evils are in fact, on this view, things which reduce well-being by producing intrinsically bad effects. Had some extrinsic evil not occurred then intrinsic well-being would have been better than it in fact is. Feldman himself canvasses this argument but finds it wanting. He insists that there are genuine extrinsic evils which have no intrinsically evil effects. Extrinsic evils cannot therefore be reduced to their intrinsically evil effects.[13]

---

[12] See *KΔ* 10.   [13] Feldman 1992, 135–7.

Let us take one of Feldman's examples. He imagines that it is possible that someone born in country A might have had a better life had she been born in country B. (Perhaps the general standard of living is better in country B or country B's educational system would better suit her natural talents and she would have flourished more there.) Of course, it is also possible that the life lived in country A is not perceptibly bad nor perceptibly deficient. Nevertheless, life in country B would have been better.[14] So, having lived in country A is an extrinsic harm. The important qualification specified in the scenario is that there is no perception on the subject's part of the comparative deficiency of her life. Nevertheless, it is this comparative deficiency which is supposed to be the harm. Still, something is most clearly perceived by the subject, namely the life she is living in country A. This, we are supposed to think, has an intrinsic value. But its intrinsic value is less than the intrinsic value of the other possible life in country B. Feldman concludes that this woman has been harmed. But the extrinsic evil (her not being born in country B or her being born in country A) does not cause any intrinsic evil. Rather, the fact that she is born in country A prevents her from enjoying certain intrinsic goods which she would have enjoyed had she lived, for example, in country B. Similarly, he concludes, death is an extrinsic evil not because it causes intrinsic evils but because it prevents intrinsic goods. Hence the harm in question is constituted by the difference in intrinsic worth between the possible two lives. It is not the case that the difference between the intrinsic worth of the two lives merely reveals something that was true all along, namely that the life in fact lived (the life in country A) is a miserable one. This last point is important. It is specified that the person under consideration lives a contented life—not merely an apparently or mistakenly contented life—in order to avoid charges of question-begging and to produce a case analogous to that of death, since the real objective of the argument is to secure the claim that death can be a bad thing even for someone who

---

[14] Feldman 1992, 137–8. Honderich 2002, 8, has a table showing comparative life expectancy in various countries based on data from the World Bank, UNICEF, and the WHO. See also the discussion in Overall 2003, 7–12. McMahan 2002, 124–7, notes a number of difficulties in determining what is a normal, average, or maximum human life span for such comparative evaluative purposes.

until death lives a subjectively contented life.[15] The dialectical pressure on this argument requires it to produce examples in which the subject perceives no direct harm. Any direct harm which is perceived can be pounced upon by the Epicurean opponent, who can merely point to this perceived intrinsic harm as the true reason for thinking the subject harmed in any way at all. In the terms of Feldman's example, the Epicurean could therefore claim that the harm is constituted merely by the person's living in country A—perhaps by the discomfort felt while living this life—and that this is an intrinsic harm. The harm is not constituted merely by the fact that she could have lived in country B and that this life would have been better.

Both sides in this debate agree that death is not an intrinsic harm. To be relevantly analogous to the case of death, therefore, the subject in any such example can suffer no intrinsic harm. But given this constraint, it becomes more difficult to construct an example in which the person in question is subject to purely extrinsic harm without once again falling into question-begging. Feldman wants to avoid this by insisting that he does not want us to conclude that living in country A is in any sense miserable. Rather, he insists simply that living in country B would have been better. Another popular way of expressing the harm of death amounts to much the same thing as this comparative account. What we may call the 'counterfactual account' of the harm of death says that death is a harm in so far as it robs the deceased of goods he *would have* experienced had he died later.[16] In essence, this is just like the comparative account. Both assert that the life which was in fact lived is deficient in comparison with an alternative, in this case one in which the subject dies later and, in the intervening period between the new alternative death and the actual death, experiences some goods such that this new life is better than and preferable to the one actually lived.

These accounts must tread a fine line. They do not want to fall into the trap of including any non-relational or non-comparative intrinsic harms at any point of the analysis (hence the insistence

---

[15] Feldman 1992, 137: 'Suppose he spends four happy years at college A... He goes to his grave never realizing how much enjoyment he missed... Suppose she is reasonably satisfied, thinking that she has lived as a woman ought to live. She goes to her grave never realizing what she has missed.'

[16] See e.g. Glannon 1994, 235.

that living in country A is not itself miserable) but they want to say that nevertheless there is some harm being done through the prevention of a better life. There are the seeds here for a dilemma. On the one hand, even these theorists agree that the person in question can live a happy and fulfilling life. If so, then what sense is there in maintaining in addition that death can be for them a harm? (This is another way of saying that there is something unsatisfactory about purely extrinsic harms.) Alternatively, one might ask whether these theorists believe that their analysis ought to cause us to think about our lives differently, plan things differently, or be concerned with different things? Presumably not, since they agree that these lives—namely, the lives they want to claim are deficient—can be perfectly happy. On the other hand, if they want to say that the realization that death can be a harm should alter how we live then it seems that they have after all introduced some intrinsic harm into the analysis—namely, the cause of the concern or anxiety which would lead one to change one's life. In other words, if Feldman's imaginary woman realized that her life would be better in country B, would this not cause intrinsically harmful worry, concern, regret, and so on? If it did not—if she maintained that despite it being true that a life in country B would be better, nevertheless her life in country A is indeed a fine and fulfilled one—then there seems little substance in the claim that she is harmed by not being in country B.

Another immediate difficulty with such comparative or counter-factual accounts of the harm of death is that they threaten to prove too much since they threaten to make nearly everyone's life harmed by death. In their search to find at least one case in which death is a harm, they may have shown that all deaths are harms. It can nearly always be said that had death occurred later one might have experienced some further goods or that had certain circumstances been different one would have lived a better life. I say 'nearly everyone' and 'nearly always' since there are unfortunate cases of people whose only prospects are continued prolonged pain and suffering. There is no possibility that such people could be benefited from prolonging life. With these exceptions, is it therefore true that everyone is harmed by death? After all, it turns out that on this kind of account we may all be assailed perpetually by extrinsic harms. Given the thought that death may rob us of goods we would have experienced were we to die later, it is difficult to resist the thought that *any* death will fit this description, or at least any death except those of people who have no possibility whatsoever of any future positive experiences. Similarly, if it is possible for death to be an extrinsic harm since it means that the subject will not live an alternative life, then once again this appears to fit every person's death. It is possible that this bleak consequence is in fact the truth of the matter—everyone's death is a harm. But this is not the conclusion which the proponents of these accounts of the harm of death intend. Rather, they are trying to offer an account which allows that death can be a harm but is not always a harm, in which case they surely intend to limit the range of possible *comparanda* for the life which is in fact being led.

Clearly, the counterfactual account needs to add some notion of the limits of expectation within which it is possible to count death as a misfortune if it is to avoid the depressing conclusion that we are all, mortal as we are, destined to be harmed even if we live to a ripe old age.[17] Some such notion of the limits of expectation would be provided if it were possible to offer some description of what a complete human life might be.

The comparative account of the harm of death faces similar, if not more serious, worries since it always seems fair to say that even a happy life could have been better. If death can harm someone by making their life deficient or revealing that it is deficient in comparison with another life they could have lived had they not died then, is it also true that while alive I am harmed because my life is deficient in comparison with another possible life I could be living (whether or not I have the slightest notion of the possibility of my living that other life)? Just a little thought could conjure up a huge variety of ways in which my life could be better than it is. The comparative harm approach, if left unrestricted, invites an enormous range of other lives in comparison with which my current life is better or worse and—in consequence—by which comparisons I seem to be being harmed and benefited. The notion

---

[17] See Nagel 1979, 9–10. Kaufman 1999, 10: 'Possibility is a condition of deprivation since no one is deprived of impossible things'. It then remains to be specified what the limits of possibility are in this case. Cf. Suits 2001, 72: 'To be deprived is to fail to get good things that were in some sense expected. It is akin to being defrauded or cheated'. A similar view is proposed by Feit 2002. McMahan 2002, 133–5, discusses what he dubs a 'Realism Condition' for such comparisons.

of harm and benefit now appears to have been stretched too far to be very intelligible or instructive.[18] In comparison, Epicurus' conception of harm, while certainly narrow, is at least clear and can function as a clear guide to decision-making.[19]

There are therefore two sorts of difficulties with this kind of account. First, there are some indeterminacies and unclarities internal to the account which threaten unwanted and unpalatable consequences, such as the conclusion that every life is comparatively harmed because there are innumerable other better lives which could have been led. Second, this account of the harm of death does not seem to have a great deal of force in persuading a staunch sceptic such as Epicurus that death is in fact a harm at all. It does not address directly the central claim of the Epicurean argument that the only harms are perceived harms—specifically pains—other than by constructing scenarios designed to draw from us the intuition that one can be harmed but not realize it. Whether or not that intuition itself is correct is not addressed.

Lucretius and the 'deprivation' of death

In the course of his assault on the fear of death Lucretius offers a picture of someone who thinks that death is a deprivation. These lines, in the form of an address to the deceased, list all the things he might be thought to 'miss out' on and also produce a new riposte. Let us first consider the sort of deprivations which the bystanders at the deceased's funeral are thought to have in mind.[20]

---

[18] See Donnelly 1994, 154; Draper 1999; Suits 2001, esp. 70–77. McMahan 1988, 40–56, and at much greater length in 2002, 98–188, provides a detailed discussion of the problems faced by any such comparative account.

[19] Glannon 1994, 239 and 242, therefore argues that even if it is allowed that death is an extrinsic harm along the lines proposed by Feldman, this should make no difference to our rational planning for our continuing lives nor does it show that it is rational to fear such a harm. Kaufman 1999, 4 responds that such a restriction on what it is rational to care about is too narrow. It would seem to prevent someone caring at all about events which are necessarily *post mortem*. I argue that this is in fact a consequence of the Epicurean position when I discuss Epicurus' will in Ch. 5 below.

[20] West 1969, 28–9, rightly rejects the possibility of using such lines as these as signs of lingering anti-Epicureanism in Lucretius' mind: 'Surely these pathetic rhetorical figures and astonishing rhythms are meant as sarcastic caricatures of the mawkish clichés used by such *stulti* and *barbari*.' Also on this passage see

'iam iam non domus accipiet te laeta neque uxor
optima, nec dulces occurrent oscula nati
praeripere et tacita pectus dulcedine tangent.
non poteris factis florentibus esse, tuisque
praesidium. misero misere', aiunt, 'omnia ademit
una dies infesta tibi tot praemia vitae'.

They say, 'Never again will a happy house or wonderful wife welcome you, nor will your children rush to steal kisses and touch your heart with deep joy. No longer will you be able to enjoy prosperity and look after your household. Poor, poor man. A single hateful day has stolen away all your many rewards of life.'

DRN 3.894–9

There is a marked concentration on the joys of a happy home life, which death is supposed to steal away.[21] This is not accidental. Whereas some may bemoan death since it puts paid to high ambitions, political or military promise, here Lucretius considers people whose values are not so far removed from proper Epicurean concerns in order to show that even those things which an Epicurean can consider to be goods during life are not things of which the deceased is deprived. The mourners correctly identify certain goods but incorrectly persist in thinking that death curtails their enjoyment. Indeed, in their expression, death robs (*ademit*) this person of the rewards of life (*praemia vitae*), emphasizing that these are goods which belonged to him and to which he should be entitled. Should that cause concern? Not at all, Lucretius explains.

illud in his rebus non addunt: 'nec tibi earum
iam desiderium rerum super insidet una'.
quod bene si videant animo dictisque sequantur,
dissolvant animi magno se angore metuque.

But they do not add: 'Nor do you have any remaining desire for those things in addition'. If they were to see this in their minds and be consistent with it in what they say then they would free themselves from much mental anguish and fear.

DRN 3.900–3

Reinhardt 2002, 293–4, who argues that Lucretius moves from focusing on one's own death to that of another in order to obfuscate the difference between fearing being dead and fearing premature death. In Reinhardt's opinion, Lucretius tackles this latter fear by using arguments pertinent only to the former.

[21] One might compare Hector's address to Andromache at Hom. *Il.* 6.441–65.

Lucretius simply asserts that the deceased will not be deprived of these goods since after death he will have no desire for them. It is certainly not the case that the deceased will 'miss' seeing his home and family. So he is not to be pitied.[22]

To be deprived of something, Lucretius implies, one must possess a desire, presumably a desire that is not or is no longer satisfied. Deprivation, in other words, is analysed as a loss; one must originally possess some object of desire and then lose it, retaining the desire. But, in the case of death, the desire disappears along with its possessor. There simply is no longer any desire, fulfilled or otherwise, and so it makes no sense to say of the deceased that, for example, he is being deprived of the love of his family. It is just about acceptable to say that Marcus, for example, will no longer enjoy the love of his family (provided we understand this to be mere shorthand and do not mistakenly allow ourselves to think that Marcus persists in any way at all). But it is certainly not true to say that Marcus will *miss* the love of his family.

Lucretius' riposte might appear to turn on the Epicureans' staunch insistence that all harms and goods must be perceived, precisely the aspect of their thought questioned by Nagel's example of the unknowing slandered man or the comatose accident victim (Mr A and Mr B). On Epicurus' account, what matters to a person is what they can perceive, and this can ultimately be analysed in terms of pleasure and pain. To an extent this notion is shared by Lucretius' mourners. After all, when the mourners give their account of what Marcus will no longer have, they stress the pleasure he used to take in his family, and it is certainly true that Lucretius will think that Marcus cannot be said to *perceive* any loss. But just as the argument to establish that 'death is nothing to us' has two aspects—one which stresses the absence of perceived harms during death and another which stresses the bare absence of any subject of harm—so too this account of what is wrong with thinking that the dead are deprived of something may be cast in two ways. In the second reading of the argument, Lucretius insists here merely on the weaker thesis that a person's well-being should be measured in terms of the level of fulfilment of that person's desires. This need not be a subjectivist account. Someone's desire may be fulfilled although they

---

[22] The correct Epicurean attitude to another's death is the subject of pp. 39–41.

themselves do not recognize it; similarly someone might think that their desires are fulfilled when in fact they are not. In death, however, the situation is clear: there is no person, so there are no desires, so there can be no unfulfilled desires. The question of whether the deceased can recognize the loss is entirely secondary. There is no loss to perceive. And there is no one to perceive a loss. Only from the perspective of one of the mourners might it be possible to think of the person's unfulfilled desires, but then only by mistakenly considering the person still to exist in some sense.[23] Note Lucretius' emphasis of the lingering identification in these mourners' minds of the corpse with the deceased. Strictly speaking, they should not be able to use the second-person form of address but they nevertheless persist in such expressions.[24] If they were more scrupulous about this perhaps they would be less inclined to identify any form of deprivation here.

There is an alternative account which would be able to see the absence of joys of life such as the happy home life depicted here as something which death causes and which can be noted as a lack. Aristotle, for example, is prepared to entertain the possibility that one's well-being (*eudaimonia*) can be adversely affected after death even though he agrees with the Epicureans that there is no *post mortem* survival. The main tactic for this sort of position is to detach the person's desires from their continued existence so that a desire can be fulfilled or unfulfilled even if the person himself no longer is alive. Some make a distinction between a desire or interest being fulfilled and its being satisfied; a desire is satisfied only if it is believed by the possessor of the desire to have been fulfilled.[25] This detaches the fulfilment of desires from the desirer's perception of their fulfilment and is one step towards

---

[23] But cf. Cockburn 1990, 188: 'Of course, there are those who say that the attitude which we characteristically have towards the dead body of a loved one is simply an emotional hangover: an expression of how we, understandably, *feel* rather than of a *recognition* of what we are confronted with. Reason needs to be given, however, for thinking that matters *must* be viewed in this way.'

[24] This is a mistake to which they are prone throughout this section, even when they take a more positive attitude to death. Cf. 3.904–5: *tu quidem ut es leto sopitus, sic eris aevi | quod superest cunctis privatu' doloribus aegris* ('You indeed, as you are now asleep in death, so you will be for all remaining time, free from all bitter pains').

[25] See Ross 1939, 300. Cf. Feinberg 1984, 84.

arguing that there can be a value to the desirer also in the fulfilment, not only the satisfaction, of these desires. To be sure, there is something quite strange about disembodied desires, so such theories tend to concentrate not on desires but 'interests'. Their account can then proceed by identifying well-being with the promotion of certain interests—the well-being of one's family, for instance—and then by saying that such interests can prosper or not, be fulfilled or not, even in the absence of the original holder of those interests. Certainly these interests cannot be said to die with the subject quite so easily as the subject's desires.

In lines 909–11 Lucretius turns to offer an *ad hominem* argument against one of the mourners who addresses the deceased as 'lulled to sleep by death' (*leto sopitus*, 904). This mourner, at least, is more accurate in his assessment of the deceased's well-being since he accepts that death brings about an absence of all evils (905).²⁶ But in that case, Lucretius asks, what sense is there in mourning the deceased since death on this account is like sleep, which is more likely to be a quiet rest than torment. This possibility had, of course, been canvassed by Socrates in the *Apology* (40c10–e4) and similarly found to reveal death to be not harmful.²⁷ Indeed, a long—in fact, everlasting—sleep might even appeal. The argument here is that even if the deceased is agreed to survive death, if death is a kind of sleep as popularly conceived, then it is still not something which we should fear nor something which should cause us to feel sorrow when it comes to others. At 912–30 the analogy between death and sleep is pursued, but now turned into an *a fortiori* argument based on the idea that death is like sleep in being a dispersal of the constituent atoms of the soul. In death, the dispersal is much larger and is irreversible.²⁸ If, as is the case, during sleep

---

²⁶ See Segal 1990, 69–70.

²⁷ For a recent reading of this section of the *Apology* see Rudebusch 1999, 65–79. Cf. Nagel 1986, 226, who insists that the prospect of complete unconsciousness is quite different from the prospect of death: 'Unconsciousness includes the continued possibility of experience, and therefore doesn't obliterate the here and now as death does.'

²⁸ Contrast 3.112–16, where Lucretius argues against the harmony theory of the soul by showing that the soul may continue to function and move even when the body's constitution is static. During sleep, he argues, we may continue to be

people feel no pain nor are they racked with thoughts of unfulfilled wants, so much the less will they feel pain and anxiety in death.

By using these two examples of confused mourners, Lucretius successfully shows that if either of two conditions are met, it is wrong to think of death as a harm and feel sorrow for the dead. First, if death is agreed to be the end of the person's existence then death cannot be a harm. Second, if death is agreed to be the absence of sensation (like sleep) then death cannot be a harm. Not surprisingly, these two mourners therefore offer Lucretius the opportunity to rehearse the two major supports for the Epicurean arguments that death is nothing to us. They also, more interestingly, allow him to show that these two arguments can be seen as independent. At least, the Epicureans could even if necessary grant that there is some sort of *post mortem* survival but still conclude that death is not to be feared.[29] Further, these examples allow Lucretius to show that, contrary to expectation, elements of the apparently revisionary Epicurean point of view can be found, albeit in a confused and implicit manner, in the common opinions that death is the absolute end of the person and that death is an absence of sensation.

We can supplement these Epicurean pictures of incorrect or confused attitudes to the death of a friend with an account of the correct attitude. Commemoration of the dead was acceptable and could even be beneficial, provided it was always remembered that such practices had no effect whatsoever on the deceased. (We might here compare the Epicurean attitude to religious practices generally. Epicureans could participate in religious events, and might even benefit from them, provided it was always remembered that the gods themselves had no interest in and were not affected by such practices.) The Epicurean Carneiscus' work, *Philista*, named after a dead friend, the second book of which is partially preserved on *PHerc.* 1027, appears to have offered some

---

assailed by joys and cares. The explanation of sleep at 4.907–53 stresses once again its soothing effect. For the idea that sleep is like death see also Herac. B26 DK, Leucipp. A34 DK (Aëtius 5.25.3).

[29] Lucretius also uses the tactic of granting a premise to his opponent but nevertheless securing his desired conclusion at *DRN* 3.843–6: even if the soul continues to perceive after it has left the body, this is no concern to us since we are a combination of body and soul.

recommendations during its polemic against the Peripatetic Praxiphanes' view of friendship.[30] More extensive evidence comes from Plutarch's *Non posse*. At 1101A–B Aristodemus begins his objection that the Epicureans, in removing any fear of the gods, also remove the possibility of humans receiving any pleasure from religious practice since they expect neither benefit nor harm from them. He likens their position on this matter to that of the mourning of friends, but notes that in this latter case the Epicureans do allow some grief since not to do so would be the sign of a much worse position, that of being entirely without emotion (τὸ ἀπαθές). Not to grieve at all at a friend's death is the sign of a cruel disposition (ὠμότης) and an irrational concern for winning a reputation (δοξοκοπία). Aristodemus refers to letters written by Epicurus on the death of one Hegesianax to the father and brother of the deceased as evidence of the Epicureans' recognizing that grief is a natural emotion.

Certainly, the Epicureans placed a great deal of significance on the ties of friendship between fellow followers of Epicurus' teaching and here the grief at the loss of some such friend seems to be caused by the loss of such a valuable tie. However, such grief as the Epicureans do allow is certainly compatible with their view that the dead are not themselves to be pitied. What pain there is at such a loss is most certainly the pain felt by those still alive at the new absence in their lives.[31] It is also clear that Epicurus stressed the pleasure the living might receive in remembering deceased friends, and prominent deceased Epicureans were commemorated with monthly and annual feasts in the Epicurean garden.[32] Once again, the emphasis is on the life and feelings of those still living. The lives and achievements of the

---

[30] See Capasso 1988 for text and commentary. See also Philodemus *Epig.* 29 Sider (*AP* 9.412) with Sider's commentary ad loc.

[31] Compare the discussion of grief in Nussbaum 2001, 19–88, as part of her 'neo-Stoic' conception of emotions as value judgements. She insists, rightly, that even if grief is essentially a value judgement, it is not merely—and perhaps not at all—a judgement about some harm that has affected the now deceased. Rather, it is a judgement about the value of the loss of the deceased from one's life. See Cockburn 1990, 155–8, for a further illuminating discussion of grief.

[32] Plut. *Non Posse* 1105E: ἡδὺ πανταχόθεν ἡ φίλου μνήμη τεθνηκότος ('The recollection of a dead friend is pleasant in every way'). Cf. Clay 1986. Sen. *Ep. Mor.* 99.25 includes a piece of advice from Metrodorus which claims that there is

dead were models which the living might use as they might also use the paradigmatic tranquillity of the gods as a model for their own progress towards the perfect life.[33] But never is it suggested that the deceased themselves are benefited or harmed by the attitude of those who survive them.

Locating the time of the harm of death

Now let us turn to the second major Epicurean argument against the possibility of death being a harm. Death cannot be a harm, this argument concludes, since there is no subject for which it could be a harm. Death itself removes any possible subject for harm since death is the destruction of the individual who dies. We might offer the argument as follows:

	1.	Death is nothing to us.
since	2.	Death is the dissolution of the soul.
and	3.	A person is a combination of soul and body.
therefore (by 2 and 3)	4.	Death is the destruction of the person.
and therefore	5.	When death is present, the person is not.
	6.	For X to be a bad for a person, the person must exist at the time of X.[34]

a certain pleasure to be found even in mourning a loved one. Margalit 2002, 91–4, suggests that the expectation of being remembered after death is partly constitutive of certain 'thick' relationships such as friendship.

[33] *Sent. Vat.* 32, 66: ΚΔ 40: ὅσοι τὴν δύναμιν ἔσχον τοῦ τὸ θαρρεῖν μάλιστα ἐκ τῶν ὁμορούντων παρασκευάσασθαι, οὗτοι καὶ ἐβίωσαν μετ᾽ ἀλλήλων ἥδιστα τὸ βεβαιότατον πίστωμα ἔχοντες, καὶ πληρεστάτην οἰκειότητα ἀπολαβόντες οὐκ ὠδύραντο ὡς πρὸς ἔλεον τὴν τοῦ τελευτήσαντος προκαταστροφήν ('All those who had the ability to take special precautions against enemies both lived most pleasantly with one another, in the most sure confidence, and also enjoyed the fullest intimacy such that they did not mourn as pitiful someone's dying before them'). Cf. Lucr. *DRN* 6.68–79 and Warren 2000b, 257–60.

[34] See Lucr. *DRN* 3.862–4 (following the line numbering after Lachmann's transposition).

Notice that put in this way there is no need for the Epicureans to rely on their notion that there are only perceived benefits or harms. Premise 6 makes no reference to whether the person perceives the harm. Rather, it merely requires that the person and the supposed harm must coincide temporally. This condition is certainly met by Nagel's example of the unperceived betrayal (Mr A), and perhaps by the example of the road accident victim (Mr B). However, it seems unlikely that it is met by the case we are really interested in, that of a person who dies (Mr C).[35] Also, this Epicurean argument will have to be answered by any theory which accepts premises 5 and 6. There is no need for premise 5 to be generated by the peculiarly Epicurean premises 2 and 3.

There are two possible points of attack for anyone wishing to resist this argument. First, it is possible to question the notions of death in 2 and of the person contained in 3 in such a way that death turns out not to be the destruction of the person. What we might term the Platonic account, for example, would deny 2 and redefine death as the separation of the soul from the body. In addition, it might identify the person—or the 'real self'— with the soul alone. In that sense, therefore, the real self can survive death.[36]

But let us grant to the Epicureans some account of the nature of death and personal identity which does yield 5: we do not survive death in any sense. Death is the destruction of the individual. This, at least, is a principle shared by the vast majority of modern critics of the Epicurean argument, who nevertheless wish to resist the Epicurean conclusion. In that case, attention must focus on the second possible area of assault, namely 6—the principle which asserts that for anything to be a harm it must be contemporaneous with the subject of that harm. The Epicureans argue that if this principle is true then since death can never be contemporaneous with the purported subject of its harm then death can never be a harm.[37] (But a person's death can obviously be a harm for others, namely those who survive the deceased.)

[35] Cf. Mitsis 2002, 17.

[36] For a discussion of such a Platonic view with reference to the prohibition of suicide in the *Phaedo* see Warren 2001c. See also ps. Pl. *Axioch.* 370c–d.

[37] *Ep. Men.* 125. This argument is attributed to Prodicus by ps. Pl. *Axioch.* 369b–c. Compare also the argument attributed to Diogenes at

I should begin with some preliminary attempts at clarification. 'Death', as we know, is an ambiguous word. Does it refer in this argument to the process of dying, the instant of ceasing to live, or the period after one's life has ended? Not the first, I think, since it is clearly the case that when dying—when passing from being alive to being dead—it is at least possible to argue that the subject still retains some life and some existence. If dying is a protracted process then it occurs at a period at the end of a life. The end of the process of dying is identical with the last moment of life, and therefore one is still alive while dying.[38] The second and third possible meanings of 'death' here are both possible. The third, however, namely 'death' meaning the period of time after life has ceased, would give the most plausible sense to the argument. It is true by definition that death in this sense is never contemporaneous with the person's life, whereas it is at least arguable that 'death' in the sense of the instant which divides a person's life from a period in which it is true to say he is no longer alive, ought to be considered contemporaneous with the very end of a life.[39]

It might be argued that there are clearly harms not contemporaneous with the subject of the harm. A baby, for example, may rightly be said to have been harmed by environmental factors which affected the health of its mother prior to conception or prior to its birth. Similarly, it is often claimed that we are harming future generations by our current burning of large quantities of hydrocarbon-based fuels. In both these cases the cause of the harm and its victim are not contemporaneous. Are they, therefore, counterexamples to the Epicurean principle offered in 6 above? Perhaps not, since in both cases it might plausibly be claimed that the specific cause of the harm is not the earlier event itself, but rather the persisting effects of that event (the mother's altered constitution, the adversely affected climate), which are in fact contemporaneous with the supposed victims. Such examples, at least, would not worry the Epicurean particularly since in any

---

D.L. 6.68: ἐρωτηθεὶς εἰ κακὸν ὁ θάνατος, 'πῶς,' εἶπε, 'κακός, οὗ παρόντος οὐκ αἰσθανόμεθα;' ('Asked if death is an evil, he said, "How can it be evil which we do not perceive when it is present?"')

[38] For the Epicureans' engagement with their atomist predecessor Democritus' discussions of the nature of the process of dying see Warren 2002a.

[39] See Van Evra 1971.

case they are dealing with harms which precede their victims—
and death most certainly is not that kind of harm.

Before passing to some more sophisticated discussions of the
problem, let us pause to consider one ancient reaction. Cicero's
first *Tusculan Disputation* contains an argument which tries to
counter the Epicurean position by claiming that rather than the
non-existence of the dead being an obstacle to viewing death as a
harm, it is precisely the fact that the dead do not exist—more
precisely, the fact that they no longer exist—which constitutes
the harm of death. The character sometimes designated in the
manuscripts as A. is trying to sustain the thesis that death is an
evil (1.9).[40] However, he is quite clear in his insistence that the
dead do not exist. In fact, he makes clear that this is what he
considers the evil of death to be—the fact of non-existence—or
rather, since when prompted by M. he recognizes that those yet
to be born are not *ipso facto* subject to the same evil (1.13),[41] the
evil of death is non-existence when one has previously existed:

A. immo, quia non sint, cum fuerint, eo miseros esse.

No. I say that they [the dead] are miserable for this reason: because they
are not, although they have been.

Cic. *Tusc.* 1.13

This account may be thought a close relative of the deprivation
account since it points to some loss as the evil of death. However,
it points specifically to the loss of existence itself rather than to
the loss of some goods or the opportunities for achieving some
goods. Of course, existence is a necessary condition for the
enjoyment of goods and indeed for the possession of the
opportunity to achieve some goods, but that is not A.'s meaning
here. Rather, the bare fact of *no longer* existing is what makes the
dead wretched.[42] This is a complete reversal of the Epicurean
argument. For the Epicureans death cannot be a harm precisely

---

[40] I retain the designation of the speakers as M. and A. merely as a
convenience. It is unlikely that they appeared designated as such in the original
versions of the *Tusc.* They appear only sporadically in the surviving MSS.

[41] So A. denies the Epicurean 'symmetry principle' which I will explore in
Ch. 3.

[42] Kamm 1993, 19, extracts something more interesting from the 'nothingness'
thesis: 'I believe a basic criticism of the Deprivation Account of why death is
bad lies buried in the "nothingness" thesis, insofar as it implies that death is bad

because death is the non-existence of the purported subject of
the harm. For A., death is a harm precisely because death is the
non-existence of a previously existing subject.

In Cicero's text, A.'s position is swiftly rubbished by his inter-
locutor, M. M. presses the obvious objection that A. is committed
to a self-contradiction, saying both that the dead are, for they 'are'
wretched and also that they are not, for they 'are no longer'.[43]
A. tries to wriggle out of this simply by dropping the verb 'to be'
from his formulation, no longer saying the dead *are* wretched,
but merely saying 'wretched',[44] but this is a doomed effort.
M. insists that he must assert something of the dead which can be
true or false and this requires him to reintroduce the offending
verb. A. then concedes defeat, accepting the principle that those
who are wretched must at least exist (*extorsisti ut faterer qui
omnino non essent, eos ne miseros quidem esse posse*) and moves
on to a fall-back position: we, the living, are wretched since we
are mortal (1.14).

A.'s new thesis that mortality, or 'the fact of future death', is
something which ought to cause concern is an example of a
concern which Epicurus addresses through other considerations
which I will canvass below.[45] For now, it is worth noting how
difficult it is to phrase the first thesis, namely that the loss of
existence is itself an evil, without falling into A.'s tangle of self-
contradiction. To talk of the 'loss' of existence is potentially
misleading since one might suppose, as the Epicureans do, that
to lose something one must at some time have that something
and then at a later time not have it. But this is to allow the subject
to persist *through* the loss—and A.'s proposed loss, of existence
itself, rules out there being any such persistent subject. Had A.
not previously rejected the idea that non-existence itself is an evil,
then he would not have become tangled in the difficulties of

because it means everything for oneself is *all over*. Since we could prefer to
postpone things being all over, even if this did not increase the total amount of
goods in our life, we must be trying to avoid something about death other than
that it diminishes the amount of goods of life we have.' She pursues this thought
in Kamm 1993, 49–54.

[43] Cic. *Tusc.* 1.13: M. *pugnantia te loqui non vides?* ('Don't you see that you
are saying incompatible things?').

[44] This manoeuvre is not possible in English, but Latin would often drop the
verb 'to be' from such accusative and infinitive constructions as used by A. here.

[45] See p. 124.

expressing his position in terms of a loss: non-existence would be an evil whether that non-existence is pre-natal or *post mortem.* But this extreme position entails that those yet to be born are harmed by not yet being born, a thought which it is indeed hard to find plausible. (If it is accepted it rapidly provokes further difficult questions. Are we obliged to help the not-yet-alive by rushing them into existence as quickly as possible?)

We are therefore left with the need to offer a formulation of A.'s view which avoids the pitfalls associated with expressing it in terms of a loss. At best, talk of the 'loss' of existence can be only elliptical or metaphorical and we ought to be able to offer the same thought in a more precise manner if we are to escape M.'s accusation that such thinking is simply confused. One way to achieve this is simply to reinterpret the 'loss of existence' in terms which make it an equivalent of the counterfactual account of the harm of death. The subject 'loses existence' in the sense that by dying when he does he will not enjoy the life he would have lived had he died later.[46]

A.'s strange thesis, therefore, can either be dismissed as non-sensical or reinterpreted as a further example of an already familiar alternative position to the Epicurean account. On either alternative, the Epicurean can move on to press the following question to anyone wishing to argue that death is a harm. If death is a harm, when does this harm occur? All possible responses to the question are then dismissed. There are a number of possible replies.

   a. Death is a harm before the person dies.
   b. Death is a harm at the instant of death.
   c. Death is a harm after the person has died.
   d. Death is eternally a harm for the person who dies.
   e. Death is a harm for the person who dies but 'at no definite time'.

---

[46] So, Quinn 2001, 77 n. 19, in the course of arguing that abortion can be an extrinsic harm to the aborted foetus: 'It is clear ... that those who with me speak of "loss" of life through, for example, accident or illness mean to call attention to the difference for the worse from the point of view of the subject that the accident or illness makes by causing it to be true that he will not have the life he would otherwise have had, and do not mean to imply that the subject will subsist in some existentially deprived state. Since it seems perfectly intelligible, it is perhaps not important to establish whether this usage constitutes a metaphor or an ordinary sense.'

Is it not obvious, asks the Epicurean, that death cannot harm a person before death? For the person has not yet died, and what kind of harm is it that can precede its cause? Also, death cannot harm someone after he has died, since there is no person after death and therefore no potential subject for harm. It is not so easy to construct an account of why death cannot be a harm at the instant of ceasing to live, but it is possible that the Epicureans would question what sense can be given to something being an instantaneous harm, a harm of no duration.[47] Remember that this account does not claim that the harm occurs instantly, rather that it is present only for an instant (since at the very next instant the argument against possibility c becomes relevant and at the very preceding instant that against argument a is still relevant).

Along with the famous 'Symmetry Argument', the subject of Chapter 3 below, the Epicurean dilemma about the non-existence of any subject for which death can be a harm has exercised a large number of modern critics. The large body of literature which has grown up in the discussion of this question provides a wide array of possible responses and also subjects each of the other options to intense scrutiny. I do not wish to repeat here the content of all of these discussions, but will instead offer examples of the major options in the debate and attempt to show whether in fact they have much force against the Epicurean position.[48]

Nagel is attracted to option e. Death is a harm for the person who dies, but it is not a harm which occurs at some particular time.[49] We should not, he says, be overly concerned by Epicurus' challenge to offer a temporal location for the harm of death. Attempting to answer Epicurus' challenge unnecessarily forces

---

[47] Levenbook 1984, 410–17, offers a defence that death can be a harm at the moment of death and that, if this first possibility is allowed, there may also be harm after the moment of death.

[48] The Epicurean concerns may be part of a larger ancient debate on causation in general. SE *PH* 3.25–8 and *M* 9.232–6 offer an argument that causes can neither precede, nor be simultaneous with, nor follow their effects. See Barnes 1983, esp. 180–2. Compare also Diog. Oin. 33.V–VIII.6 where he argues that causes may indeed precede, coincide with, or follow their effects. Cf. Sedley 2002.

[49] Nagel 1979, 6–7. Compare the interpretations of Nagel's claim in Silverstein 1980, 415–17; Lamont 1998; and Grey 1999. Grey seems to me to be correct.

us into regarding the harm of death as a non-relational harm, whereas it is instead one of the goods and harms which are 'irreducibly relational; they are features of the relations between a person, with spatial and temporal boundaries of the usual sort, and circumstances which may not coincide with him either in space or in time.'[50] We have already seen how Nagel tries to convince us of the existence of such harms, and that the Epicurean response might be simply to reject them. Again, there is something of a stalemate. Nagel asserts that there are irreducibly relational harms and that therefore there is no need to locate them temporally and spatially, or at least no reason to demand that their location should coincide with that of the subject of the harm. Epicurus, on the other hand, rejects such harms and therefore can press his demand for an account of when death could be a non-relational harm.

Feldman emphasizes another of Nagel's suggestions, that death is a comparative harm. For Feldman, then, the question of when death can harm its victim is best answered by option d. Death is eternally a harm, since the harm of death on his account is 'a complex fact about the relative values of two possible lives'.[51] In so far as Feldman's account also relies on relational and comparative harms it too generates the same dialectical stalemate as Nagel's.[52]

Other commentators have at least tried to locate the harm of death at a time contemporaneous with the subject of the harm, sharing to this degree at least what is a premise of the Epicurean argument (premise 6, above p. 41). Since they also agree that death is the total destruction of the subject, the most plausible remaining option is a: death is a harm before the person dies or, in other words, death harms the *ante mortem* person. Clearly, the danger for this view is that it locates temporally the effect of the harm before the cause of the harm. It threatens to allow

---

[50] Nagel 1979, 6.   [51] Feldman 1992, 154.

[52] For further discussion and criticism of Feldman's position see Mitsis 1996, 811–12; Lamont 1998, 199–202; Feit 2002, 362–5; McMahan 2002, 98–185. Feit proposes a version of c: death is a harm after death but stops being a harm once it stops depriving the deceased of goods he would have enjoyed had he lived longer. (So death is no longer a harm one thousand years after a person's death. The deceased could not have lived that long.)

retrospective causation. But the causation in question may be innocuous. Death at a particular time can, on this account, make it true that the subject's life was harmed, either by making it true that certain interests were defeated or by making it true that his life was comparatively worse than it otherwise could have been.[53] It is, of course, possible to say that in fact it had always been true that the subject's life would be harmed, the truth-value of the statement 'X's interests will be thwarted by the manner of his death' was always true throughout X's life; its truth-maker is the fact of X dying in the manner he does. X's death merely *reveals* it to have been true. Therefore there is no need to worry either that there is something peculiar about a later event causing something earlier to have been true. Nor should we worry that it always having been the true that 'X's interests will be thwarted by the manner of his death' somehow ushers in a kind of determinism.[54] The argument from the bivalence of propositions of all tenses to a kind of determinism was, of course, familiar in antiquity since at least Aristotle's famous discussion of 'tomorrow's sea battle' in *De Interpretatione* 9. In the Hellenistic period, in particular, it was the cause of considerable debate.[55] To avoid what he thought were determinist consequences, Epicurus himself seems to have taken the view that it is not necessary that one of a pair of contradictory contingent future-tensed propositions is true and the other false.[56] On this view, once X's manner of death is clear it will be possible to say truly that 'X's interests were thwarted by his death' but it will not be possible to claim without contradiction in retrospect that 'it *was* true that X's interests *would be* thwarted by his death' since it has already been agreed that back then it was not true that X's interests would be

---

[53] See e.g. Feinberg 1984, 90–2, and Pitcher 1984. This view is also discussed by Donnelly 1994, 154–9, and Lamont 1998, 202–5.

[54] Cf. Lamont 1998, 203–4, and Grey 1999.

[55] For a good introduction see Frede 1990. Carneades seems to have been clear-headed on this matter: see Cic. *Fat.* 19–20 and compare Ryle 1954. The denial of bivalence to some future-tensed propositions is not a particularly fashionable view now and particularly not among those who hold a tenseless or B-series view of time. It is, however, defended by Tooley 1997, 309–17.

[56] For the evidence for this view see Cic. *Acad.* 2.97, *Nat. Deorum* 1.70, *Fat.* 37. The example in each case is *aut vivet cras aut non* ('Either he will be alive tomorrow or not') where the subject is either Epicurus or Hermarchus.

thwarted.[57] So at no time during X's life is it possible to say truly that his life *will be* harmed by his death.[58]

There is no evidence that the Epicureans ever produced an argument to show that there is no time at which death could harm a living subject on the basis of their view of the truth-value of contingent future-tensed propositions. Even so, that logical doctrine would provide a further reason for Epicurus to be reluctant to accept any account of the harm of death being visited from the future on the still living person. Once again, this account of the timing of the harm of death also relies upon the counterfactual or comparative account of the nature of the harm of death.

At this point we should turn to perhaps the most fertile ancient discussion of the possibility of harming the dead, which is found in Aristotle's *Nicomachean Ethics* 1.10–11.[59] At first glance, Aristotle appears to defend a version of option c: death is or at least can be a harm after the person has died. But it would be surprising if this were in fact Aristotle's view, since he appears to share two important beliefs with Epicurus. First, the dead can have no consciousness of *post mortem* events. Second, death is the end of the person; there is no kind of personal *post mortem* survival.[60] The first belief is not as significant for Aristotle's own ethical view as it is for Epicurus, since Aristotle does not restrict what can affect one's well-being to what one perceives. The second belief, however, is all that is needed to generate the problem of locating the time of the harm of death.

[57] See also Bobzien 1998, 82–3; Ferrari 2000. If every death is *ipso facto* harmful then it will always be true that 'X will be harmed by his death', but this will no longer be a merely contingent future-tensed proposition.

[58] Plut. *Pyth. Orac.* 399A has the Epicurean Boethus claim that a contingent future proposition is now false, even if events should turn out in the future just as it describes. This relies on the notion of temporally relativized truth-values. So there is no contradiction if at t^1 (before A's death) it is not true that 'A will be harmed by death' (it is false or merely 'indeterminate'—this being a further, third, truth-value), whereas at t^2 (after A's death) it is true that 'A was harmed by his death'. For a defence of this approach see Tooley 1997, 125–56.

[59] For discussion, see Solomon 1976, Prizl 1983, Gooch 1983, Scott 2000.

[60] Aristotle allows that 'active *nous*' is immortal (*DA* 430^{a}22–5) and, at *NE* 1177^{b}26–1178^{a}8, that the life of contemplation, a life in accordance with *nous* (1177^{a}6–7) allows a person to become immortal 'in so far as it is possible for a human' (1177^{b}33). Cf. Sedley 1997, 335–9. This notion is entirely absent from his discussion of the possibility of *post mortem* harm in *NE* 1.10–11.

Aristotle repeatedly talks about posthumous events affecting the dead, which *prima facie* suggests that the time at which the harm is supposed to occur is *post mortem*,[61] and accepts that it would be difficult to reject this thought completely (1100ª29–30, 1101ª22–4). But he recognizes that this particular common view appears to conflict with the view that well-being, *eudaimonia*, should be something stable (1100ª27–9). It also conflicts with his view that well-being consists in virtuous activity, something which the dead are not able to do. Part of his solution is that although posthumous events can affect a person, they will not affect their *eudaimonia*; no one who was *eudaimōn* will be prevented from being so by posthumous events, nor will anyone achieve *eudaimonia* posthumously (1101ᵇ1–5: but notice that this is still hypothetical: 'If there is any affect, then it will not remove or produce *eudaimonia*'). The particular question at hand is whether Aristotle wishes to locate the time of such, admittedly small, effects before or after the person's death. There are good reasons for thinking he could not, whether or not this is contrary to the way in which he presents the common view of the matter, think that the time of these harms is in fact *post mortem*. It makes no sense in Aristotle's view to consider the well-being of the dead. The dead are no longer; they are engaging in none of the activities which would constitute well- or ill-being. Even if we accept the suggestion that Aristotle in 1.11 is asking not whether a person's *eudaimonia* can be affected, but whether *a person* can be affected after their death, there still seem to be difficulties in locating the time of the harm after death.[62] In what sense can Aristotle argue that there is a person to be harmed after death, let alone a *eudaimōn* person?

One answer is that in fact Aristotle intends no such thing, but is instead offering a close relative of one of the more recent favoured accounts of when death can be a harm, namely option c. On this view, Aristotle in fact believes that since a person's actions when alive can have long-lasting effects, effects which may be located after the person's death, and since a person's well-being depends in part on the success of those actions, then

---

[61] e.g. 1100ª19–20, where he claims that this is like unperceived harms which affect the living (much like Nagel's analogies); 1100ª22–7.

[62] Cf. Scott 2000, 218–20.

how a person's descendants fare, for example, finally determines in the fullness of time the value of the person's life. So it becomes true that Priam's life, for example, was not so successful as it initially seemed, once the fate of his various descendants is settled. Let us distinguish this view from a close relative. This related view would not say that only after the descendants' fate is settled does it become true that Priam's life was successful, say, but rather that the fact that the descendants fared as they did is the reason why it was true all along that Priam's life was successful. In the first view, while Priam is alive it is simply neither true nor false that his life is a success; that will not be settled until later. In the second, related view, it is already true that Priam's life is a success, even while he is living it, but that truth is not evident until the descendants' fate is also known. This second view, therefore, is a version of option d: Priam's death is eternally a harm for him. How are we to decide between these two options as possible interpretations of Aristotle's view?[63]

Both interpretations avoid assigning to Aristotle any un-Aristotelian sounding notions about personal *post mortem* survival or the like. However, to the extent that it relies on Aristotle's apparent insistence that truths are indeed temporally relativized, the first view—that later events make true what was at the time not merely unclear but in fact indeterminate—would be at least consistent with his famous discussion of the sea battle in *De Interpretatione* 9, where he is uncomfortable with assigning a determinate truth-value to members of at least some pairs of contradictory future-tensed propositions (19^a28-^b4).[64] There is no guarantee, of course, that Aristotle's views as expressed in the

---

[63] See Scott 2000, 226: '[I]t is possible for Aristotle to explain how posthumous events may affect the ante-mortem person in the following way: the good actions of protégés and descendants make it true that the life of the ante-mortem person was a success in productive terms'. This way of putting the case is compatible with both the alternative interpretations I outline. However Scott 2000, 226 n. 25 likens this position to that of Pitcher 1984 in that he uses the expression 'makes true' in a non-mysterious way innocent of any backwards causation. In that case Scott's position is an example of the second of my alternatives.

[64] The interpretation of this famous section of argument is controversial. See, for examples of various lines of interpretation: Waterlow 1982, 79–109; Frede 1985b; Whitaker 1996, 109–31. White 1992, 93–4, seems to think that Aristotle's view in *De Int.* 9 will allow just the sort of analysis of the harm of death offered by Pitcher (see above n. 63).

De Interpretatione were put into practice in the *Nicomachean Ethics*, but the resulting consistency commends this general interpretation. A consequence of this interpretation, however, is that Aristotle must agree that at no time during the person's life is it in fact true that his death harms him; the matter is simply not resolved. (Contrast the alternative interpretation according to which it is always true but simply not evident that his death harms him.) As such, it would presumably leave it open for an Epicurean critic, for example, to point out what to him would be the absurd result that the harm supposedly caused by death and the person supposed to be the subject of the harm never coincide temporally.

An alternative approach to the interpretation of *NE* 1.10–11 concludes that in fact, however difficult this may be to square with other opinions Aristotle expresses, there is some sense in which the person persists after death, perhaps in the products she creates during life (including, importantly, her descendants). It is when these products are affected, *post mortem*, that the person is affected.[65] In that case, Aristotle would stand as a prominent example of an advocate of my option c: death is a harm after the person has died. However, he is able to offer this opinion only because he denies, in effect, that death is the total destruction of the person. The person persists in an ethically relevant sense after his own death.

It would be helpful to know if Epicurus had read and thought through this Aristotelian discussion, but it is controversial whether the Aristotelian 'esoteric' texts which we read were at all widely circulated or known of in the Hellenistic period.[66] I find no reason to think he would not have read the *Nicomachean Ethics* and, had he done so, this passage would appear to be one he would have found particularly thought-provoking as he constructed

---

[65] Scott 2000, 227–9, concludes that this may in fact be the 'more exotic' option favoured by Aristotle. He notes, 229 n. 27, a possible Platonic heritage in Diotima's suggestion that a low-grade kind of immortality may be found in the production of physical and intellectual offspring (*Symp.* 207^{a}6–209^{c}4). We might compare this position with that of Velleman 2000, 67–8, who considers the question of the harm of death in terms of what difference death will make to a person's 'life-story' (on which see below pp. 120–2), which may also contain events which are later than a person's death (67 n. 24).

[66] See e.g. Sandbach 1985.

his own system.[67] Both ask the same question: How can we think that posthumous events affect a person if we agree that there is no *post mortem* survival? Aristotle wants, clearly, to save the common opinions to some degree and is therefore pulled towards asserting some kind of *post mortem* survival, whereas Epicurus is happy to demand that we revise our commonly held views.

In sum, all reactions to the Epicurean account which want to assert that there is a possibility of *post mortem* harm without a *post mortem* subject must rely on some relational or comparative analysis of the nature of the harm of death in order to give any plausibility to their claims about the timing of the harm of death.[68] For death to be a harm, therefore, given that death is the destruction of the subject, that harm must be relational or comparative. If we reject such harms then Epicurus seems to be on very strong ground. The debate over the timing of the harm of death, therefore, leads us back to the opening exchanges on the nature of harm. If Epicurus has secured that there are only perceived harms, then he can add this argument over the timing of the harm of death in order to press his point. But anyone convinced of the possibility of unperceived harms will be able to offer some kind of analysis of the timing of the harm of death compatible with that particular and opposing view.[69]

I will return to these issues when I consider what the consequences might be of adopting an Epicurean view of death in Chapter 5. In particular, the rejection of the possibility of *post mortem* harm will have, or so I will argue, profound effects on how we should conceive of the time after our deaths and will seriously limit the sense in which it is possible to have any rationally conceived desires for what should happen after we die.

---

[67] I cannot argue extensively here for Epicurus' knowledge of the *NE* and there is no direct evidence which will prove that contention, but there seem to me to be some important similarities between, for example, the Aristotelian and Epicurean discussions of pleasure, which make such a claim more plausible. See also Gigante 1999.

[68] There are other suggestions that I will not canvass in detail here. For example, Silverstein 1980 argues from a four-dimensional conception of space-time that temporally distant events can harm a subject just as spatially distant ones can.

[69] I will not pursue here the validity and strength of the Epicureans' own arguments for the truth of hedonism. For discussion of these see Brunschwig 1986, Mitsis 1988b, Striker 1993, Sedley 1996.

Already in antiquity, ancient critics pressed this objection against the Epicureans. Why, they asked, did Epicurus write a will? Some find the revisions required of us were we to take up the Epicurean view sufficiently great that they themselves constitute an argument against the Epicurean position.

3

Symmetry Arguments

τὸ μὴ γενέσθαι τῷ θανεῖν ἴσον λέγω

I say that not being born is the same as being dead.

Euripides, *Troades* 636

The second Epicurean argument which has commanded the attention of recent commentators is found in two sections of Lucretius' poem. The Symmetry Argument, as it has become known, is sometimes cited as a new 'Lucretian' argument which adds an important dimension to the arguments canvassed in the previous chapter (which are sometimes attributed to Epicurus himself to distinguish them from these new Lucretian arguments) by offering a reason for us not to feel distress at the fact that we are going to die.[1] *KΔ* 2, it is claimed, addresses only the fear we might have of 'being dead', of the state of no longer living, and therefore leaves an important area of residual worry entirely untouched. The Symmetry Argument, therefore, has been interpreted as patching this otherwise gaping hole in the Epicurean account. However, it is not in fact the case—or so I will argue—that this Symmetry Argument is designed to produce a conclusion in any way different from that produced by the arguments of *KΔ* 2. If the Epicureans did provide any argument against the thought that we might feel anxiety looking forward from within a life to its eventual end, then it is to be found elsewhere.

The two relevant passages of Lucretius, in which he invokes a symmetry of past and future non-existence, are the following. I call them Texts A and B for ease of reference.

---

[1] See e.g. Kamm 1993, 25. We may in any case be suspicious of the ascription of any major innovations to Lucretius if we accept the general conclusion of Sedley 1998 that Lucretius works solely with Epicurus' *On Nature* as his philosophical source. The overall impression is that Lucretius was reluctant to alter in any significant way Epicurus' own original argumentation.

Text A (*DRN* 3.832–42)

> et velut anteacto nil tempore sensimus aegri,
> ad confligendum venientibus undique Poenis,
> omnia cum belli trepido concussa tumultu
> horrida contremuere sub altis aetheris auris,
> in dubioque fuere utrorum ad regna cadendum
> omnibus humanis esset terraque marique,
> sic, ubi non erimus, cum corporis atque animai
> discidium fuerit, quibus e sumus uniter apti,
> scilicet haud nobis quicquam, qui non erimus tum,
> accidere omnino poterit sensumque movere,
> non si terra mari miscebitur et mare caelo.

And just as in the time that went before we felt no pain—when Carthaginians came from all sides to wage war, and the world struck by the disturbing upheaval of war shook and quivered under the high vault of heaven, and it was unclear to whose kingdom should fall all men on land and sea—so when we are [lit. 'will be'] no more, when the body and soul from whose combination we are formed have come apart, then you can be sure that we (who will not exist then) will be able to have nothing whatsoever happen to us or move our senses in the slightest, not even if earth and sea and sea and sky are mixed together.

Text B (*DRN* 3.972–5)

> respice item quam nil ad nos anteacta vetustas
> temporis aeterni fuerit, quam nascimur ante.
> hoc igitur speculum nobis natura futuri
> temporis exponit post mortem denique nostram.

Look back similarly at how the stretch of unending time before we are born has been nothing to us. Nature, therefore, offers this reflection to us of the time to come after our eventual death.

The first step in establishing just what Lucretius' argument conveys is to distinguish two similar but different claims. I shall call them P (for 'past') i and ii.

> Pi.   Our pre-natal non-existence was nothing to us before we were born.
>
> Pii.   Looking back from within a lifetime, our pre-natal non-existence is nothing to us.

Pi deals with a state of affairs during the period before our birth, and asserts that *at that time* our non-existence was nothing to us.

We felt no pain, loss, or distress. This relies on the generally accepted claim that since before our birth we are not, that is to say we have not (yet) come into existence, it makes absolutely no sense to consider our relative state of well- or ill-being at that time. There is no subject to consider. Pii makes a different claim. It considers a point of time within a life and asserts that looking back from the present our pre-natal non-existence is 'nothing to us'. We can further explain the distinction between the two by reintroducing two senses of non-existence being 'nothing to us' (see above pp. 17–18). Non-existence can be nothing to us in the sense that in fact it is not harmful and in the sense that the thought of it causes no distress. The Epicurean task is to marry these two, to make us accept the true belief that non-existence is in fact not harmful and therefore feel no distress at the thought of it. Unfortunately, most people have a false opinion about the harmfulness of *post mortem* non-existence. They think it harmful (and in that sense it is 'something to them') although it is not.

Clearly, the Epicureans want to claim that pre-natal non-existence is nothing to us in both senses. It is not harmful and should not be thought to be harmful. They also want to use people's prevalent true beliefs about pre-natal non-existence as a means of showing that they ought to take a consistent view about *post mortem* non-existence. Most people are correct about past non-existence but mistaken about future non-existence. In terms of Pi this amounts to the thought that not only *was* it the case that pre-natal non-existence was nothing to our pre-natal selves, but also it is the case that we do not think that pre-natal non-existence *was* harmful to our pre-natal selves. In terms of Pii, the thought is that not only *is* our pre-natal non-existence nothing to us now—we are not harmed now by our lives extending only finitely far back into the past—but also that it is the case that we do not think that pre-natal non-existence *is* harmful to us now.

The general form Symmetry Argument takes as a premise an assertion about pre-natal non-existence and then claims that there is no relevant difference between this period and its 'reflection' in the future, our *post mortem* non-existence. This latter is, of course, the period which must be the object of any fear of death. If it can be shown that we have no reason to take a different view of *post mortem* from pre-natal non-existence, and further that pre-natal non-existence is universally and justifiably not considered a source of distress, then it follows that to fear death is irrational and unjustifiable.

This general form holds whether the major premise is proposition Pi or Pii. However, the force of the argument and its conclusion are certainly affected by the choice of premise, since the symmetrical relation upon which the argument relies will generate conclusions about the rational attitude to take towards *post mortem* non-existence which are symmetrical to the starting premises and therefore distinct in the same way as those premises. In other words, if the premise is Pi, then the claim generated by the argument about the future will be F (for 'future') i:

> Fi. Our *post mortem* non-existence will be nothing to us after our death.

But if Pii is the premise, then the claim generated about the future will be this:

> Fii. Looking forward from within a lifetime, our *post mortem* non-existence is nothing to us.

The acceptance of these claims will result in a change in our view of the harmfulness of *post mortem* non-existence. Accepting Fi we come to believe that *post mortem* non-existence *will* not be anything to us and will therefore remove any present distress caused by the thought that we *will* be harmed after death by non-existence. Accepting Fii we come to believe that *post mortem* non-existence *is* nothing to us and therefore remove any present distress at the thought that we *are* harmed by our lives extending only finitely far into the future. Fi deals with the period after our death and asserts that at that time we *will* feel no pain or distress. This, of course, is the conclusion also generated by the famous Epicurean *dictum* distilled into the second *Kyria Doxa*:

ὁ θάνατος οὐδὲν πρὸς ἡμᾶς· τὸ γὰρ διαλυθὲν ἀναισθητεῖ, τὸ δ' ἀναισθητοῦν οὐδὲν πρὸς ἡμᾶς.

Death is nothing to us; for what has been dissolved has no sensation, and what has no sensation is nothing to us.

As is familiar by now, in Epicurean terms, death is the disruption of the atomic complex of body and soul which constitute a person, and since no further sensation can be experienced, no pleasure and pain can be experienced and therefore no well- or ill-being in Epicurean terms. This is the argument, therefore, that in order for something to count for or against well-being there must be a subject of that well- or ill-being who stands in an appropriate relationship to the supposed good or bad.[2] For an Epicurean this relationship is the perception of pleasure or pain. In any case, after death there is no subject at all (just as before birth there was no subject) and therefore death, as a matter of fact, does not harm us. Again, the argument of *KΔ* 2 shows only that in the period after death we cannot be harmed. However, it can still conclude that death 'is' nothing to us (and Lucretius can make this explicit by writing *nil mors est ad nos* at 3.830) in the sense that we now are not distressed by thoughts of harms to come after our death. If we accept this conclusion fully, death becomes 'nothing to us' in that we will not feel now any distress at the thought that we will be harmed after death, since we cannot be harmed after death. (We will see later, pp. 101–5, that *Ep. Men.* 125 makes explicit this move from a conclusion about what will not be harmful to a present lack of distress at the thought of what is to come.) If this is the force of the Symmetry Argument, then it adds nothing significant to the major Epicurean claim about death.

Fii, however, makes a different claim. It asserts something about our present attitudes as we look forward from the present to a point in time after death. It claims that just as when looking back we feel no distress at the thought of pre-natal non-existence, so we should in the present feel similarly about *post mortem* time. This offers a new dimension to the Epicurean discussion of the fear of death. Whereas *KΔ* 2 and Fi dealt merely with the state of affairs after death, this argument deals directly with our present attitudes during our lifetime. It reflects on to the future the retrospective attitude we supposedly have now as we look back through the past to the period before that life began, asking us to take a symmetrical prospective attitude. So Pii and Fii concern our attitudes to whether our present state is harmed by the fact that there was a period of pre-natal non-existence and there will be a similar period of *post mortem* non-existence, while Pi and Fi concern our attitudes to whether we *were* harmed at the time by pre-natal non-existence and *will be* harmed by *post mortem* non-existence when it comes. Let me call the version of the argument

[2] Lucr. *DRN* 3.862–4.

which starts with Pi and generates Fi, version 1, and the version which starts with Pii and generates Fii, version 2. I set them out here:

Version 1:

Pi. Our pre-natal non-existence was nothing to us before we were born.

SYM Prenatal non-existence is relevantly like *post mortem* non-existence.

Fi. Our *post mortem* non-existence will be nothing to us after our death.

Version 2:

Pii. Looking back from within a lifetime, our pre-natal non-existence is nothing to us.

SYM Prenatal non-existence is relevantly like *post mortem* non-existence.

Fii. Looking forward from within a lifetime, our *post mortem* non-existence is nothing to us.

It is perfectly understandable why it might be preferable to find in the Lucretian Symmetry Argument a new and otherwise missing area of discussion and therefore why version 2 of the argument has been adopted by a number of commentators. First, unless it is interpreted in this way, this apparently sophisticated argument, which invokes the intriguing notion of a symmetry between pre-natal and *post mortem* time concludes with little more than a restatement of the now familiar assertion that death is annihilation and therefore since after death there is no subject, death cannot be a harm.[3] Second, a criticism is sometimes levelled at the Epicureans that they *ought to have* produced an argument

---

[3] Mitsis 1988a, 306 n. 6 appears to disagree with Furley's 1986 assessment of the argument (see below n. 6), but in his own description of the argument at p. 306 expresses it clearly in the form Pi/Fi: 'We felt nothing in the time before we were born; just so, we will feel nothing when we are dead'. His general attitude throughout the article, however, is that this argument is part of an Epicurean concern to address worries about the duration of a life—and presumably this concern must be part of a prospective vision of one's lifetime from the point of view of the present. Sorabji 1983, 176 is uncertain whether Lucretius intends the 'more interesting' argument from Pii to Fii. Kamm 1993, 25, also offers version 2 as 'Lucretius'' argument, distinct from 'Epicurus'' argument in *Kyria Doxa* 2: 'Lucretius recognises that we *are* not disturbed much about the fact of our non-existence prior to our creation. If so, he asked, why *are* we so disturbed about our non-existence after death?' (my emphasis). Belshaw 1993, 103, also gives a version 2 argument.

along the lines of the second form of the Symmetry Argument. $K\Delta$ 2, it is claimed, is fine as far as it goes, but it fails to address perhaps the primary sense in which people fear death, namely the prospective fear that their lives are going to end. Whether or not after death there will be a subject to experience pleasure or pain does not matter. What does matter is what can be called the fear of *mortality*, or alternatively 'distress at the thought that one's life is going to end' (which was designated as fearing death in sense 2*, above p. 4). This source of distress can be distinguished from the fear of death addressed by $K\Delta$ 2, since it is entirely conceivable that someone might well agree that 'being dead' is neither pleasant nor painful, but nevertheless feel distress as he looks forward from some point in his life to a time when that life will cease.[4] A critical reading of $K\Delta$ 2 would emphasize this error, and claim that Epicurus is wrong to state as his conclusion that 'Death *is* nothing to us'. He is entitled to conclude only that death *will be* nothing to us at some future time, namely when we are dead. He has said nothing so far to counter the distressing prospect that my life will cease at some time. The second form of the Symmetry Argument, of course, does address this second type of concern, since it is concerned with a present prospective attitude to eventual future non-existence.[5] In that case, in a spirit of charity we should see these Symmetry Arguments providing the extra and otherwise missing element in the Epicureans' armoury against the fear of death.

Which version of the argument is to be found in our texts? Unfortunate as this might be for the assessment of the efficacy of Lucretius' therapy, the two texts from the *DRN* tend to favour the first version of the Symmetry Argument (namely Pi → Fi).

---

[4] This distinction is arrived at by A. and M. in Cicero's first *Tusculan Disputation*. At *Tusc.* 1.14, A. asks: *age iam concedo non esse miseros qui mortui sint quoniam extorsisti ut faterer, qui omnino non essent, eos ne miseros quidem esse posse. quid? qui vivimus, cum moriendum sit, nonne miseri sumus? quae enim iucunditas, cum dies et noctes cogitandum sit iam iamque esse moriendum?* ('Come now, I agree that those who are dead are not miserable, since you have wrenched from me the concession that those who do not exist at all cannot be miserable. But so what? We who are alive, are we not miserable since we must die? What joy is there, when day and night we must think that at any time now it is necessary to die?')

[5] Note, however, that this second Symmetry Argument although it addresses the prospective fear of death still does not address the further fear of *premature* death. These two are well distinguished by Striker 1988.

At least, text A certainly offers this argument and text B probably does.

That text A offers little beyond the familiar claim that death removes a possible subject for harm has been pointed out before. but given the frequent misreadings of this section of Lucretius, the conclusion should be restated.[6] The tenses of the verbs which Lucretius employs are quite clear. First, Lucretius establishes Pi: 'previously we *felt* no harm' (*anteacto tempore nil <u>sensimus</u> aegri*, 3.832). The verb is clearly aorist. Lucretius might still be accused here of being loose in his expression in this line, though. We might be tempted to think that Lucretius' expression here implies that we were there and had the potential to feel pain, but did not. But this cannot be Lucretius' claim, since the point he wishes to convey is of course not that we were present at that time and felt something *other than pain*, but that we were not there at all and therefore could not experience anything, a point he makes explicitly a little later (3.862–4). In any case, the period of time in question is clearly pre-natal: we did not suffer any pain *then*. Nothing is said about the present, nor about our present attitude to the past. Text A then goes on to invoke a symmetry between this period and the time *post mortem* (*sic* 838), and the symmetrical claim it produces about the future is clearly Fi, not Fii.

> sic, ubi non erimus...
> scilicet haud nobis quicquam, qui non erimus tum,
> accidere omnino poterit sensumque movere...
>
>   3.838–41

---

[6] Furley 1986, 76: 'The tenses of the verbs are conclusive about this; there is no statement at all about our present attitudes'. Rosenbaum 1989b, 358 takes issue with Furley, although he recognizes that Furley is certainly correct about the tenses of the verbs in the relevant Lucretian texts. Nevertheless, he argues that Epicurus is certainly concerned with present attitudes since, for example, *KΔ* 2 holds that 'death *is* nothing to us'. Rosenbaum goes on (359–60) to offer a version of the Symmetry Argument which has as its first premise: 'No one fears the time before which one existed', and concludes: 'Therefore it is not reasonable now for one to fear one's future non-existence'. These are clearly versions of Pii and Fii. If Rosenbaum is right that Epicurus was concerned with present attitudes, he is nevertheless wrong in claiming that this is the particular argument by which he set out to alleviate them. Aronoff 1997, which was brought to my attention by one of the readers for the Press, comes to some conclusions very similar to my own and offers some telling criticisms of Rosenbaum.

Lucretius is describing a state of affairs at a time after death ('we *will* not be then', 'it *will* not be able to affect us': *non erimus tum...haud poterit*), not our present state. He insists that *post mortem* non-existence will not harm us, not that it does not harm us. Text A, therefore, gives what I called version 1 of the Symmetry Argument and confirms *KΔ* 2. It does not address the thought that someone may presently be harmed by the fact that their life will come to an end.[7]

Text B is more complicated and its conclusions less clear, but ultimately it offers little if any more support for proponents of version 2 of the Symmetry Argument (Pii → Fii).

> respice item quam nil ad nos anteacta vetustas
> temporis aeterni fuerit, quam nascimur ante.
> hoc igitur speculum nobis natura futuri
> temporis exponit post mortem denique nostram.

Initially we might think that these lines do indeed describe a present attitude to pre-natal time. At first glance, the metaphor of viewing might be thought to invite just such an interpretation. After all, in the first line of the argument we are invited to 'look back' towards the past, and presumably the only point from which we may currently look back to the past is the present. Further, the metaphor of a mirror which these lines introduce might also point in this direction. The image is of a viewer who looks back in time at a mirror in front of him.[8] The mirror displays an image of what is behind the viewer, namely the future. So as the viewer looks back to his past non-existence, he is in fact seeing before him a

---

[7] For my reading of the *palingenesis* argument which immediately follows this passage, see Warren 2001a.

[8] The image of someone looking backwards in time conforms to the ancient image of us 'backing into the future'. We can 'see' (i.e. remember) the past but the future is not visible. Compare the use of the Greek ὀπίσω to mean 'hereafter' (LSJ s.v. II). Also see Kenney 1971 *ad* 974. He insists that *speculum exponit* should be understood as 'shows a reflection', not 'holds up a mirror', since this allows *hoc* (974) to refer to *anteacta vetustas temporis aeterni*. '[T]hat is what Nature shows us as the mirror-image of *futurum tempus*, and it is, of course, a blank, a reflection of nothing.... Naturally there is nothing *horribile* or *triste* (976) to be seen, because there is nothing *at all* to be seen.' This last remark is an overstatement. Of course, Lucretius is not denying that nothing at all happened before our birth, merely that whatever did happen, it caused us no pain.

mirror image of what is to come.[9] And since nothing in the image causes any distress (976–7), the future presents nothing to fear.

A proponent of version 2 of the Symmetry Argument must place a lot of weight on this metaphor, and must insist that it implies a viewer located in the present looking at a mirror image of what he could see clearly if he looked over his shoulder. On this understanding the viewer is considering the relationship between himself located in the present and the object in the mirror—a reflection of *post mortem* time. Hence the argument is thought to concern our present prospective attitude to death. This picture offers the strongest indication that Lucretius is concerned with our present attitudes to past and future non-existence, rather than the state of affairs at some time before or after our lifetime.[10]

However, despite the intuitive attraction of such an understanding, the tenses of the verbs used here suggest again that in fact—and despite the metaphor of viewing—Lucretius is offering version 1 of the Symmetry Argument. Above all, the tense of the form of the verb 'to be' here (*fuerit*, 973) suggests that this is the case: 'pre-natal time *was* nothing to us'. This is another expression of premise Pi of version 1 of the Symmetry Argument. Admittedly, this phrase might carry a perfect sense: 'pre-natal time *has been* nothing to us'. In that case it might be understood as a form of premise Pii of version 2 of the Symmetry Argument, if it is understood that 'has been' here means in effect: 'pre-natal time has been [sc. during our life, up to the present] nothing to us'. But if Lucretius wished to make clear that he is talking about it presently being the case that our pre-natal non-existence causes us no distress, then he could have done so easily by writing the present tense of the same verb (*sit*).[11] This would have

---

[9] Lucretius explains in his discussion of mirrors at 4.269 ff. why the image in the mirror appears to be twice as far away as the viewer is from the mirror itself. We need not think that in this passage in book 3 Lucretius wishes to imply that the subject is at a temporal point half-way through his life, equidistant between birth and death, although his vision in the mirror makes it look as though he is.

[10] Feldman 1990, 23, points to this passage in order to produce an argument beginning from the premise: 'The fact that he didn't exist for an infinitely long period of time prior to his birth is not bad for anyone' (a species of Pii).

[11] *nascimur* is, of course, present tense, but this offers no support for version 2. Kenney 1971 ad loc.: 'The tense shows that *nascimur* refers to all successive generations, not merely this one'.

produced the following translation, which would convey the point without ambiguity:

'Look back at how all the immense amount of time before we were born is nothing to us.'

Whereas, with *fuerit*, the translation is more naturally:

'Look back at how all the immense amount of time before we were born was nothing to us.'

Both these versions construe 'before we were born' (*quam nascimur ante*) as amplifying 'the immense amount of previous time' (*anteacta vetustas*) in the previous line. This is compatible with both understandings of the argument. However, it is also possible, I think, to take *quam nascimur ante* as an adverbial phrase qualifying *fuerit*, in which case the translation would read:

'Look back at how all the previous immense amount of time was nothing to us before we were born.'

This is incompatible with a version 2 understanding of the argument, since in this case it is made clear that the time being considered at which pre-natal non-existence caused no harm is precisely the time before birth. On this construal Lucretius gives a version of proposition Pi. Most current translations seem to understand *quam nascimur ante* in the first of these ways, amplifying *anteacta vetustas*, so this alone cannot decide the issue in favour of a version 1 reading of the argument.[12] But such an interpretation is in any case strongly supported by the tense of *fuerit*.

It is also perfectly possible to understand the metaphor of looking into a mirror in a way which is consistent with version 1 of the Symmetry Argument. Rather than focusing on the

---

[12] Latham's Penguin translation gives: 'Look back at the eternity that passed before we were born, and mark how utterly it counts to us as nothing.' Smith's revised Loeb has: 'Look back also and see how the ages of everlasting time past before we were born have been to us nothing.' Bailey (Oxford, 1947): 'Look back again to see how the past ages of everlasting time, before we are born, have been as nought to us.' Brown (Warminster, 1997): 'Look back in turn and see how the eternity of everlasting time that elapsed of old before our birth was absolutely nothing to us.' Melville (Oxford, 1998): 'Look back upon the ages of time past | Eternal, before we were born, and see | That they have been nothing to us, nothing at all.'

relationship between a viewer, located in the present, and the period of time at which he is looking (namely a reflection of future time), we should consider ourselves, as Lucretius tells us to do, in the place of the viewer. After all, Lucretius here instructs the reader to look back (*respice*), not to consider some other person looking at an image in a mirror. We are being told to focus on the image in the mirror held up before *us*. Is there anything to fear in it? No. But it is merely a reflection of how things will be after death. So since we are happy to accept that at that time before birth there was nothing which could cause any pain, we must agree that there *will be* nothing which can cause pain after death. Therefore, although Lucretius' striking image of the mirror perhaps tempts us towards version 2 of the Symmetry Argument. it does not require us to think along those lines.[13]

Neither of the two texts which might be offered by proponents of version 2 of the Symmetry Argument can sustain such a reading. Text A certainly cannot, and Text B certainly does not in any unambiguous way. It should be concluded, therefore, that Lucretius does not in these passages offer a clear argument against the fear of mortality, if this is distinguished from the fear of 'being dead'.[14]

Other ancient Symmetry Arguments

Symmetry Arguments appear regularly in ancient texts from the Hellenistic period through to Imperial Greek and Latin texts. The first of these (and one of the earliest surviving examples of the argument)[15] comes from the pseudo Platonic *Axiochus* (365d7–e2).

---

[13] Bailey 1947, *ad* 974 comments that this section is merely reinforcing what was said in 3.832 ff., and by doing so rounds off a particular set of arguments in this book. before Lucretius goes on to offer his thoughts on the genesis of particular myths about punishments in the Underworld.

[14] Again. when Lucretius points out the irrationality of those who, while protesting that they do not fear being dead. are nevertheless concerned about the treatment of their corpse, the focus is on the appropriate attitude for a state of affairs *after* death (*DRN* 3.870–75).

[15] There is a chance that the argument was anticipated by Anaxagoras, if this report in Stobaeus 4.52b.39 (A34 DK) is accurate: Ἀναξαγόρας δύο ἔλεγε διδασκαλίας εἶναι θανάτου, τόν τε πρὸ τοῦ γενέσθαι χρόνον καὶ τὸν ὕπνον

ὡς οὖν ἐπὶ τῆς Δράκοντος ἢ Κλεισθένους πολιτείας οὐδὲν περὶ σὲ κακὸν ἦν—
ἀρχὴν γὰρ οὐκ ἦς, περὶ ὃν ἂν ἦν—οὕτως οὐδὲ μετὰ τὴν τελευτὴν γενήσεται·
σὺ γὰρ οὐκ ἔσῃ περὶ ὃν ἔσται.

Just as in the time of Draco or Cleisthenes there was no harm to you,
since you were not there to be affected in the first place, so too will it be
the case after death. For you will not be there to be affected.

It clearly gives version 1 of the argument, and offers as a reason
for the conclusion that these periods of pre-natal and *post mortem*
time should not concern us the fact that *at those times* we do not
exist. A similarly clear version 1 of the Symmetry Argument
appears in an extremely brief form in Cicero's *Tusculans* 1.91:[16]

ut nihil pertinuit ad nos ante ortum, sic nihil post mortem pertinebit.

Just as nothing was of concern to us before birth, so too nothing will be
of concern to us after death.

Pliny the Elder also uses a recognizable Symmetry Argument
during his discussion of what he considers to be the foolish belief
in an afterlife or in some sort of immortal soul. He too uses a
form of version 1.[17]

('Anaxagoras said that there are two lessons for death: the time before birth and
sleep'). This differs from texts which assert that death is similar or identical to
not being born (such as Andromache in Euripides *Troades* 636) in so far as
Anaxagoras appears explicitly to make pre-natal time *instructive* for how we
ought to view death. An argument from Teles' *Peri Apatheias* (61.2–4 Hense)
may be roughly contemporary with the *Axiochus*. See below n. 27.

[16] *Tusc.* 1.90 comes close to a version 2 argument by asking why someone
should now feel pain at the thought of the capture of Rome in the far future
given that he does not feel pain at the thought of the capture of Rome in the
time of Camillus. Cf. Cic. *Fin.* 1.49: *sic robustus animus et excelsus omni est liber
cura et angore, cum et mortem contemnit, qua qui adfecti sunt in eadem causa sunt
qua antequam nati* ('Just so a strong and noble spirit is free from all care and
pain, since it even looks down on death. For those who are touched by death are
in the same position as before they were born'); *De Rep.* 6.23: *quid autem
interest ab iis, qui postea nascentur, sermonem fore de te, cum ab iis nullus fuerit
qui anti nati sunt?* ('For why does it matter that there should be some talk about
you among those who will be born later, when there was none among those who
were born before?').

[17] Pliny's argument is quoted by Hume in his *On the immortality of the soul*
with the comment: 'Our insensibility before the composition of the body seems
to natural reason a proof of a like state after dissolution.' Hume also seems to
have been impressed by the Epicurean symmetry argument. Boswell 1777 relates
Hume's understanding of the argument: 'I asked [Hume] if the thought of
annihilation never gave him any uneasiness. He said not the least; no more than
the thought that he had not been, as Lucretius observes.'

omnibus a supremo die eadem quae ante primum, nec magis a morte
sensus ullus aut corpori aut animae quam ante natalem . . .
at quanto facilius certiusque sibi quemque credere, specimen securitatis
futurae antegenitali sumere experimento.

Everyone, from their last day will be in the same state as before their
first and there will be no more sensation of body or soul than there was
before birth.

But how much easier and more sure for everyone to believe in himself,
taking as an example of the tranquillity to come what was undergone
before birth?

NH 7.188, 190

Seneca too uses similar arguments on a number of occasions,
most of which also conform to my version 1 of the Symmetry
Argument.[18] There is, however, a related passage in *Ep. Mor.*
77.11 which offers a rather different perspective on these issues.

nonne tibi videtur stultissimus omnium qui flevit quod ante annos mille
non vixerat? aeque stultus est qui flet quod post annos mille non vivet.
haec paria sunt: non eris nec fuisti; utrumque tempus alienum est.

Doesn't the person who wept because he had not been alive a thousand
years ago seem to you an utter fool? Equally foolish is he who weeps
because he will not be alive in a thousand years' time. These two are the
same: you will not be, nor were you. Neither time belongs to you.

Rather than a single subject or addressee as in the Lucretian
texts, two characters are described, one concerned with past
non-existence and one with future. The tenses of the verbs used
also complicate the issue, since Seneca does not maintain a strict
equivalence between the two characters he is comparing. The

---

[18] Sen. *Cons. ad Marc.* 19.5: *mors dolorum omnium exsolutio est et finis, ultra
quem mala nostra non exeunt, quae nos in illam tranquillitatem, in qua antequam
nasceremur iacuimus, reponit. si mortuorum aliquis miseretur et non natorum
misereatur* ('Death is the release and end of all pains beyond which our evils
cannot pass, which places us back into that tranquillity in which we lay before
birth. If anyone pities the dead he ought also to pity the unborn'). *Ep. Mor.*
54.4: *id quale sit iam scio: hoc erit post me quod ante me fuit. si quid in hac re* [sc.
morte] *tormenti est, necesse est et fuisse antequam prodiremus in lucem; atqui
nullam sensimus tunc vexationem* ('I now know what sort of thing it is: after me
will be just what was before me. If there is anything painful in death then
necessarily there also was before we came into the light; but we felt no
disturbance then'). *Ep. Mor.* 65.24: *nec desinere timeo (idem est enim quod non
coepisse)* ('I am not afraid to cease (for it is just the same as not having begun)').

first wept (*flevit*) because he had not been alive (*vixerat*) a thousand years previously;[19] the second weeps now (*flet*) because he will not be alive a thousand years in the future. This suggests that in this passage at least Seneca is indeed interested in retro- and prospective attitudes, but not so much in a strict symmetry between past- and future-directed attitudes. It is therefore dif- ficult to tell whether Seneca is indeed making a specific claim about the exact relationship between retrospective and prospect- ive attitudes.[20] What is more evident is that Seneca intends here to portray two *absurd* examples of regret. It is important that these two characters are weeping over the thought of not experiencing things in the very distant past and future.[21]

Even those who would wish to accept that death can be a harm since it robs us of goods which we would otherwise have enjoyed (the counterfactual account of the harm of death) might shrink from the claim that death robs us of goods located a thousand years in the future. (This extreme position is a possibility, how- ever. In Cicero's *Tusculans* 1.9, the character A. begins with the claim that both the dead and those who are going to die are wretched (*miseri*). It is pointed out that this would lead to the radical conclusion that everyone is always subject to eternal misery.) A more moderate position will concede that death is only a harm in so far as it robs us of time and goods we could reasonably have been expected to experience. This trades on the idea that we can reasonably expect to live a full life of perhaps eighty years or so, and so dying before this time is up robs us of something to which we should feel entitled. Such a counterfactual account of the harm of death obviously loses its force in the far future, since we cannot reasonably hope to live for a thousand years. While it might be right for a twenty-year-old to feel regret

[19] Madvig emended to: *flebit quod ante annos mille non vixerit. vixerit* appears in one of the codices.

[20] Cf. Rosenbaum 1989b, 357: 'For Seneca, the thought is clearly directed against negative feelings about future non-existence.' This may be so, but it remains to be explained exactly how the example of an absurd retrospective attitude is meant to be instructive.

[21] Here, as elsewhere, Montaigne shows that he is a keen reader of Seneca: *That to philosophise is to learn to die* (*Essais* 1.20), 'As our birth brought us the birth of all things, so will our death bring us the death of all things. Wherefore it is foolish to lament that we shall not be alive a hundred years from now as it is to lament that we were not alive a hundred years ago.'

if he is assured he will die before the age of thirty, it is less plausible to claim that a Roman senator of the first century AD should have felt aggrieved at the thought that he would not participate in the millennial celebrations on 31 December 1999.[22] There is considerable room between the acceptance that Seneca's examples of regret are absurd and the conclusion that it is absurd to weep at the thought of non-existence *however near or far* in the past or future that non-existence may be.[23]

Seneca does close this gap, and the crucial step in his argument comes in the final phrase of the section just cited: 'neither of these periods of time belongs to you' (*utrumque tempus alienum est*). On this basis Seneca grounds his assertion that such feelings about future non-existence are not justifiable. This Stoic premise is rather stronger than the Epicurean claim that before birth and after death we 'are not', since not only do the Stoics think that before birth and after death we are not, but they also are adamant that that time does not *belong* to us (since the times of our birth and death are fated), and therefore its absence from our lifetime cannot be a loss to us.[24] Those times were never ours to lose. Seneca uses the Stoic notion of fate to underline his point (77.12).

in hoc punctum coniectus es, quod ut extendas, quousque extendes? quid fles? quid optas? perdis operam. desine fata deum flecti sperare precando (=Verg. *Aen.* 6.376). rata et fixa sunt et magna et aeterna necessitate ducuntur: eo ibis quo omnia eunt.

You have been placed at this point. If you want to make it longer, how far will you? What are you weeping for? What are you searching for? You are wasting your energy. Give up hoping that the divine fates can be bent by prayer. They are considered and sure and great and ever-lasting, and led by necessity. You will go to where everything goes.

---

[22] Cf. Striker 1988, 327. Lucretius himself emphasizes that the period of *post mortem* non-existence will extend infinitely far into the future, no matter when we actually die (3.1073–5).

[23] Malcolm Schofield suggested to me that it might be possible to perform a *sorites*-like argument beginning with the acceptance that it is absurd to weep at far-future non-existence and ending with the conclusion that it is equally absurd to weep at any future non-existence. There is no suggestion that Seneca has such an additional move in mind here.

[24] These two periods of time are *aliena*. In some Latin Stoic texts this word describes objects which are the object of the opposite of *oikeiōsis* (e.g. Cic *Fin.* 3.16: *alienari*).

This additional move provides the missing extra step. Not only is it absurd to weep at non-existence in the far future, it is equally absurd to feel the loss of any lifetime which one does not in fact enjoy. Given Stoic determinism, Seneca can head off any residual possibility that death at some particular time might be thought a harm by depriving the person of time he might have expected to live.[25] The period immediately following someone's death is no more theirs to be deprived of than some time a thousand years into the future. Given that the time of one's death is predestined, death cannot deprive one of anything—not even a second.

The next example comes from Plutarch's *Consolatio ad Apollonium*. At 107D Plutarch outlines three possibilities for the nature of death, and attributes the identification of these possibilities to Socrates. Either death is like a deep and dreamless sleep, or it is like a journey, or it is the extinction of body and soul. Each possibility is then examined in turn, and it is shown that on each account death is not to be feared. The first two possibilities are familiar from Socrates' final address in Plato's *Apology* (40c5 ff.), and the third—the destruction of body and soul—may simply be an expansion from the idea of death as a complete lack of perception, which is of course the major force of the analogy with a dreamless sleep. The *Apology* is unconcerned to make a decision between death as annihilation and death as the absence of sensation.[26] Nevertheless, Plutarch treats the two as distinct positions and in his discussion of death as annihilation uses arguments familiar from Epicurean contexts.

εἴ γε μὴν ὁ θάνατος τελεία τίς ἐστι φθορὰ καὶ διάλυσις τοῦ τε σώματος καὶ τῆς ψυχῆς (τὸ τρίτον γὰρ ἦν τοῦτο τῆς Σωκρατικῆς εἰκασίας), οὐδ᾽ οὕτω κακόν ἐστιν· ἀναισθησία γάρ τις κατ᾽ αὐτὸν γίγνεται καὶ πάσης ἀπαλλαγὴ λύπης καὶ φροντίδος. ὥσπερ γὰρ οὔτ᾽ ἀγαθὸν ἡμῖν ἔπεστιν οὕτως οὐδὲ κακόν· περὶ γὰρ τὸ ὄν καὶ τὸ ὑφεστηκὸς καθάπερ τὸ ἀγαθὸν πέφυκε γίγνεσθαι, τὸν

---

[25] Such arguments that death is an evil tend to trade on the idea that while the time of a subject's birth must be fixed (since date of birth is essential to that subject's identity), the time of death is contingent and therefore a counterfactual account of the harm of death is possible. If in addition the time of death is agreed to be necessary (as in Stoicism), then this possibility is removed. See Sedley 1993, 316–18, for further discussion of the Stoic view.

[26] Of course, the *Phaedo* characterizes death as a διάλυσις or ἀπαλλαγή of body and soul (e.g. 64c4–8, 88a10–b2) and as a release from care and pain, but it most certainly does not allow that death involves the φθορά of the soul.

αὐτὸν τρόπον καὶ τὸ κακόν· περὶ δὲ τὸ μὴ ὂν ἀλλ' ἠρμένον ἐκ τῶν ὄντων
οὐδέτερον τούτων ὑπάρχει. εἰς τὴν αὐτὴν οὖν τάξιν οἱ τελευτήσαντες
καθίστανται τῇ πρὸ τῆς γενέσεως. ὥσπερ οὖν οὐδὲν ἦν ἡμῖν πρὸ τῆς γενέσεως
οὔτ' ἀγαθὸν οὔτε κακόν, οὕτως οὐδὲ μετὰ τὴν τελευτήν. καὶ καθάπερ τὰ πρὸ
ἡμῶν οὐδὲν ἦν πρὸς ἡμᾶς, οὕτως οὐδὲ τὰ μεθ' ἡμᾶς οὐδὲν ἔσται πρὸς ἡμᾶς.

Even if, however, death is some kind of complete destruction and dissolution of both body and soul (for this was the third of Socrates'
guesses) then even on this account it is not an evil. For, so he says, there
comes about some kind of absence of perception and a release from all
pain and care. Just as there is no good to us then, so too there is no evil.
For just as what is good comes about by nature for what is and what
subsists so too does what is bad. Neither of them is present for what is
not and has been removed from what exists. *So the dead are in the same
state as they were before birth, and so just as there was no good or bad for
us before birth, so too will there be none after death. Just as those things
before us were nothing to us, so too those after us will be nothing to us.*

The section italicized in my translation contains Plutarch's
version of the Symmetry Argument, and this again is cast in terms
of version 1, not in terms of retro- and prospective attitudes.

Ancient examples of an argument concerning the symmetry or
asymmetry of prospective and retrospective attitudes to past and
future non-existence are extremely rare.[27] It is therefore very
unlikely, although not impossible, that the Epicureans themselves
offered any such argument.[28] If they did offer some such argument then there is no clear sign of it in our sources. In that case
the criticism that Epicureans omitted to give an argument against
the most debilitating species of fearing death can be restated.

---

[27] The closest examples I know are Cic. *Tusc.* 1.90 (see above n. 16) and
Teles' *Peri apatheias* (*ap.* Stob. 4.44.83, Hense vol. 3, 990.21–91.3), but this
latter example is complicated by being about someone's attitude to another's
pre-natal and *post mortem* non-existence. Teles answers someone who is pained
by the thought that his loved-one will cease to be: οὐδὲ γὰρ ἦν μυριοστὸν ἔτος, οὐδ'
ἐπὶ τῶν Τρωικῶν· οὐδὲ γὰρ κατὰ τοὺς προπάππους σου. σὺ δὲ ἐπὶ μὲν τούτῳ οὐκ
ἄχθῃ, ὅτι δὲ εἰς ὕστερον οὐκ ἔσται, δυσχεραίνεις ('For he was not alive ten thousand
years ago, nor during the Trojan Wars, nor in your great grandfathers' time.
But you do not grieve at that, although you are pained that he will not be in the
future'). Cf. Wallach 1976, 17.

[28] The extant sections of Philodemus *De Morte* contain no mention of the
Symmetry Argument. However, since the only extant texts are scraps of the
fourth book I do not think we can conclude, as Armstrong 2004, 53 would wish,
that Philodemus 'spurns the symmetry argument as poor therapy and only
usable in an ancillary role'.

Nothing we have canvassed so far suggests that there was an Epicurean Symmetry Argument dedicated to attacking the particular concern which might arise at the thought of one's life coming to an end.

Reverse Symmetry Arguments

A reverse Symmetry Argument takes as a premise the claim that 'everyone fears future non-existence', and uses the symmetry of past and future sustained by both version 1 and 2 of the original argument to conclude that it is reasonable to regret one's past non-existence. If the two periods of non-existence are truly symmetrical then we are as justified in seeing both as a loss as in seeing neither. The dialectical strength of this move is that it uses the work expended on maintaining the similarity of both periods and turns it to produce quite the opposite conclusion. In other words, it accepts the symmetry of the two periods, but swaps the first premise. It uses the premise that pre-natal and *post mortem* non-existence are relevantly alike and a modified premise about future non-existence to create a new and unwelcome conclusion about past non-existence.

There are therefore two reverse Symmetry Arguments, distinguished by whether their starting premise is *Fi or *Fii:

Version 1*

    *Fi: Our *post mortem* non-existence will harm us after our death.

        Pre-natal non-existence is relevantly like *post mortem* non-existence.

Therefore   *Pi: Our pre-natal non-existence harmed us before birth.

Version 2*

    *Fii: Looking forward from within a lifetime, our *post mortem* non-existence causes us distress.

        Pre-natal non-existence is relevantly like *post mortem* non-existence.

Therefore   *Pii: Looking back from within a lifetime our pre-natal non-existence causes us distress.

Seneca offers version 1 of the reverse Symmetry Argument in conditional form as rhetorical support for the conclusion that death is not to be feared. The alternative, he argues, is absurd:

si mortuorum aliquis miseretur et non natorum misereatur.

If anyone pities the dead, then he should also pity the unborn.[29]

Seneca *Cons. ad Marc.* 19.5

The symmetry principle is relied upon implicitly. To my knowledge there are no examples in ancient texts of this sort of argument being offered positively as proof that the unborn are harmed. However, its presence as dialectical support for the more usual 'forwards' Symmetry Argument shows that in many ways the most important component of that argument is not the Symmetry Principle (SYM) itself, but rather the starting premise about the harmlessness of pre-natal non-existence (Pi or Pii). The comparison of the 'forwards' and reverse versions reveals the relative plausibilities of the starting premises, of Pi compared with *Fi and Pii compared with *Fii. It is certainly the case that the Epicureans feel that the starting claim about the harmlessness of pre-natal non-existence is sufficiently robust and unquestionable that they feel unthreatened by the possibility of a reverse Symmetry Argument being used against them.[30]

Criticisms of the Symmetry Argument

Perhaps the fact that the Symmetry Argument is not designed to bear the weight of securing freedom from this particular fear is a

[29] Cf. Schopenhauer 1958, vol. 2, 466: 'If what makes death seem so terrible to us were the thought of *non-existence* we should necessarily think with equal horror of the time when as yet we did not exist. For it is irrefutably certain that non-existence after death cannot be different from non-existence before birth, and is therefore no more deplorable than that is.'

[30] See also Rosenbaum 1989b, 368–71, who thinks that a possible defence is available in Seneca's version of the argument at *Ep.* 77.11. This begins not with the simple claim that one does not regret one's past non-existence, but that it is not reasonable to do so. The relevant 'backfire' argument would therefore have to begin by showing that it is reasonable to fear future non-existence. In the *palingenesis* argument of 3.843–62 Lucretius also (at 852–8) uses the observation that in fact we feel at present no concern for past selves to bolster his claim that we should feel no concern for future selves. For my reading of this argument see Warren 2001a.

beneficial result for the Epicureans. At least, the discussion which has been provoked by the suggestion of a symmetry between pre-natal and *post mortem* non-existence suggests that it is not a principle to which they could expect everyone to agree. Those who object to Fi or Fii (and therefore think that *post mortem* non-existence is or will be 'something to us') sometimes happily grant Pi and Pii (that pre-natal non-existence is or was 'nothing to us'). By doing so these objectors deny the very symmetry of past and future upon which both versions of the argument rely. There are two reasons which are generally given to support this denial. They are:

A. The time of birth is a necessary condition of personal identity, whereas the time of death is merely contingent (i.e. I could not have been born earlier than I was, but could die later than I will).[31]

B. Within a lifetime our attitudes to past and future experiences are inevitably asymmetrical.[32]

The majority of the present literature devoted to this topic takes these two positions as starting points, and while much of interest and use has been produced which involves discussions of personal identity, and the rationality of future-biased reasoning, the discussion has drifted away from the original structure of the Epicurean argument. Indeed, if the Epicurean argument is indeed version 1 rather than 2, then it does not invoke present attitudes to past and future experiences. Therefore, the strand of objection encompassed by B cannot strike directly at the heart of the Epicurean position, since it is clearly considering the attitudes of a subject from a 'temporally located perspective' to things which he did experience and will experience.[33] It assumes, therefore, that version 2 is the Epicureans' argument.

Objection A therefore seems to have a better chance against Epicurus, since it can also strike against version 1 of the

---

[31] The 'classic' statement of this position is offered (although tentatively) by Nagel 1979, 8. More recently see Glannon 1994, 240–1, Williams 1995, Brueckner and Fischer 1998.

[32] The 'classic' statement of this position of asymmetrical attitudes is in Parfit 1984, 165 ff., although he is appropriately cautious about the extent to which he wishes to endorse this position. More recently, see Brueckner and Fischer 1993a, Kaufman 1999.   [33] Fischer 1993, 26.

Symmetry Argument. It argues that Pi (or Pii) might be true, but that this attitude cannot and should not be transferred to the future, because attitudes about pre-natal non-existence can be explained by the bare fact that a particular individual could not have been born earlier than the actual date of birth. In other words, date of birth is essential to personal identity, whereas the date of death is not. This is offered as a relevant distinction between past and future non-existence.

This objection is sometimes supplemented by what we have already encountered as the counterfactual account of the harm constituted by death. Death is an evil because it deprives one of goods which would have been enjoyed had death occurred later. But pre-natal non-existence is not also an evil, because the relevant symmetrical claim about birth (namely that being born at a particular time deprives one of goods which would have been enjoyed had one been born earlier) does not express a real possibility; the *comparanda* (person born at t_1 and person born at t_2) are not the same person living two possible lives. Consider the following diagram.

1925	1950	1975	2000	2025

P ――――――――――――――――――――――――――

Q ············ ―――――――――――――――― ············

R ――――――――――――――――――――――

P, Q, and R represent three lives. The solid line in each case represents the period of time during which each life persists. Clearly, life Q is shorter than both life P and life R by twenty-five years. The dotted lines at each end of life Q represent these two comparative deficiencies. Let us further assume that these three lives are as similar to each other as possible. So lives Q and R, for example, are identical for the period 1950–2000 (so life Q is life R 'cut short'). We can also stipulate that (although historical circumstances may change) the period in life P of 1925–75 is *as like as possible* the period 1950–2000 in the other two lives and that—with the same proviso—that life P is as like life R as possible.

In essence, Nagel—and anyone else who wishes to deny the Symmetry Principle but maintain the deprivation account of the harm of death—will argue that although it is true to say that life Q is deprived of the twenty-five extra years which life R contains, life Q is not deprived of the twenty-five extra years that life P contains. A proponent of pre-natal and *post mortem* symmetry, on the other hand, claims that if life Q is truly deprived of one of these twenty-five year periods then it must be deprived of both, and if life Q is truly not deprived of one of these periods then it cannot be deprived of either. Nagel claims that lives Q and R share the important characteristic of beginning at the same time, which he takes to be at least a necessary condition of their indeed being alternative lives for one individual. They are identical for fifty years and then one comes to an end while another continues. In that case, says Nagel, it is true to say that life Q is deprived of the extra twenty-five years contained in life R. But, he also argues, it is not true to say that life Q is deprived of the extra twenty-five years contained in life P. There is a strong intuitive plausibility to this claim. After all, we have seen that it is reasonable to say that lives Q and R can be *identical* throughout the period of life Q, whereas lives P and Q cannot. How do we account for this?

This is clearly a matter of the criteria of personal identity. The most concise way to express the thought is to say that the time of birth is a necessary condition of personal identity. But why should this be? Nagel is clear: 'The direction of time is crucial in assigning possibilities to people or other individuals. Distinct possible lives of a single person can diverge from a common beginning but they cannot converge to a common conclusion from diverse beginnings.'[34] That the time of birth is a necessary condition for personal identity is then usually explained either in terms of genetics or in terms of psychology. It is sometimes contended that only at the particular time of conception do the two specific gametes come together to create the unique

---

[34] Nagel 1979, 8 (cf. Williams 1995, 225). Nagel 1979, 8 n. 3, confesses some reticence over this argument but maintains that 'while it would be a cause for regret that one had been deprived of all those possible years of life by being born too late, the feeling would differ from that which many people have about death. I conclude that something about the future *prospect* of nothingness is not captured by the analysis in terms of denied possibilities.'

individual.[35] However, it now seems possible at least to delay someone's birth or conception. Particular gametes may be stored for some time (even beyond the death of one of the parents) before they are brought together. Similarly, a particular zygote may be stored for some time before implantation. In both cases it may reasonably be claimed that someone who develops from such stored cells could indeed have been born earlier.[36] Alternatively, the account is based upon the notion of psychological continuity.[37] Lives Q and R are psychologically identical until the end of life Q. So they share, for that period, concerns, hopes, plans, and so on. Life P, however, begins earlier and the formative years are quite different—attachments are formed to people not alive during lives Q and R, for example. Life P, therefore, is sufficiently psychologically distinct from lives Q and R that it cannot be an alternative life for someone who might otherwise live life Q or R. So someone who does live life Q, for example, could not have been born earlier and live life P.[38]

Since it relies on a certain view about personal identity, this argument can be disarmed given certain alternative assumptions. I have already shown, for example, how Seneca uses the Stoic notion of strictly determined times for birth and death in *Ep. Mor.* 77.11 to remove the possibility of death being a deprivation of goods.[39] Unfortunately, the Epicureans' position on the question

---

[35] This is sometimes called the 'Zygotic principle'. See Parfit 1984, 351 ff., where he terms this the 'Time dependence claim' or the 'Origin view', and Williams 1995. If maintained, it produces some interesting problems for cases of pre-natal harm. See Feinberg 1992.   [36] Cf. Rosenbaum 1989b, 362.

[37] See Belshaw 1993, 109–12.

[38] For this sort of account see Kaufman 1995 or 1996. Brueckner and Fischer 1998 reply. Similar views can be found in Belshaw 1993, 109–12 (cf. the response by Brueckner and Fischer 1993b), and Glannon 1994, 241: '*Whether* one might have been born ten, twenty, or even thirty years earlier than he actually was born, or *whether* one might have lived for the same number of years if he had not died when he actually did does not really matter. Rather, what matters is *when* one actually is conceived and *when* one actually is born. Specifically, what matters are the conditions that obtain at those times and how they bear causally on what one will actually experience between the present and the time of death.'

[39] Kamm 1993, 28, argues that even if we imagine that the future is totally determined then we would still be more concerned about the loss brought about by death than pre-natal non-existence. This is a special sense of 'loss', which allows one to consider something to be lost which there is no possibility at all of having. Compare the other sense of 'loss' discussed above, p. 44 ff.

of what constitutes personal identity is not particularly clear, and it is not easy to imagine what reaction they would have had to this view. There is no sign, however, that they share Nagel's intuition that the time of one's birth is a necessary condition of identity. True, *Sent. Vat.* 14 claims that it is not possible to 'be born twice' (δὶς δὲ οὐκ ἔστι γενέσθαι), but this still falls short of the claim Nagel needs that it is necessary for my being me to have been born when I in fact was.[40]

In any case, it is important to clarify what position has been reached in the dialectic. We should remember that the Epicureans will claim to have shown that death does not constitute a deprivation on grounds other than the Symmetry Principle. In that case, they do not—as Nagel does—need to find some way of distinguishing pre-natal and *post mortem* non-existence, nor will their major conclusion that 'death is nothing to us' be irrevocably damaged if the Symmetry Principle is found to fail. Nagel offers this view of personal identity as a 'solution to the problem of temporal asymmetry, pointed out by Lucretius'.[41] But *whose* problem is it? It is not a problem for the Epicureans, since, although recognizing it as widespread, they simply regard the asymmetrical view as irrational and easily avoided once the inconsistency is disclosed. It is, however, a problem for Nagel since unless he can account sufficiently for, and indeed justify, the asymmetry which people do tend to exhibit then his deprivation account of the harm of death will also apply to the time before birth. In this sense, therefore, the burden is on Nagel and his supporters to show this asymmetry in order to maintain their own view of the harm of death, and the Epicureans—as we have already seen (p. 34ft.)—have reasons for rejecting the deprivation account of death which do not rely on the Symmetry Argument. On the other hand, however, if Nagel can justify the asymmetrical attitude to pre-natal and *post mortem* non-existence on these grounds, then he has constructed a powerful objection to the Symmetry

---

[40] For relevant discussion see Alberti 1990, Warren 2001a. Kaufman 1996, 309, claims support for the notion that 'what matters' in this context is not 'biological' or genetic identity, but identity of biography or psychological continuity from Lucr. *DRN* 3.851, 859–60. On the question of 'what matters' in such discussions of the metaphysics of personal identity, focused on the repercussions of a Parfitian approach based on psychological continuity, see Wolf 1986, Parfit 1986, and McMahan 2002, 39–94.   [41] Nagel 1979, 7.

Argument itself and the Epicureans ought to be careful not to
rely too heavily on it providing any new and independent reasons
for the conclusion that 'death is nothing to us'.[42]

Parfit's patient and asymmetrical preferences

Let us leave aside, for the moment, the historical question of
which version of the Symmetry Argument is promoted by
Epicurean and other ancient texts and consider objection B,
primarily as a counter to version 2 of the argument. Perhaps the
best-known starting-point for this general area of discussion is
an example constructed by Derek Parfit, which I will call 'Parfit's
patient'.

I am in some hospital, to have some kind of surgery. Since this is completely safe, and always successful, I have no fears about the effects.
The surgery may be brief, or it may take a long time. Because I have to
co-operate with the surgeon, I cannot have anaesthetics. I have had this
surgery once before and can remember how painful it is. Under a new
policy, because the operation is so painful, patients are now afterwards
made to forget it. Some drug removes their memories of the last few
hours.

I have just woken up. I cannot remember going to sleep. I ask my nurse
if it has been decided when my operation is going to be, and how long it
must take. She says that she knows the facts both about me and another
patient, but that she cannot remember which facts apply to whom. She
can tell me that the following is true. I may be the patient who had his
operation yesterday. In that case, my operation was the longest ever
performed, lasting ten hours. I may instead be the patient who is to have
a short operation later today. It is either true that I did suffer for ten
hours or that I shall suffer for one hour.

---

[42] Benn 1998, 210, suspects that the fact that those who have died can be
specifically referred to *post mortem* whereas those yet to be born cannot offers
some support for this attempt to produce an asymmetry. But see Nozick 1981,
645 n. 6: 'Also, we should avoid the answer that before you exist, in contrast to
afterwards, you cannot even be referred to; in consequence, no one could have
said earlier that *you* did not exist then, while after your death that can be said.
First, why is it not sadder that not only did you not exist earlier, but you could
not even be referred to then? (There could have been a list of everyone who
existed earlier, and that list would not have included you.) Second, you can be
referred to now, and so now we can say that you did not exist then.'

I ask the nurse to find out which is true. While she is away, it is clear to me which I prefer to be true. If I learn that the first is true, I shall be greatly relieved.

Parfit 1984, 166[43]

Parfit's primary concern in producing this example is not to offer it as an objection to a Symmetry Argument, although he does recognize its relevance to such questions. Rather, this discussion takes place within a general examination of what Parfit calls 'S' (Self-Interest theories). The theory under discussion is a hedonist version of the self-interest theory which holds that all that should matter to us is that we experience pleasure rather than pain. Examples such as 'Parfit's patient' are supposed to erode the view that the only ethically relevant factor is the subject of the pleasure/pain, which would imply that when the pleasure or pain is experienced is irrelevant. If we intuitively agree with the preference which the patient expresses at the end of the story, then some additional factor besides the subject of the pleasure/ pain and the amount of pleasure/pain experienced has been agreed to be relevant. It matters *when* the pleasure/pain takes place. More specifically, we always prefer pleasures to be in the future rather than the past, and pains to be in the past rather than the future. If this is so, then the S-theorist will find it hard to maintain a further thesis to which he is committed, namely that it is irrational to be biased towards the near future, solely on the basis of a general attitude which he assumes of temporal neutrality.[44]

When the intuitive reaction to the story of Parfit's patient is applied to version 2 of the Symmetry Argument, it is claimed that we have now found good reason to think that future non-existence is not relevantly similar to past non-existence simply in virtue of the fact that it is in the future and that in fact we have temporally asymmetrical attitudes to the past and future.

The defender of the Symmetry Argument claims that he can tell us how we *should* look at these periods, not that this is how we do in fact consider the past and future. If, therefore, the proponent of this Parfit-inspired objection is to pass from this descriptive account of our current intuitions to a normative

---

[43] Cf. Nozick 1981, 744 n. 6.   [44] Parfit 1984, 169.

account of how we ought to or must inevitably look at the past and future, he owes us one of the following:

i. An account of how our asymmetrical attitudes themselves can be used to show that the two periods of non-existence are not of equal value; in other words, an account of the rationality of that asymmetrical attitude. In order to avoid question-begging, this would require him to show that pre-natal and *post mortem* non-existence are in fact not of equal value independently of the attitudes we happen to have towards them.

OR

ii. The demonstration that such an asymmetrical attitude is inescapable, whether or not it is justifiable. We simply cannot perform the required change of mind; it is impossible to think of the past and future in the required symmetrical manner. It remains an open question whether pre-natal and *post mortem* non-existence are in fact of equal value, but such a question is irrelevant in practice since we cannot alter our concerns as the Symmetry Argument recommends.

Parfit himself is instructively cautious about making such claims and wonders how we are to account for the asymmetry he has uncovered.[45] He considers a number of possible options.

a. 'The direction of causation'

We can affect the future but not the past (indeed we can affect the *post mortem* future but not the pre-natal past), so there is a good reason to be biased towards the future. But there is no such distinction to be made between the near and far future, so there is no reason to be biased towards the near future. The obvious response to this proposal is to show that we are in fact biased towards the future even when the relevant event is entirely out of our hands. The patient in the example has no ability to alter what will happen. Nevertheless it is easy to see how he would prefer already to have undergone the surgery.[46]

[45] Nagel 1986, 229, wonders if it is 'a fact perhaps too deep for explanation'.
[46] Parfit 1984, 168.

In the specific case of death, however, it is possible to argue that we do have the power to affect matters. Although it is impossible for someone, once born, to affect the past and be born earlier (even provided that the chosen view of personal identity allows that one and the same person *could* be born earlier) it is perfectly possible for him to take pains to die as late as possible. Future non-existence is something which it is in our power to try to postpone.[47] Similarly, it is in our power to attempt to experience more future pleasures and fewer future pains whereas it is not in our power to alter the number of pains and pleasures felt in the past. If it is agreed to be in our interests to experience pleasures and avoid pains, then this might offer a prudential basis for maintaining an asymmetrical attitude to past and future.

A future bias towards even events which cannot be altered could offer a response to the form of the Symmetry Argument found in Seneca and discussed above (pp. 70–3). There, Seneca relied on the Stoic thesis of pervasive determinism to show that death does not deprive us of anything, since there was never the possibility of us living any longer. (Just as being born later does not deprive us of anything.) On this model, being born and dying are a pair of events which—although one is past and the other future—we can do nothing to alter. Does Parfit's example of the patient therefore offer a reason for feeling unsatisfied with Seneca's argument even if we accept the determinist principles on which it relies? Again, the patient in the example is unable to affect which of the alternative scenarios is the case but nevertheless would prefer one over the other. Just so, were we unable to affect the times of our birth and death, it could be argued, there would be a similar future bias. It is unclear how plausible a view this is, perhaps, since it is difficult to imagine being committed to the relevant kind of deterministic outlook. Seneca's claim is that it is a necessary consequence of accepting the true Stoic determined view of the world that one should not even begin to think that one's time of death is alterable. Even if we do not know when we are going to die, our lives have a pre-determined length and we are pre-destined to die at some fixed point in the future. Indeed, coming to accept and live in accordance with nature's rational plan is a necessary part of living a virtuous Stoic life.

---

[47] Cf. Ewin 2002, 16.

b. 'The direction of time'

A related attempt to offer an independent reason for rejecting the symmetry of past and future non-existence invokes the A-series of time.[48] Indeed, some philosophers have relied upon the presence of asymmetrical attitudes to the past and future as a reason for concluding that the A-series must be real.[49] The A-series builds into time a directionality, or flow, by asserting that at any moment all events have the property either of pastness, presentness, or futurity. If it is agreed that the A-series is real, i.e. that pastness, presentness, and futurity are indeed real characteristics of times, then one might suggest that past and future non-existence differ in this very sense: one is past and the other is future. In that case our asymmetrical attitude might be grounded in an independently established fact about the nature of things. The futurity of future events is an objective characteristic of those events (i.e. not a merely relational property dependent on the point of view of the present observer) which might then be used as the grounds of the asymmetrical attitude. Unfortunately, this approach suffers from two important flaws. First, it is highly controversial whether the A-series of time is in fact real, and therefore this dialectical move opens up huge new areas of metaphysical disagreement which would have to be fought over and secured. Second, even if it could be shown that the A-series is real, the further question has to be broached of just how this is relevant. Even if future non-existence has the property of futurity, why should this alone serve to justify my taking an attitude to its value different from that I take towards the other period of non-existence which frames my life, which now has the property of 'being past'? More work will be needed to show the required relationship between these temporal properties and our present attitudes.

---

[48] See e.g. Yourgrau 1993, 156: 'The futurity of death, therefore, is its distinguishing feature, as opposed to prenatal non-existence, and this is a feature invisible to the spatialized time of the B-series'. Cf. Parfit 1984, 178–81; Gallois 1994; Dainton 2001, 335 n. 3: 'In a block universe this fear [sc. of death] is misplaced, for if all times and events are equally real, death does not bring absolute annihilation, lives do not cease to exist, they simply have beginnings and ends.'

[49] See e.g. Schlesinger 1980, 34–6, who considers our past and future attitudes to pain and non-existence. Also note Prior 1959 and the B-theorists' need to be able to account for statements of the kind 'Thank goodness that's over!' Cf. Mellor 1998, 40–6.

Nevertheless, a similar tactic is available which has the benefit of avoiding these tricky metaphysical problems concerning the nature of time. It may be argued that, whether or not they are themselves relying on a B-series or 'tenseless' conception of time, the proponents of the Symmetry Argument fail to recognize the importance of the first-person perspective in matters of this kind. This first-person perspective, the perspective adopted by each person as they consider their life from within, is just that highlighted and explored by examples such as that of Parfit's patient. It is also arguably the perspective from which issues such as the fear of death ought primarily to be addressed since 'fear' is also an attitude taken up by individuals to future events from a temporally located personal perspective.

> The fact that we live our lives within time . . . provides some reason to think that the temporally situated perspective is at least as important as the atemporal . . . with respect to the generation or recognition of values.
>
> Brueckner and Fischer 1993a, 42

David Cockburn offers similar sentiments:

> The sense in which physical pain is thought of as an evil is revealed as fundamentally in our fear of future pain as in our aversion to present pain (and, one might add, in our concerns about the past, present, and future pains of others). Similarly, the sense in which death is thought of as an evil is revealed in a *fundamental* way in a person's fear of her own death.
>
> Cockburn 1997, 138

It is somewhat unclear how we are to understand the claim that attitudes reveal 'in a fundamental way' the value of their objects. Perhaps the claim is that the value of objects of concern is generated or caused by the concern itself; *post mortem* non-existence 'matters' because we are concerned about it, not vice versa. For Cockburn, this claim is related to a more wide-ranging concern about the relative priority given to questions of value and questions of ontology or metaphysics more generally in discussions such as this.[50]

---

[50] Cockburn 1997, 140: '[I]f we do not think of the transformation from one tense to another as being a common operation on a range of different propositional cores we will find no incongruity in the idea that something which is a matter of complete indifference when it lies in the past should be a matter of deep concern when it lies in the future.' Compare also Cockburn

c. 'The bias to the future is an inevitable evolutionary product'

This explanation claims that we have as a species developed to have a functional and/or instinctive attitude which fits with the necessity to act so as to affect what is about to happen. Again, however, such a response might fail adequately to distinguish between a bias to the future (which the S-theorist wishes to retain) and a bias to the near future (which he wishes to discard). Presumably, there are good grounds for thinking that the near future is more significant for the sort of prudential reasoning which is meant to be accounted for as an 'evolutionary product'.

These general approaches are alike in so far as they attempt to offer an account of an asymmetrical attitude to the past and future. Such an attitude is then said to be prudential or instrumental in some way. In addition, this instrumentally advantageous attitude may be given an evolutionary basis—in the hope that this basis adds to the notion that the asymmetrical attitude is a non-negotiable piece of human psychology.[51] They also share a weakness. Although they may be successful in offering an account of the origin of the apparently intuitive asymmetrical attitude, they are much less successful in showing whether and in what way that attitude can be justified, especially in the case of past and future non-existence. Indeed, they might even be thought to offer a circular argument. The asymmetrical attitude requires some sort of justification independent of the mere claim that past and future non-existence do in fact differ in value, since otherwise the only reason offered for why it is true that past and future non-existence differ in value is the supposed asymmetrical attitude itself. In other words, it ought not to be the case that denial of the symmetry of past and future non-existence is the reason for thinking that the asymmetrical attitude must be maintained, if the denial of the symmetry of past and future non-existence is based in turn upon the fact of us holding asymmetrical attitudes to them.[52]

1998. For an example of the kind of view Cockburn wishes to criticize see Nagel 1970, 61.

[51] Brueckner and Fischer 1986, cf. Haji 1991, 177.

[52] For a criticism of Brueckner and Fischer's 1986 application of Parfitian asymmetries to the question of past and future non-existence, see Haji

In fact, the supporter of the Symmetry Argument is quite at liberty simply to claim that we can and ought to discard this evolutionary inheritance or prudential attitude in this case, especially if there can be shown to be clear benefits of taking a symmetrical attitude. Eliminating the prospective fear of death is certainly a benefit, and therefore can itself be relied upon as a reason to struggle against any proposed psychological attitude produced as part of our evolution. (Parfit himself argues that there are good reasons to think that a symmetrical attitude not only towards pre-natal and *post mortem* non-existence but also to pleasures and pains within a life would yield beneficial results.)

If they are to counter this kind of reasoning, the objectors to the Symmetry Argument must do one of two things. First, they could show not only that we do have a future bias, but that we *should* have a future bias or, at least, that we cannot live without a future bias and they ought to do this without relying merely on a supposed difference in value in past and future non-existence. They could do this by showing either that the benefits of the future bias outweigh any benefits of a symmetrical view (and therefore even if we could change to a symmetrical attitude we have reason not to) or that the Symmetry Argument is calling upon us to effect an impossible psychological reordering (and therefore even if we can see a benefit in changing to a symmetrical view, the whole argument is beside the point: such an attitude cannot be held). Second, they could show that past and future non-existence do in fact differ in value without relying as proof of this difference on any asymmetrical attitude we happen to take towards them.[53]

It is important to ask what the upshot would be of accepting Parfit's examples as demonstrating a certain and—perhaps—permanent asymmetry in an agent's attitudes to the past and future. Does this help those who wish to object to the Epicurean position? First, we should note that if these examples show anything they show that this temporal asymmetry holds only for goods and evils which the particular agent in question has or will experience. Whatever conclusions are drawn about our

1991. Brueckner and Fischer 1993a respond to Haji's criticisms and clarify their own position.

[53] An approach recommended by Kaufman 1999, 9.

respective attitudes to past and future experiences, it remains to be seen how these are relevant to the question of whether it is rational to take a particular view about things which cannot be experienced, whether they are in the past or the future. Much of the discussion of this question is centred on the rationality or otherwise of an apparent intuitive preference for pains to be in the past and pleasures to be in the future, but the Symmetry Argument, on either version, is considering not two experiences, but two *absences* of experience. The reason we do not display equanimity with regard to pre-natal events is not that, although they were distressing at the time, they are now in the past. They simply were not ever distressing to us because they happened when we did not (yet) exist. So, for example, the conclusion that we have a 'future bias' when it comes to our pleasures is not of direct relevance.[54] It can be argued, for example, that there is no similar asymmetry to be found in an agent's attitudes to some other person's benefits or harms; what matters there is not when they happen but the size of the benefit or harm. (Ask whether you would prefer your mother to have undergone a greater amount of pain or to be about to undergo a smaller amount. It seems more reasonable here to prefer the latter, and any preference for the former may be diagnosed as caused by a temporary sympathetic identification of oneself with the person in question.)[55] If this is so, then those who wish to retain the asymmetry must restrict it to an asymmetrical attitude with respect to those pleasures and pains which the agent whose attitudes are in question will expect to experience. An important note of subjectivity is therefore introduced. But this can be seen to play into the Epicureans' hands to the extent that it is in tension with the arguments offered by Nagel, for example, for the claim that non-experienced goods and evils can benefit and harm. The Parfitian asymmetry depends on a subjectivity which the Epicureans can

---

[54] The cases considered by Parfit 1984, 165–7, by which he generates an intuitive 'future bias' are different from the case of death in so far as they are cases in which pain has been or will be experienced, although the memory of this pain is subsequently removed by induced amnesia. In this case, it would appear, Epicurus would happily concede that such future painful experiences might be feared. Death, however, is not painful when it is present. Cf. Glannon 1994, 237–8, who criticizes both Parfit and Brueckner and Fischer for not realizing this important distinction.   [55] See the examples in Parfit 1984, 181–4.

counter by falling back upon their claim that death is by its very nature not something which can be experienced by the deceased. Death is not to be feared since we will not experience it, and even if there is some asymmetry in our attitudes to the past and future this holds if at all only for experiential goods and evils. It therefore is irrelevant to the question of the value of death. The Epicurean can therefore construct the following dilemma:

Either (a), we agree that the goods and bads in question are perceived goods and bads in order to retain the asymmetrical attitude (therefore avoid the Symmetry Argument), but thereby fall foul of the 'existence requirement' argument;

Or (b), we do not accept that the goods and evils in question are necessarily perceived goods and bads, but by doing so are less well equipped to argue against the symmetry of pre-natal and *post mortem* non-existence from the presence of an asymmetrical temporal attitude to past and future goods. (In that case, in order to secure the asymmetry between the two periods a critic following Nagel must rely on the admittedly tentative claim that the fixity of time of birth but contingency of time of death can generate the required distinction between the two periods of non-existence.)

Would a symmetrical attitude be better for us?

Parfit has a generally positive view of how we would be if we did not have this intuitive asymmetrical attitude to past and future goods and evils. He conjures up a temporally neutral man 'Timeless'.[56] Timeless views his own past and future suffering with the same neutrality as displayed towards the sufferings of others by those who remain temporally biased in matters of their own suffering or benefit. So when faced with the position of the patient who may either already have undergone a long and painful operation or who might be about to undergo a shorter, less painful operation, Timeless prefers the option which involves the least pain, *whenever it may be*. In this case, he will prefer to be about to undergo surgery. Parfit himself seems to think that this attitude is

[56] Parfit 1984, 174.

not entirely possible since it is it difficult to see how essentially future-directed activities such as planning and hoping would play much of a role in a 'timeless' life. A Timeless person would certainly be a passive type of person, as content to relive past enjoyments as to do anything to strive for future ones. Nevertheless, Parfit does find something positive in such a 'timeless' existence, however implausible or impracticable it might prove to be.[57]

> We would be much happier if we lacked the bias towards the future. We would be much less depressed by ageing and the approach of death. If we were like Timeless, being at the end of our lives would be more like being at the beginning. At any point in our lives we could enjoy looking back or forward to our whole lives.

> Parfit 1984, 177

This picture of Timeless is reminiscent of the picture of Epicurus himself on his deathbed (see above pp. 9–10). Epicurus too claimed that his very last day was enjoyable, despite physical discomfort, since he was able to recollect past pleasures. Indeed, one of the significant differences between Epicurean hedonism and that of their major contemporary hedonist rivals, the Cyrenaics, was the Epicurean claim that it is possible to enjoy through anticipation and recollection mental pleasures whose intentional objects are located temporally other than in the present. (They also claimed that in many ways looking back allows one to edit out any past painful experiences simply by choosing not to recollect them, whereas the uncertainty of the future makes a similar, forward-looking practice less promising.)[58] However, the Epicureans would certainly want to resist the claim that by taking such an attitude to the past and future they would have to maintain a certain detachment from themselves and their future lives, which is one of the consequences often stressed by those who find Parfit's Timeless character inconceivable.[59]

---

[57] Cf. Wolf 1986, 719. Similar points can be found in e.g. Williams 1976. Kaufman 1999, 7–9, constructs another character, Prior, who is biased to the past. He argues that Prior is no less conceivable than Timeless but that in fact on closer inspection Prior's complete indifference to the future makes such a life inconceivable. In that case Timeless too is inconceivable.

[58] For more on this see Warren 2001d. Compare Sen. *De Brev. Vitae* 10.5.

[59] This notion of 'detachment' can be explored further through the contrast between a 'subjective' or first-personal and 'objective' or third-personal view of oneself, and the relationship and possible conflicts between the two. This

Certainly, the Epicurean would not seem to be indifferent to the future in the sense that he will make no effort whatsoever to ensure that his future is a secure one in which he can continue to live a happy life. Epicurus offers some advice on how best to plan for the most pleasant future at *Ep. Men.* 129–30, even counselling on occasion that a pleasure should be avoided in order to secure some greater more distant good.[60] Nevertheless, we will see later a powerful objection to the Epicurean position on the question of premature death which claims that in order not to be subject to the potential frustration of future-oriented goals and projects, an Epicurean will have only a very restricted set of aspirations.[61] If this objection has any force, it would seem correct to think that an Epicurean would differ psychologically from most people in significant ways, even if not in such an extreme way as Parfit's Timeless.

Joseph Raz's Symmetry Argument

It may appear that my discussion of the Symmetry Argument has taken a mainly negative tone, and has shown that Lucretius does not in fact offer the interesting argument which others have taken from the text. But there is an important lesson to be drawn from that conclusion. It is easy to be mistaken about the exact intention and force of an argument, particularly an argument found in an ancient source. It is easy to be misled and rely on second-hand interpretations of the argument.

If my interpretation of the Symmetry Argument found in Lucretius is correct, there are two mistaken views of what it is intended to show. The first and more common mistaken view is that it is designed to show that it is irrational to hold a prospective fear of death, a fear of mortality. A second, less common, mistaken view is that the Symmetry Argument is designed to

---

interplay is the topic of Nagel 1986, who considers how this affects how one conceives of one's own death at 223–31. Cf. Cockburn 1990, 193–5. Long 1997 pursues similar themes in Lucretius.

[60] See Warren 2001d and the discussions of the future at *Ep. Men.* 127 and *Sent. Vat.* 33.

[61] This is the argument of Luper-Foy 1987. See below pp. 210–12.

show that we ought not to hold the view that longevity is valuable, or, in other words, that life is intrinsically valuable and the more of it we have the better. I have already discussed some examples of the first kind of mistaken interpretation since they advocate reading what I called version 2 of the Symmetry Argument. Let me offer as an example of this second kind of mistaken interpretation Joseph Raz's 'Lucretian' argument.[62] In the course of a careful and lucid discussion of the question of whether life is intrinsically valuable, Raz comes to consider what he takes to be a Lucretian argument for the thesis that life has no intrinsic value. On Raz's view, Lucretius argues indirectly for this thesis by arguing that death cannot be bad for the dead and that in fact our own asymmetrical attitudes to past and future non-existence show this to be the case. The argument which Raz constructs is as follows.

If death is bad, it is bad because it deprives us of life we *could have lived.* But a person could have been born earlier just as he could die later. Therefore, late birth and early death are similar in so far as they deprive us of time *we could have lived.* But no one thinks that being born later is a bad. Therefore, being deprived of time we could have lived is not regarded as a bad. So death is not a bad.

Raz explains the argument—and the confusion he detects in it—by distinguishing between two kinds of preference, which he terms 'the longevity preference' and the 'time-location preference'. The first simply is a wish to live for as long a time as possible. The second is a wish to live during some particular time. The two kinds of preference are independent but related. It is possible to wish to live at some particular time in the world's history (here I use 'history' in a very broad sense which would include both the future and the past) without wishing to lead a longer life than one in fact will live. I suppose it might even be possible to wish to live at a particular time in history and live a shorter life than one will in fact live. They are related because, clearly, if one lives a longer life *ipso facto* one lives 'through' a larger stretch of history than one would if the length of life were shorter. So one way to ensure that one fulfils a time-location preference would be to extend one's lifetime (forwards or backwards) so

---

[62] Raz 2001, 88–99.

that it extends to include the events one would wish to be around to experience. Whether this is the only way in which one can fulfil a time-location preference would depend upon whether it is in fact true that the same individual could live at different times, in short, whether one's personal identity is necessarily related to one's date of birth. If it is the only way, then it is impossible for me, for example, coherently to wish to have lived in fourth-century Athens (sc. rather than in twenty-first-century England), since whatever person I imagine living at that time would not share my actual time of birth, and by this criterion is therefore necessarily not me 'living another possible life'.

Raz also thinks that Lucretius intends to show through this argument that we ought not to hold a longevity preference. He thinks that the implicit general form of Lucretius' argument, therefore, must be something like the following: 'We cannot hold both a longevity preference and an asymmetrical time-location preference. Since, if our time-location preference is asymmetrical this shows that it is not the length of lifetime itself that we wish for, but rather we wish only for more future lifetime. But our time-location preference is always asymmetrical. So we cannot consistently hold a longevity preference.' Already there is something surprising about this formulation. Here Raz's Lucretius appears to be relying upon an asymmetrical attitude as a reason for rejecting the longevity preference, rather than acting as an advocate of adopting a symmetrical attitude towards the past and future. The asymmetry is used as a standard against which Lucretius tests the longevity preference. Finding an inconsistency, Lucretius discards not the asymmetry but the longevity preference itself. (Perhaps, then, this ought rather to be called the Asymmetry Argument.)[63] In any case, this is how Raz diagnoses the mistake in Lucretius' argument:

Lucretius is wrong in thinking that people's preference for longevity is unwarranted because it manifests an unwarranted post-mortem/pre-natal asymmetry. It manifests no such asymmetry, for it involves

---

[63] This is in fact how Raz introduces it at Raz 2001, 88. Contrast the argument constructed by Haji 1991, 172, who considers the case of a person he calls 'Past'. His proponent of a Symmetry Argument reasons: 'Since more life is better than less, it does not matter *when* you enjoy the extra years'. Raz's proponent argues: 'Since it *does* matter when you enjoy the extra time, more life is not better than less'.

no location preference, only a preference regarding longevity. Only a location preference, however, can manifest the asymmetry, and no such preference is necessarily involved in the preference for greater longevity.

Raz 2001, 91

For Raz, Lucretius thinks that people display a particular asymmetrical attitude to the past and future. They want their lives to continue into the future and regard a loss of such continuation as an evil, but do not similarly regret that their lives were not extended into the past. But if people are instead simply concerned that they will die at twenty rather than eighty, for example, then Raz thinks that this need imply no such asymmetrical attitude.

The connection between the two sorts of preference, which Raz himself makes clear, can come to Lucretius' rescue. Raz assumes, I think, that the Symmetry Argument concerns past- and future-directed concerns, that it addresses someone looking backwards and forwards from within a life. I have already explained why I think this is not the force of the argument as it appears in Lucretius' text. But, allowing for the moment that 'Lucretius' does have in mind past- and future-directed attitudes, given that the argument therefore concerns someone in the process of living a life, it is possible to argue that a longevity preference cannot fail also to involve location-preference.

If one were to ask someone living a life, 'Would you like your life to be longer rather than shorter?', it is quite possible that he will answer 'Yes'. What is meant by this? Not, or at least not at all commonly, that this person thinks simply that longer lives are better than shorter ones, and would prefer a longer life whenever that extra time would be and whenever the life takes place. Rather, this surely means that he would like to die later rather than sooner. In other words, if the argument is indeed concerned with the attitude of a person looking backwards and forwards in time then it cannot fail to involve such A-series conceptions, and this in turn involves asymmetric location-preferences.

Raz anticipates this response and argues that this does nothing to show that the longevity-preference itself necessarily manifests any of the irrational asymmetry which Lucretius wishes to eradicate. It is not possible to change the past, and therefore if one wishes to fulfil a longevity-preference then the only way to do so is to extend one's life into the future. But this does not mean that in doing so one is in fact committed to the thought that extra future lifetime is better than extra past lifetime. Indeed, Raz goes so far as to claim that people do not generally have an asymmetric location preference. I am not sure that I understand how he could substantiate this claim. It may indeed be true that people generally consider longer lives to be better but the very difficulties of dissociating such thinking from the distinct supposition that extra future lifetime is better lead me to doubt that we can rely on any such intuitions about what people generally believe. It is also true that some people might sincerely wish to have been born earlier than they were or to have lived at some particular time in the past, presumably free of any disturbing concerns about the metaphysical implications of such wishes for their personal identity.

Raz next introduces a distinction between two kinds of location preference. He interprets the reply to his argument as saying that Lucretius moves from establishing that we all have an asymmetrical 'indexical location preference' (we want our lives to carry on later but do not want them to have begun sooner) to a 'relational location preference' (we want our lives to be longer). Lucretius assumes an asymmetry in the first, indexical, location preference and argues that this is incompatible with a relational location preference. We do not want our lives to have begun sooner, so cannot be concerned merely with living as long a life as possible.

But, Raz argues, we can show that the indexical preference does not entail a preference for longevity; the two are independent but merely coincide in the case of most people given the practical impossibility of extending one's lifetime in any manner other than by trying to extend it into the future. But if other possibilities were opened up, our preferences might be different. For example, if it were possible to 'trade in' past lived time for lifetime in the future, some people might want this, perhaps even trading in ten years of past life for a mere five to come (again, sidestepping any difficulties this may produce for personal identity).[64] This shows a mere indexical location

---

[64] This side-step is rather difficult. Raz 2001, 93–4 (and especially n. 11, relating a suggestion by Nagel) has to introduce a special 'Genie' able to overcome the problems in altering the past, and must build in various safeguards to evade further metaphysical worries.

preference.[65] But it would then also become possible for someone to choose to have lived ten years more by trading in five of the years to come. In this case all that is of concern is longevity; the longer the life the better, no matter when the extra time occurs. Some people, it is true, might sincerely wish to have been born earlier than they were or to have lived at some particular time in the past, in order for their lifetime to overlap some particular event they wish they could witness.

Once the discussion moves into the realms of such examples I find that the strength of any intuitions I might have is greatly weakened. But Raz's point is clear. The Lucretian argument cannot claim a victory against the preference for longevity since this turns out to be quite compatible with an asymmetrical indexical location preference.

At this point it is worth stepping back and asking whether in fact Lucretius wished to show—as Raz assumes he does—that a preference for longevity is irrational. My preceding interpretation of the argument has shown that in fact Lucretius is instead concerned with demonstrating that the state of non-existence is not an evil. This leaves room for further questions about whether it is rational to prefer to live a longer rather than a shorter life, but those questions are left entirely untouched by the Symmetry Argument. The version of the Symmetry Argument which emerges from my own interpretation of the text of Lucretius' poem and Raz's Lucretian argument nevertheless clearly have certain elements in common. They are both concerned with pointing out inconsistencies in most people's attitudes to life and death. My version of the Symmetry Argument shows that people tend to have inconsistent beliefs about the period of non-existence before birth and that after death. Raz's Lucretian argument tries—but fails, in Raz's eyes—to show that people inconsistently hold that longevity is something to be preferred and also that they wish their lives to be extended further into the future but not into the past.

Raz's interpretation of the argument therefore takes a different view from those other interpretations which think it is

---

[65] Compare here Parfit's discussion of a 'future bias' with regard to pleasures and pains: Parfit 1984, 165–84, and above p. 82 ff. Raz's overall concern is with the value or not of life itself so his example differs appropriately.

directed against the fear of mortality—the prospective fear of future non-existence. Rather, Raz takes it to be aimed at the view that life ought always to be lived for as long as possible: the longer the life the better. Raz comes to Lucretius' argument after a brief discussion of the question whether immortality is something we ought to hope for. Raz concludes that there is no conclusive reason why we ought not to wish for immortality, since he agrees that other considerations being equal it is in fact better to live a longer rather than a shorter life because a longer life allows greater opportunity for enjoying various goods.[66] He takes Lucretius to be arguing here for what he calls 'the thesis': 'life is a precondition for good, and normally a conditional good, but it is not unconditionally and intrinsically a good'.[67] Of course, simply arguing that death—the state of non-existence which follows life—is not an evil is not enough to show that I ought not to wish my life to be as long as possible. Raz thinks that Lucretius offers this Symmetry Argument to secure that second conclusion. I do not. If anywhere, the Epicureans' arguments against the value of prolonging a life are to be found in their characterization of a complete life.

In my view, Raz's conclusion that Lucretius cannot show that we cannot consistently retain a desire for longevity and that therefore his argument fails, simply misunderstands what the argument as it appears in the poem is designed to show. It is not Lucretius' intention, at least not here, to show that longevity ought not to be desired. So Lucretius' argument cannot therefore be considered to be a failure. Part of the confusion is caused by the fact that Epicurus does indeed subscribe to 'the thesis', as Raz himself points out. That much is made clear by the Epicurean apology offered by Sextus Empiricus at *M.* 1.285:

εἶτα οὐδὲ κατὰ τοῦτο ἔφησεν ὁ Ἐπίκουρος τὸν θάνατον μηδὲν εἶναι πρὸς ἡμᾶς, καθὸ ἀδιάφορον ἐστιν ἢ ζῆν ἢ μή· πολλῷ γὰρ αἰρετώτερον τὸ ζῆν διὰ τὸ

---

[66] He is clear that he does not consider life *per se* to be a good. On whether immortality is something to wish for, see the influential paper by Williams 1973a, and the reply by Fischer 1994. Cf. also p. 110 ff. on Epicurean arguments against the desirability of immortality.

[67] Raz 2001, 77. Cf. Sen. *Ep. Mor.* 99.12: *vita nec bonum nec malum est: boni et mali locus est* ('Life is neither good nor bad, but is a condition of goodness and badness'). Also compare Lucr. *DRN* 3.862–4.

αἰσθανομένων εἶναι τὸ ἀγαθόν· ἀλλ' ἐν ἀναισθησίᾳ οὔτε κακόν τι εἶναι οὔτε ἀγαθόν.

Moreover, Epicurus did not say that 'death is nothing to us' in the sense that it does not matter at all whether we live or not.[68] For it is far preferable to be alive since what is good belongs to perceivers, and there is neither good nor bad in the absence of perception.

S.E. *M.* 1.285

However, that Epicurus did indeed hold that living is not *per se* good, but rather is a precondition of any good (or bad, for that matter), does not require that all of the related arguments about the value of death which modern philosophers have lifted from Epicurus and Lucretius argue for that very thesis. The Symmetry Argument is instead intended to bolster the—albeit related— claim that 'non-existence is not an evil'. Of course, all this leaves untouched Raz's own concerns about the cogency of the particular argument which he himself has constructed against the thesis that we ought not to hold a longevity preference. But that argument is Raz's own construction. It is not an argument which appears in the Epicurean texts and, although the conclusion would win their approval, a criticism of this argument is not a criticism of Epicureanism.

An Epicurean argument against feeling distress at the thought of life coming to an end

My general conclusion so far has been that the Symmetry Argument found in Lucretius' poem offers the same conclusion as the argument distilled into *KΔ* 2. It does not, contrary to some more recent interpretations, offer a new argument to tackle the fear of mortality, the troubling thought that one's life is going to come to an end. However. all is not lost so far as the Epicureans are concerned. since although there is an important distinction between the conclusions of the two versions of the Symmetry Argument (which I labelled Fi and Fii above, p. 60), they are

---

[68] This distances the Epicurean claim from that made by Epicharmus, cited at S.E. *M.* 1.273, and suggested by some as the ultimate source of the Epicurean thesis. See above, p. 5.

nevertheless related. Indeed, Fi can be used as a premise in a secondary argument which then produces Fii, so long as a further premise is inserted. And that premise, while missing from Lucretius' presentation of the Symmetry Argument, is prominent in Epicurus' brief summary of his ethical teachings, the *Letter to Menoeceus*.[69] Here again are the two claims.

Fi: 'Our *post mortem* non-existence will be nothing to us after our death.'

Fii: 'Looking forward from within a lifetime, our *post mortem* non-existence is nothing to us.'

Fii can be derived from Fi by using the following principle:

Whatever causes no pain when present, causes only empty distress when anticipated.[70]

This principle can be extracted from a section of Epicurus' letter which explicitly deduces that a fear of future non-existence is irrational since, when it comes, death is annihilation. It is worth quoting this in full.

ὥστε μάταιος ὁ λέγων δεδιέναι τὸν θάνατον οὐχ ὅτι λυπήσει παρών, ἀλλ' ὅτι λυπεῖ μέλλων. ὃ γὰρ παρὸν οὐκ ἐνοχλεῖ, προσδοκώμενον κενῶς[71] λυπεῖ.

So, foolish is he who says that he fears death not because it will cause pain when present but because it causes pain as a prospect. For that

---

[69] Lucretius does give examples of empty pains caused by false anticipatory fears of death, e.g. *DRN* 3.31–93.

[70] Cf. Cic. *Tusc.* 1.16: M.: *quia, quoniam post mortem mali nihil est, ne mors quidem est malum, cui proximum tempus est post mortem, in quo mali nihil esse concedis: ita ne moriendum quidem esse malum est: id est enim, perveniendum esse ad id, quod non esse malum confitemur* ('Since there is nothing harmful after death, then not even death is an evil—which is immediately followed by a time after death in which you agree there is nothing harmful. So it is not even a harm to have to die. For this is merely to have to arrive at that point which we admit is not harmful').

[71] The combination κενός—μάταιος recurs in Epicurus' works. In the letter to Anaxarchus, quoted in Plutarch *Adv. Col.* 1117A, Epicurus uses both adjectives to describe the virtues, which 'filling us with hope of rewards, are empty and pointless and bring us trouble'. The force of κενός seems to be 'empty' in the sense of irrational, or without justification—as in the Epicurean term κενοδοξία, used of ill-founded beliefs which tend to cause suffering. The sense of μάταιος is 'foolish' or 'vain' and when used of persons generally means that what they are doing is futile. Compare *Ep. Men.* 127 where someone appears who claims that it is bad to be born, but when one is born it is best to die as quickly as

which when present causes no distress produces only empty pain when anticipated.[72]

Ep. Men. 125

An imagined objector replies to Epicurus that he agrees with *KΔ* 2 that being dead is no evil. Death 'will not cause pain when it is present'. Nevertheless, he argues, this does not remove his fear since he feels distress now at its approach. Epicurus carefully distinguishes these claims with two similar verb + participle phrases (λυπήσει παρών; λυπεῖ μέλλων), but in doing so makes clear how small is the distance to be travelled between agreement with the first, and acceptance of the second. The transformation of one phrase to the other requires two changes. The tense of the verb must switch from present to future (or vice versa), while the participle must change from παρών to μέλλων or vice versa. If the verb alters from present to future, then the participle changes in the opposite direction, from one which implies 'presentness' to the prospective μέλλων. The overall effect is to enact the confusion exhibited by the objector by making the two claims he is trying to keep so distinct as like each other as possible. In this way Epicurus tries to point out that any pain caused by anticipating death is 'empty', since it is based on false opinions or faulty understanding and can and should easily be removed.

Of course, Epicurus is aware that there is a real distinction to be made between causing pain when present and causing pain through anticipation, and is not trying to obliterate this distinction. Rather, his concern is to show that someone trying to retain the distinction *and* agree to *KΔ* 2, cannot do so consistently. The reason for this is given in the second sentence of the quotation,

---

possible. Epicurus claims that if this is said with conviction, the person should immediately commit suicide. If it is said in mockery, then the person is μάταιος since no one would believe him.

[72] Compare this with the fragment of Arcesilaus, cited with approval by Plutarch at *Cons. ad Apoll.* IIOA: τοῦτο τὸ λεγόμενον κακὸν ὁ θάνατος μόνον τῶν ἄλλων τῶν νενομισμένων κακῶν παρὸν μὲν οὐδένα πώποτ' ἐλύπησεν, ἀπὸν δὲ καὶ προσδοκώμενον λυπεῖ ('Death, this so-called evil, is the only thing considered an evil which when present hurts no one but when absent causes pain even when anticipated'). The closeness of the wording of the two passages suggests Arcesilaus is echoing this Epicurean principle. Arcesilaus is presumably making the point that this general conception (νόμος) about death is indeed inconsistent.

which contains the principle required to pass from Fi to Fii. The argument in full is as follows:

Fi: 'Our *post mortem* non-existence will be nothing to us after our death.'

Ep. Men. 125: 'Whatever causes no pain when present, causes only empty distress when anticipated'.

Therefore: Since death causes no pain when present, it causes only empty distress when anticipated (and empty distress is no real distress at all).

Conclusion: Fii: 'Looking forward from within a lifetime, our *post mortem* non-existence is nothing to us.'

A symmetrical argument could, if wanted, be constructed to derive Pii from Pi, by using the symmetrical principle (call this *Ep. Men.* 125*): 'Whatever causes no pain when present, causes only empty pain in retrospect'. Nowhere is this principle evoked, perhaps since Pii is not controversial as is Fii. Pi is also relatively uncontroversial. No one has argued seriously that pre-natal non-existence was an evil, although as we have already seen (above pp. 75–6) this thesis has been advanced as an absurd conclusion to a reverse (or 'Backfire') form of the Symmetry Argument. Even so, there is further reason to wonder whether the *Ep. Men.* 125* is true, let alone plausibly true. Is it not the case that there are events which at the time they occur are not painful but are nevertheless later regretted and therefore cause pain in retrospect? As time passes various consequences of the act may emerge, or the agent may alter in such a way as to regard something now as painful which at the time was not. If so, perhaps this should lead us to reassess the truth of the principle offered in *Ep. Men.* 125 itself. However, one could plausibly argue that in such cases of regret the retrospective pain is caused not by the past painless event itself but rather by its consequences, that is to say, by present painful states of affairs which result from the original—now past—painless event. The Epicureans, of course, were appropriately careful to warn people when considering a particular course of action to take into account the various consequences which may ensue and to take these into account when making a choice between different courses of action.[73] In that case, this is one case

---

[73] See *Ep. Men* 129–30 and Warren 2001d.

in which the temporal direction is very significant: in the case of the prospective perspective of the principle in *Ep. Men.* 125 there is no analogue of these consequences. A future painless event cannot itself produce painful 'precursors' in the way in which a painless past event may produce painful consequences. So far, I hope to have shown that Epicurus did provide an argument which concludes that our present fear of future non-existence is irrational, but he did so through this addition to his original claim of *KΔ* 2, not through the Symmetry Argument, at least not in the form presented by Lucretius and other ancient authors.

If my interpretation is correct, the Epicureans themselves did not see the Symmetry Argument as an independent argument against the fear of death. In version 1 this argument merely generates the same conclusion as *KΔ* 2. This same conclusion, therefore, can be reached by a route which does not invoke the symmetry of past and future non-existence, and any counter-argument which does deny this symmetry is presumably offered on the mistaken understanding that the Epicureans are offering version 2 of the argument as their only available attack on the prospective fear of death. Perhaps it might therefore be asked at this point just why Lucretius provided a Symmetry Argument, if it produced a conclusion no different from that of *KΔ* 2, and if in doing so it has to invoke the principle of the symmetry of past and future non-existence—which would need to be defended against a number of strong objections. In the structure of the argument against the fear of death, version 1 of the Symmetry Argument produces no new conclusions. However, it does produce the same conclusion as *KΔ* 2 on different grounds, namely on the basis of our attitude to pre-natal time, and therefore perhaps should be seen as playing a role in Lucretius' attempts to persuade us of those conclusions. It points to a particular attitude we have to the time before we were born which is thought to be sufficiently robust to be unquestionable, and asks us to view the future in the same way. By doing so, it is providing further evidence for someone who is trying to 'accustom himself' (as Epicurus tells us we must) to the thought of *KΔ* 2. The Symmetry Argument has a confirmatory and persuasive role rather than the task of establishing a new and independent conclusion. It takes a true belief which we all seem to share about the value of pre-natal non-existence and uses it to correct the prevalent false belief that *post mortem* non-existence is a potential source of harm.

Conclusions

It remains to be observed that most recent discussions of the Symmetry Argument tend not to tackle explicitly the principle invoked in *Letter to Menoeceus* 125, which, if I am right, must stand as an important part of Epicurus' argument against the prospective fear of death.[74] The principle must surely be true in the sense that if someone truly thinks that when some state of affairs comes about, it will not cause any pain, it is indeed irrational nevertheless to fear in anticipation being in that state. If this person persists in fearing going to the dentist, say, then this surely must be because he thinks that when he is in the dentist's chair he will experience pain. If he knows that there will be no pain, then it does not seem rational to fear in anticipation painless dental work. This allows, of course, that one might mistakenly believe that some future state of affairs will be painful and therefore fear it in anticipation, but this simply underlines how crucial it is for Epicurus to convince us of the truth of $K\Delta$ 2.

By bridging the distance between fearing being dead and fearing future non-existence in the way I have suggested here, Epicurus can try to force the discussion back to his central claim that the state of being dead is not painful in any way (and is therefore not an evil). Perhaps this explains what might otherwise seem a strange omission on Lucretius' part, namely the lack of the further argument against the present fear of future non-existence found in *Letter to Menoeceus* 125. If Epicurus saw this

---

[74] Furley 1986, 76, is again a notable exception. Nussbaum 1994, 202 n. 9, 203 n. 11, rightly sees that this is the crucial premise for Epicurus' argument, although she seems to agree with Mitsis that my text B deals with present attitudes to death, whereas text A does not. Cf. Alberti 1990, 170–1. Rosenbaum 1989b, 370, entertains the idea that this might be the basis for Epicurean arguments against fearing death, but later rejects it since then (371) 'the symmetry argument would not really be the ingenious, novel contribution to Epicurean thanatology which many have thought... [It] would at bottom rely logically on already well-established and defensible Epicurean ideals and would quite simply be superfluous, except perhaps as a rhetorical flourish.' This begs the question.

prospective fear as derivative from the fear of the state of being dead, and was convinced that it was on this latter fear that his attention should be concentrated, then Lucretius may well also have been so convinced that he went so far as to omit the brief argument retained in *Letter to Menoeceus* 125, thinking that it was merely an optional supplementary step. All his attention was directed, even in the supposed Symmetry Arguments, towards establishing the conclusion of *KΔ* 2, a version of which, as we have seen, opens Lucretius' discussion of the topic as a whole.

> nil igitur mors est ad nos nec pertinet hilum,
> quandoquidem natura animi mortalis habetur

Therefore, death is nothing to us, nor does it concern us in the slightest, since the nature of the mind is held to be mortal.

3.830–1

It might even be suggested that *KΔ* 2 itself contains an implicit use of the principle invoked in *Letter to Menoeceus* 125. I noted above (p. 63) that a critical reading would object to Epicurus' conclusion that death *is* nothing to us, since what follows only shows that death *will be* nothing to us. A more charitable reading would invoke the idea contained in *Letter to Menoeceus* 125 as understood within the argumentation of *KΔ* 2 to generate a conclusion about how we presently should view the period of our future non-existence.

Again, however, it should be emphasized just what Epicurus has shown so far—and what he has not. The combination of *KΔ* 2 and the argument of *Letter to Menoeceus* 125 shows that the state of being dead is not to be feared even in prospect since it will not be painful. But this still does not tackle directly the fear of mortality—the fear which some critics of Epicureanism found left intact by *KΔ* 2. The critic might claim that by talking of a fear of death, he is not claiming to justify the fear of not-being (and so could allow Epicurus the claim in *KΔ* 2), but rather this fear of mortality. In other words, the fear is not based on an inconsistent dread of 'being dead', but rather in the prospective concern that one's life, plans, and projects might be curtailed prematurely.[75] If

---

[75] See Striker 1988. Cockburn 1997, 137, is also unconvinced that Lucretius is correct in identifying the sense in which people fear the prospect of death: 'Lucretius adds: the fear can only be in place in so far as there will be an evil to

this is a criticism specifically of the argument of *KΔ* 2, and of the Symmetry Argument as I have interpreted it, then it is a reasonable one. Nothing here explicitly tackles the problem of fearing that a life will end incomplete. The critic of Epicureanism might also complain that even with the addition of the argument of *Letter to Menoeceus* 125, Epicurus again misses the point. He might well claim that fearing death is not at all like fearing an impending painful event—it is rather a concern with the shape and completeness of a life.

This could even be expressed in hedonistic terms, again using the counterfactual account of the harm of death. Someone might be quite happy with the conclusion that being dead is not painful, and therefore agree that they should not fear in anticipation the state of being dead (in other words, they might agree whole-heartedly with *KΔ* 2 and *Letter to Menoeceus* 125), but nevertheless feel anxious at the thought that dying at some point in time will rob them of pleasure that they would have experienced had they died at a later time. Their life might be better than it will turn out to be. Their death might be *premature*.[76]

There are good reasons to think that the Epicureans did concern themselves with the question of the completeness of a life and therefore with the question of whether and when a death can be premature. But they did this via their own particular brand of eudaimonistic hedonism, not through the specific arguments we have surveyed so far. Just how they attempted to remove this residual fear is the topic of Chapter 4 below, but, in short, the Epicureans try to dissociate the idea of a complete life from notions of temporal duration and attempt to deny any cumulative notion of pleasures. They therefore would argue that so long as you achieve katastematic pleasure, death cannot rob you of any further good which you 'would have experienced had you died later'. They try to argue that complete pleasure can be experienced in a finite time. Once Epicurus has reduced as much

---

be perceived, by the one who fears, at the time of what is feared. That is to say, the most direct characterisation of the evil of death must be one from the perspective of the time at which death is present.'

[76] Indeed, if expressed in hedonistic terms it appears that any death, even one in advanced old age, may rob me of possible pleasures. Of course, on such an account death could also be counted as a good—provided it releases me from inevitable future pains.

as possible of the complex of anxieties about death to the fear of being dead, and has countered these with $K\Delta$ 2 and the Symmetry Argument, he can set about putting in place his own positive account of a complete life which, he hopes, is immune to fears of premature death.

4

Premature Death and a Complete Life

omnia tamquam mortales timetis, omnia tamquam
immortales concupistis.

You fear everything as mortals, but desire everything
as immortals.

Seneca, De Brevitate Vitae 3.4

None of the Epicurean arguments examined so far have addressed
a remaining sense in which it is possible to fear death, namely the
fear of premature death. This fear is distinct both from the fear
of being dead and from the fear of mortality (the fear that one
will die) since it is possible to imagine someone who is concerned
neither that he will be harmed after his death nor that he will die
at some time in the future. Instead, this person fears that he will
die too soon.[1] Indeed it is possible to imagine that someone
progressing in his studies of Epicureanism may have mastered
and accepted the claims of $K\varDelta$ 2 and made the additional move of
removing the anticipatory fear of the state of being dead, but
who nevertheless has heard nothing yet to remove any possibility
of fearing a premature death. This person may still harbour
thoughts about the projected course of his life and retain certain
beliefs about what his life ought to be like which would allow the
possibility of this life being cut short. Of course, as a budding
Epicurean he does not fall into the clear absurdity of believing
that it would be a source of regret or pain to him, when dead,
that he had not achieved all that he had hoped for. But he may
still be anxious looking from within his life and considering the
sort of life he hopes for that some of his plans and projects may
be curtailed by death. So he is not worried about the fact that he

---

[1] Cf. Moore 2001, 227: 'I might be appalled at the thought that I shall live for
ever, without, at any particular time in the future, wanting *these* to be my last
five minutes. (That is, I might never want to die without wanting never to die.)'

will die, only by the possibility that his life may be cut short or left incomplete.[2] It is not immediately clear that the Epicureans address any specific arguments against this kind of fear.[3] At least, it has been claimed that what points they do make about the completeness of a life still leave room for a reasonable fear of premature death. However, it seems to me that they do offer a characterization of a complete Epicurean life which may indeed allow them to claim some immunity from the fear of premature death. Even so, the plausibility and attractiveness of the sort of life they commend is itself questionable, and we shall see later that this proposed answer to the possibility of fearing premature death will itself leave the Epicureans facing a difficult dilemma.[4]

The undesirability of immortality

The Epicureans are explicit in their claims that there is nothing desirable in immortality. Life is not made worse for the fact that it will come to an end; mortality *per se* is not lamentable.

ὅθεν γνῶσις ὀρθὴ τοῦ μηθὲν εἶναι πρὸς ἡμᾶς τὸν θάνατον ἀπολαυστὸν ποιεῖ τὸ τῆς ζωῆς θνητόν, οὐκ ἄπειρον προστιθεῖσα χρόνον, ἀλλὰ τὸν τῆς ἀθανασίας ἀφελομένη πόθον.

So a correct understanding that death is nothing to us makes the mortality of life enjoyable, not by adding infinite time but by removing the desire for immortality.[5]

Ep. Men. 124

This follows immediately from the argument that death is nothing to us since it is the absence of all sensation. It follows,

---

[2] Cf. Green 1982, 105.

[3] Honderich 2002, 2, seems to think they do not: '[J]ust going on living, living longer, is certainly more than desirable. If it does need to be distinguished from much else that we also want, it is indeed for almost all of us an intrinsic good. We want it for itself, whether or not it is a means to anything else. The ancient Greek philosopher Epicurus tells us not to worry about death, because it itself isn't experienced—where you are, your death isn't, and where it is, you aren't. Only impressionable logicians are consoled.'   [4] See below, p. 153 ff.

[5] Cf. *Ep. Men.* 135: ἀθανάτοις ἀγαθοῖς ('immortal goods'). Here the connotation might well be one of a constant supply, a persistent succession of goods.

therefore, that there is no reason to desire immortality simply to escape the inevitable state of being dead. That state is not going to be painful so there is no reason to be concerned about it, not even in prospect. This much merely articulates points we have already seen and discussed. However, here Epicurus adds a further claim that a correct understanding of death will in fact make life itself more enjoyable. Apparently, it will do this by removing the otherwise presumably damaging desire for immortality (ἀθανασία). The rather elliptical reference to time here makes clear that the kind of immortality being rejected is literally death-less-ness (ἀ–θανασία), a state in which one simply will never die.[6] Death is nothing to us, not because we will not die but because our deaths are not something to be concerned about. (We might contrast a Platonic argument against the fear of death as illustrated in, for example, the *Phaedo* and the Ps.-Platonic *Axiochus* which tells us not to fear death because we, or at least our souls, the most essential part of us, will never die.)[7]

Why should this new conception of our inevitable and painless demise make life more enjoyable? Epicurus does not make clear here just how this connection is to be made. One modern discussion of the possible value of immortality, by Bernard Williams, argues that immortality is not to be coveted since it would create an inevitable tedium. The argument for this claim depends upon the idea that there are certain 'categorical desires', the possession of which propels one forward and gives one reasons to continue to live. An everlasting life, however, seems to rule out the continued presence of any such desires. Eventually, it is claimed, such an immortal will have no such unfulfilled desires left and therefore no reason to continue living or, alternatively, will have had to change their character to such an extent in order to find new things to desire in this way that it becomes difficult to maintain the idea that the everlasting existence made up of these different characters is indeed one continuous single life lived by

---

[6] Epicurus does characterize his ideal state as one in which one becomes like a god. But for the Greeks the gods did not simply never die, they also never aged. For more discussion of the sense in which an Epicurean can become godlike see Warren 2000b, Erler 2002.

[7] The contrast is put succinctly by Williams 1973a, 83: '[D]eath is said by some not to be an evil because it is not the end, and by others, because it is.'

one particular individual.[8] Whatever the merits of such an argument against immortality, it is clear that this is not an argument which the Epicureans would offer. In particular, the pivotal notion of a categorical desire is one which seems rather to offer the distinct possibility of death being an evil since it would seem quite reasonable to be anxious that one should not die before such a categorical desire could be fulfilled. Since the role of these desires is to give one a reason for living and an over-arching structure to one's life through what have been termed 'ground projects', the Epicureans would risk the creation of a very difficult problem for themselves if they were tempted by this sort of consideration. Indeed, Williams himself constructs a powerful argument for the rationality of fearing death from the presence of just this kind of desire.[9] (Whether the absence of any such categorical desires would lead to an untenable picture of a human life, that is, whether such desires are necessary for a recognizable and attractive life is a question to which we will return below, pp. 205–12.)

However, there are other pieces of evidence which point to the Epicureans' particular brand of hedonism as the most promising source for the required arguments, both for the claim that premature death need not be feared and also for the accompanying claim that only by correctly accepting mortality can a life be properly enjoyed. They seem to have offered two sets of considerations. The first argues positively for the amount of pleasure available in a finite space of time, from which it can be concluded that there is no need on hedonistic grounds for an infinite amount of time. The second argues that in fact the prevailing opinion that the longer the space of time available for enjoying

---

[8] This argument is expounded fully in Williams 1973b. Fischer 1994 responds, wondering whether Williams is overly pessimistic about the possibilities of varying desires and generating new ones. Cf. Nagel 1986, 224; McMahan 2002, 100–3; Overall 2003, 124–82.

[9] Williams 1973b, 85: 'To want something, we may also say, is to that extent to have reason for resisting what excludes having that thing: and death certainly does that, for a very large range of things that one wants. If that is right, then for any of those things, wanting something itself gives one a reason for avoiding death. Even though if I do not succeed, I will not know that, nor what I am missing, from the perspective of the wanting agent it is rational to aim for states of affairs in which his want is satisfied, and hence to regard death as something to be avoided; that is, to regard it as an evil.' For 'ground projects' see the related discussion in Williams 1976, esp. 207–10.

pleasures the better (and therefore that an infinite amount of time is best of all) not only relies on a mistaken conception of the nature of pleasure, but also in practice causes a large amount of distress and leads one not to enjoy any pleasures one has nevertheless managed to secure. Both these arguments may appear paradoxical. After all, surely a hedonist is committed to the idea that the more pleasure there is in a life the better that life is. If so, surely a hedonist is forced to conclude that a longer life is better than a shorter life and that one might reasonably worry about a life being curtailed? Certainly some brands of hedonism are committed to these claims, but Epicurean hedonism attempts not to be.[10] In the *Letter to Menoeceus* Epicurus is at pains to stress that the wise Epicurean will not wish to extend his life indefinitely. In fact, duration is not of primary concern for him at all:

οὔτε γὰρ αὐτῷ προσίσταται τὸ ζῆν οὔτε δοξάζεται κακόν εἶναί τι τὸ μὴ ζῆν. ὥσπερ δὲ τὸ σιτίον οὐ τὸ πλεῖστον πάντως ἀλλὰ τὸ ἥδιστον αἱρεῖται, οὕτω καὶ χρόνον οὐ τὸν μήκιστον ἀλλὰ τὸν ἥδιστον καρπίζεται.

For living does not offend [the wise man], nor does not living appear to him to be an evil. Just as with food, he chooses not the greatest quantity but the most pleasant, similarly he will enjoy not the longest but the most pleasant time.

Ep. Men. 126

The sole criterion for determining the value of a life, therefore, is the pleasantness of that life. Duration *per se* certainly plays no part in any such determination.[11] Further arguments can be found in the *Kyriai Doxai* (19–21) to show that duration is not important even indirectly as allowing additional time for more pleasures to be enjoyed.

---

[10] Therefore Feldman 1992, 147–8, 156, is wrong to claim that his hedonist argument for death being an evil is constructed on Epicurean grounds since the hedonism on which he relies is not one which the Epicureans would have accepted. He characterizes his hedonist's view as follows (p. 147): 'If hedonism is true, then the value of a life for a person is determined in this way: first consider how much pleasure the person experienced throughout her life. Add it up. Then consider how much pain the person experienced throughout her life. Add it up. Then subtract the pain from the pleasure. The hedonic value of the life is the result.'

[11] Cf. Cic. *Fin.* 1.63: *neque maiorem voluptatem ex infinito tempore aetatis percipi posse quam ex hoc percipiatur quod videamus esse finitum* ('[He says that] no greater pleasure can be perceived in an infinite length of time than is perceived in this period which we see to be finite').

ΚΔ 19: ὁ ἄπειρος χρόνος ἴσην ἔχει τὴν ἡδονὴν καὶ ὁ πεπερασμένος, ἐάν τις αὐτῆς τὰ πέρατα καταμετρήσῃ τῷ λογισμῷ.

The infinite time has as much pleasure as the finite, if one measures pleasure's limits with reason.

ΚΔ 20: ἡ μὲν σὰρξ ἀπέλαβε τὰ πέρατα τῆς ἡδονῆς ἄπειρα καὶ ἄπειρος αὐτὴν χρόνος παρεσκεύασεν· ἡ δὲ διάνοια τοῦ τῆς σαρκὸς τέλους καὶ πέρατος λαβοῦσα τὸν ἐπιλογισμὸν καὶ τοὺς ὑπὲρ τοῦ αἰῶνος φόβους ἐκλύσασα τὸν παντελῆ βίον παρεσκεύασε, καὶ οὐθὲν ἔτι τοῦ ἀπείρου χρόνου προσεδεήθη· ἀλλ᾽ οὔτε ἔφυγε τὴν ἡδονὴν οὐδ᾽ ἡνίκα τὴν ἐξαγωγὴν ἐκ τοῦ ζῆν τὰ πράγματα παρεσκεύαζεν, ὡς ἐλλείπουσά τι τοῦ ἀρίστου βίου κατέστρεψεν.

The flesh takes as unlimited the limits of pleasure and an infinite time [is needed to][12] provide it. But the mind, taking the calculation of the goal and limit of the flesh and, banishing the fears brought on by eternity, makes life complete and no longer in need of an infinite time. But the mind does not flee from pleasure nor, when things bring about a departure from life, does it depart as if lacking something from the best life.

ΚΔ 21: ὁ τὰ πέρατα τοῦ βίου κατειδὼς οἶδεν ὡς εὐπόριστόν ἐστι τὸ <τὸ> ἀλγοῦν κατ᾽ ἔνδειαν ἐξαιροῦν καὶ τὸ τὸν ὅλον βίον παντελῆ καθιστάν· ὥστε οὐδὲν προσδεῖται πραγμάτων ἀγῶνας κεκτημένων.

The man who knows the limits of life knows how easy it is to produce the removal of pain caused by want and to make one's whole life complete. As a result, there is no need for competitive behaviour.

The upshot of these brief sayings is that the peculiar Epicurean view that the highest pleasure is the absence of pain may be used to bolster an argument to show that given this brand of hedonism a greater duration, indeed a greater number of pleasures, is not necessarily preferable to a shorter duration. To be sure, the argumentation is not always clear,[13] but they nevertheless can be agreed to produce a contrast between a rational understanding of pleasure which recognizes the 'limits' of pleasure and therefore somehow leads to a complete life or the best life, and the irrational tendency of the flesh which is to disregard any limits and ask constantly for more and more pleasure.[14] *ΚΔ* 19 is the clearest statement of the matter, although it lacks any internal supporting

---

[12] See Bailey 1926 ad loc.
[13] See Furley 1986, 81, for a negative view of the argumentative cogency of these *ΚΔ*.
[14] Philodemus *De morte* XIX.33–XX.1 says that the fool will never achieve true happiness even if he should live as long as Tithonus, Dawn's lover who was

argumentation, offering the claim that an infinite and finite time contain the same amount of pleasure. This is perhaps already surprising, given that one might have expected a hedonist to think that the more time to enjoy pleasure the better.[15] The same thought as expressed in *KΔ* 19 is also found in Philodemus' *De Morte* XIII.3–6 Kuiper:

ἐ[ξὸν δὲ] | ἐμ ποσῷ χρόνῳ τὸ μέγιστον αὐ[τῶν] | καὶ περιποιήσασθαι κα[ὶ] ἀπολαῦσαι κ[α]θά|περ ὑπέδειξ[α] . . .

It being possible both to achieve and enjoy the greatest [goods] in some certain period of time, as I have demonstrated . . .

This remark appears within Philodemus' discussion of the common view that death in youth is an evil, to which I will turn in more detail below. For now, we can simply state that its presence in that context offers some support for those who would see in these *Kyriai Doxai* the seeds of an Epicurean account of how one might avoid the fear of premature death by seeking a complete Epicurean life. The finer details of this account will be considered further below. First, we should construct and consider a powerful criticism of the Epicurean view outlined so far based on the idea that although it may be true that the value of a life is not necessarily compromised by its being of finite duration, nevertheless there is room for longer and shorter lives to differ in value and, therefore, for death to be able adversely to affect the value of a life.[16]

Complete lives

Perhaps Epicurus has good reason to think that he can show that the duration of a life is not necessarily linked to the pleasantness (and therefore the goodness) of that life. Certainly, he can claim

granted immortality but not agelessness (*HH. Aphr.* 218 ff.). Again, immortality is not of itself worth pursuing. What matters is correct understanding.

[15] Cicero, *Fin.* 2.87–8, seems to be thinking along the same lines as Feldman when he asserts a clear inconsistency between hedonism and the rejection of a preference for longer duration.

[16] Gosling and Taylor 1984, 356, interpret *KΔ* 19 as already implying that 'no extension of the period of a pleasure will increase it'. It seems to me that this is not necessarily the case; cf. Mitsis 1988b, 25–7. *KΔ* 19 alone may show only that an infinite time will not be preferable.

plausibly that an infinite life is no better, will contain no more pleasure, than a finite one. This alone gives a further reason for thinking that we should not be afraid of the fact that we are going to die. We have already seen (above p. 100ft.) the argument that death when it comes will not be painful and so should not be feared in prospect. In addition, now Epicurus can offer the thought that we have no reason to think that dying will seriously compromise the amount of pleasure we will enjoy. This pleasure would not be increased by living forever.[17] Nevertheless, there is a further obstacle for him to avoid, namely the charge that in fact duration is not really the issue. Rather, what causes anxiety and fear of death in this sense is not the thought that one's life might be too short, but that it might be incomplete. This argument is put most concisely and forcefully by Striker, who offers the following analogy.

The eighteen year old who wants to continue living is like someone who has watched the first act of an opera and is justifiably annoyed if the performance breaks off at this point. He is angry, not because he had thought that he was going to spend three hours instead of only one, but because he wanted to see the entire opera, not just part of it. On the other hand, the person who worries about being mortal might be compared to someone who wished the opera would never end. They want to listen as long as possible—and for such people it might indeed be irrational to insist that they want the opera to go on later, not to begin earlier.

Striker 1988, 325–6

The final comment here is directed at the same issues raised in particular by Joseph Raz's reaction to Lucretius' Symmetry Argument (above p. 93ft.). Indeed, if duration were all that mattered then it would seem odd to prefer to die later rather than be born earlier. Striker's main point here, however, is the contrast between a mere preference for duration and a desire for completeness. The reference to an operatic performance is particularly significant since it shows that Striker's position here can be likened to other discussions of the 'shapes' of lives which also argue that a human life has a number of important stages to be

---

[17] Feldman's additive hedonism, however (see above n. 10), would certainly leave open the possibility that simply being mortal prevents the greatest accumulation of pleasure.

lived through in the appropriate order. Such a conception offers a quick explanation of what is thought regrettable about the deaths of people in their youths or in middle age: they have not lived through all the stages of a human life which one should expect. Like an opera cut short before the final act, their lives lack the appropriate narrative shape and structure.

Striker wants to use these two distinct kinds of anxiety to show that although Epicurus may have offered some useful considerations against the mere preference for duration. he has little or nothing to offer in the discussion of the fear of the premature curtailment of a life. Certainly, it seems reasonable not to want an opera to go on forever—indeed, an opera that never ended would surely be worse than an opera which did. Nevertheless, there remains a concern for an opera, or a life, to exhibit a degree of completeness which death may threaten. The fear in this case is not the mere fear of dying, the fear of mortality. but the fear of dying too soon.

Let us contrast Striker's position with the similar explanation of the potential evil of death offered by Williams.[18] This analyses the evil of death in terms of the frustration of ground projects or categorical desires, fundamental wishes and desires which an agent possesses and which give that agent reason not only for acting in order to fulfil the desires but also to go on living in the hope of their fulfilment. Both Striker and Williams agree that a never-ending life would not be attractive. Both nevertheless want to argue that death could harm an agent by curtailing life either before it is complete or before these ground projects can be completed. The important difference between the two positions is that Williams would find it difficult to claim that the death of a very young infant, for example, may be thought premature since it would be difficult to claim that such an infant has any ground projects. That we may assume that had it lived it would have generated some such projects is not of much help if the central claim remains that the evil of death is the frustration of desires.[19]

---

[18] In Williams 1973b, 1976. See also above pp. 111–12.

[19] Compare Cic. *Tusc.* 1.93: *idem, si puer parvus occidit, aequo animo ferendum putant: si vero in cunis, ne querendum quidem. atqui ab hoc acerbius exegit natura quod dederat. 'nondum gustaverat,' inquiunt, 'vitae suavitatem: hic autem iam sperabat magna, quibus frui coeperat.'* ('The same people think that if a young boy dies, this should be borne with equanimity. We should not even grumble if

Although Striker's analogy has two people 'desiring' to see a complete opera there is room for her to claim that a death may be premature and a life incomplete on her account whether or not it frustrates any desires the subject may happen to have. Rather, she could rely more on the notion that human lives are to be expected to have a certain general structure (like the structure of an opera) and were that to be curtailed death could be regarded as an evil. (Of course, we might agree that the person who has no desire at all to go on living, whatever their age, is not harmed by dying, but these would be very exceptional cases and Epicurus for one would presumably not want to base his claim that premature death is not to be feared on the premise that one should not want to go on living.)[20]

There are two lessons be drawn from the operatic analogy. The first, as we have seen, is that the removal of desire for an infinitely long life does not necessarily remove the fear of premature death since it remains possible that a finite but longer life is better than a shorter life. The second lesson is that there is a strong intuition that lives should exhibit a certain kind of shape, or—to continue the operatic analogy—a plot. Other writers have suggested something similar: they claim that lives have or ought to have a kind of narrative structure, a 'life-story'. If so, then this would give us some indication of how to set about constructing an answer to the question of when a life would be complete or incomplete. A life will be complete, on this sort of account, if it exhibits a recognizably finished narrative structure and will be incomplete if it does not.

The central notion of a 'life-story', however, remains rather indistinct, and it is not immediately clear how much more

he dies in the cradle. But in this second case nature has demanded the return of what she had given even more cruelly. They say, "The infant had not yet tasted the sweetness of life. But the boy already had great ambitions which he was beginning to enjoy." ') Cf. Quinn 2001, 78–83, who wants to resist the necessity of the presence of unfulfilled desires or frustrated interests in order for death to be an evil precisely because otherwise it is hard to see how very young infants or foetuses can be thought to be harmed by death or abortion. See also Nussbaum 1994, 211 n. 26.

[20] Even so, once I have outlined what I take to be the Epicurean answer to the potential fear of premature death there will be reason to think that there is a problem for them in showing why one would want to continue to live at all. See below, p. 205 ff.

definition it can be given.[21] One preliminary possibility is the identification of a number of essential life-stages, the presence of which in a life (in the correct order) would be at least a minimal requirement for that life being complete. Something like this position would fit well with the common and intuitive presumption that a life which ends at 18, for example, is incomplete. Such a life would lack the essential stages of adulthood and, perhaps, old age which form necessary parts of a complete life. This rough-and-ready account could also try to avoid the possibly difficult task of assigning particular periods of time to the different stages and therefore to a complete life. There is no need to be concerned about whether 70 years, or 80, should count as the mark of completeness. First, there is something to be said for any such expectation of the duration of a complete life to be contingent to an extent on cultural and economic/demographic factors. Second, any proposed definite answer to the question of the age at which a life becomes complete would face possible *sorites*-style arguments pointing out the arbitrary nature of a choice of 80 over, say, 81 years.[22]

Another method of approaching the idea of a complete life is to think not necessarily in terms of duration at all, or even these 'life-stages', but rather to emphasize the notion of a complete life having to exhibit the correct narrative shape.[23] One way to approach this idea would be to compare a number of very brief biographies:

> Mr P dies at the age of 80. In his career he rose to the top of his profession before a quiet and relaxing retirement.

> Mr Q dies at the age of 80. In a prodigious early career he rose swiftly to the heights of his profession aged only 30 before a long and progressive decline in his abilities and success.

[21] Rosenbaum 1990, 34–5, takes this lack of definition to be a fatal flaw in Striker's position. It remains to be seen, however, whether some such conception can be offered which is definite enough to do justice to the strong intuition behind Striker's analogy.

[22] For a discussion of life-stages see Slote 1983, 13–37.

[23] Quinn 2001, 81, seems to combine the two approaches: 'To die in childhood or infancy is to be deprived of a natural life span; such a death makes one's life a stunted and unshapely affair. And even death in middle age denies one the right to make the right finish, the right way of tying things up and rounding things off for the best.'

Mr R dies at the age of 80. After a long career he finally reached the top of his chosen profession just before his death.

P, Q, and R all live for the same length of time, so any difference in the evaluation of these lives cannot be solely on the basis that one is longer than another. There are, however, reasons to think that we would—even on the basis of the very brief and schematized information given here—judge the lives differently. In particular, Mr Q's life may seem the least attractive of the three. But why? There appears to be something in the shape of the life. in particular in the long decline after early success, which counts against this life's attractiveness. Now a number of questions pose themselves. Is this intuitive reaction to be given some sort of justification? What does it tell us about the claim that lives ought to have some sort of shape? What does it tell us about the possibility of premature death?

The first step is to recognize that this difference of reaction to the three lives appears to show that the value of a life is not merely additive. that it is not merely a question of the addition of the levels of well-being achieved from moment to moment. We might distinguish two measures of well-being: 'momentary well-being', which is the well-being of a subject at a given moment. and 'global well-being', which is the well-being of a subject over the whole of a life.[24] (How well-being itself is to be measured would obviously be a matter of further discussion.) In addition to the sum of scores for momentary well-being a further factor, the arrangement of the levels of well-being seems also to be pertinent to the assessment of a life. In other words, global well-being cannot be reduced merely to a sum of the collection of scores for momentary well-being. Imagine that it is specified that the three lives P, Q, and R all contain the same sum of momentary levels of well-being. (So, if we were able to construct a graph showing the level of momentary well-being of these three persons throughout the period of their lives, the areas under the lines describing this changing momentary level of well-being over time for lives P, Q, and R would be equal.) Even so, it can be claimed, there is an important further reason to find one of them

[24] For this distinction see e.g. Bigelow, Campbell, and Pargetter 1990.

preferable, namely how the moments of well-being are arranged in that life.[25]

There remain a number of questions about how best to analyse this additional factor. Is global well-being merely a supervenient property of a set of momentary well-beings? Or is there a more complex relationship dependent on the memory, character, and personality of the individual in question?[26] For our present purposes this issue need not be settled definitively. In either case, the possibilty of a further global evaluation of a life offers a further reason to think that death, and premature death in particular, can be an evil. If there is some value to a life being of a particular sort, of having some sort of profile or narrative shape, then clearly death may curtail and alter that shape. So one might look at a particular biography and think that that person's life-story was adversely affected by death. (This is not only because death can come too early. It is equally possible to think that a life would have had a better shape or story had it come to an end earlier.)[27] More importantly, people are able to think about and plan for the future and take into account the shape of their lives so far. They are able to consider what sort of life-story they want; they are to an extent the authors of their own life-story.[28] So when living a life, it is possible to be concerned about how the story of that life will turn out. It seems reasonable, therefore, to be concerned about the possibility of death cutting off that life before its envisaged conclusion. In this sense, it is quite clear that a person may be anxious about a premature death—not

[25] e.g. Velleman 2000, 71: '[T]wo lives containing equal sums of momentary well-being need not be equally good lives if their momentary benefits stand in different temporal or, more generally, different narrative relations.' Yourgrau 1993, 156, argues for the necessity of A-series conceptions of time in such evaluations which can identify temporal direction or 'flow': 'A life, for example, that opens in misery and works its way to serenity is surely to be preferred to one that proceeds in the opposite direction.'

[26] Velleman 2000 argues for the latter view against Slote 1983 and Bigelow, Campbell, and Pargetter 1990. They all agree, however, that there is some sort of criterion of value beyond the mere addition of well-being from moment to moment. Compare MacIntyre 1984, 204–25.

[27] Cf. Sen. *Cons. ad Marc.* 20.4–6.

[28] This is the important contribution of Velleman 2000. Contrast this with Striker's opera analogy in which the person is a more or less passive spectator. Feldman 2004, 121–41 responds to Velleman in support of his own 'attitudinal hedonism'. Also see McMahan 2002, 179–80.

necessarily a death which simply prevents the addition of further goods, but a death which prevents a life-story being completed.[29]

Let us call this sort of account the 'Narrative Model' of a life's completeness. We will use it as a means of comparison with whatever conception of completeness emerges from the Epicurean texts as we look to understand more fully whatever it is that Epicurus meant by the references to a 'complete life' in *KΔ* 20 and 21. But before beginning on the search for this Epicurean conception let us first consider an important philosophical predecessor of the Epicurean theory. It is sometimes claimed by those who wish to support this model of life's completeness that it—or at least some relative of it—can be found in Aristotle's conception of the good life. Certainly, Aristotle often specifies that a good life should be a complete (τελείος) life.[30] Exactly what this means, however, is somewhat unclear and it is possible that Aristotle has deliberately avoided attempting to specify what this completeness amounts to since he thinks that this would be to ask for an inappropriate level of specificity for the question at hand. He makes two more specific claims to offer a small further degree of specificity. He is clear that a single day will not make a person happy (*eudaimōn*) just as a single swallow does not make a spring, so it must be the case that a complete life is a good life of some duration. He also makes it clear that a complete life is not a finished life in the sense that he is quite content for someone to be truly termed happy while still alive. This second clarification emerges from his famous consideration of the Solonic dictum that one should 'call no man happy until he is dead' in *Nicomachean Ethics* I.10. The discussion arises immediately from the claim that a good life should be a complete life. This, Aristotle recognizes, raises a puzzle. On the one hand, it seems prudent to be reticent to call anyone happy while still alive since it is possible that they may, even late in life, suffer some terrible misfortunes sufficient to overshadow whatever well-being they have enjoyed so far. The case of Priam, prosperous king of Troy whose kingdom and family were destroyed when he was an old man, shows clearly this possibility. No one would want to say that his life was

---

[29] Cf. Annas 1993, 346.
[30] *NE* 1098ᵃ18–20, 1100ᵃ5, 1101ᵃ11–13, 1177ᵇ25; *EE* 1219ᵃ35–9, 1219ᵇ4–8; *MM* 1185ᵃ1–6.

good, says Aristotle (1100^{a}5–9). Aristotle interprets Solon's dictum as a reaction to this possibility. Since any life may be marred unexpectedly at any time, we cannot safely (ἀσφαλῶς) call any man happy until he is beyond the reach of such fortune (1100^{a}14–17).[31] On the other hand, while recognizing that there is some truth in this view, Aristotle himself is concerned to retain the possibility of truly calling someone happy while they are still alive (1100^{a}33–^{b}5). In the subsequent discussion, he insists that well-being primarily depends on virtuous activity which in turn depends upon a settled condition of the soul and as a result is not the sort of thing to be jeopardized to a large degree by contingent events. Further, the virtuous person requires only a sufficient supply of external goods and so will be affected only by severe alterations of fortune (1101^{a}6–13).[32]

It is notable that during the course of this discussion questions of duration fade into the background to be replaced by questions of the stability or otherwise of happiness and the degree to which it is subject to external factors and therefore to chance. Still, comments elsewhere show that Aristotle is certain that one must be a mature adult to have attained happiness—something which in any case will follow from the fact that only mature adult males can exhibit the correct degree of rationality required for virtuous activity.[33] But there is little sign in this chapter of the *Nicomachean Ethics* of any desire on Aristotle's part to offer any more detailed consideration of this temporal requirement for a good life. He seems content to say merely that happiness can be attained only by adults and that a single day of happiness does not make a life happy.[34] This being the case, it is not entirely clear what

---

[31] This thought leads Aristotle to consider whether even after death a person may not be beyond the reach of misfortune. I have commented on his discussion of the possibility of posthumous harm above, pp. 50–4.

[32] Cf. Kraut 1989, 150.

[33] *EE* 1219^{b}5–6: no child or youth is *eudaimōn*.

[34] Irwin 1985, 103–5, argues that there is a distinction between the view of the *Nicomachean Ethics* and that of the *Eudemian Ethics* and *Magna Moralia*. In the former, *eudaimonia* can be—in extreme circumstances—lost and eventually regained (1101^{a}6–13), so cannot require the complete duration of a life. Irwin 1985, 104–5: 'Happiness is complete, and therefore requires a complete range of activity realizing human happiness. A "complete time" is time long enough for such a complete range; and since the projects of a virtuous friend or a magnificent and magnanimous person take some time to realize, a complete time will

Aristotle would have to say about the question of whether death can be premature. On the one hand, he seems to think that a good life lasts and consists in persistent virtuous activity. On the other hand, it is not clear beyond the bare specification that one must be in this state for more than a moment or a day whether he has any notion that this virtuous activity, and therefore the goodness of a life, is directly affected by its duration. It is not clear to me, in any case, what Aristotle would say if asked whether a life of thirty years of virtuous activity (or, indeed, contemplation) is better than one lasting only twenty years.[35]

Nevertheless, Aristotle is certainly an example of someone who would, it seems, wish at least to claim that a truly good life ought to last. While he might also agree that a life would not be better were it never to end, he still seems to hold a position which would allow space for death to be premature since it seems possible for someone to die and it to be true that had that person lived longer his life would have been better since he would have lived long enough to have acquired and exercised the virtues.

Epicurus and the complete life

Finally, we are in a position to begin to explain what Epicurus may have meant by a 'complete life' in *KΔ* 20 and 21. First, let us consider whether Epicurus was in fact simply ignorant of the problem of premature death, thinking instead that it was enough merely to show that an infinite duration would not be preferable to a finite one. The two major pieces of evidence for the conclusion that the Epicureans did in fact consider the fear of premature death are the extended discussions of the completeness of a life in Lucretius and in Philodemus' *De Morte*, to which I will turn in more detail below. There are, however, other pieces of evidence

not be a short time.' The *Eudemian Ethics*, however, appears to offer the view that a complete life is required (1219ᵇ4–8) and the *Magna Moralia* specifies that the time required for a complete life is a whole human life (ὅσον ἄνθρωπος βιοῖ, 1185ᵃ5–6).

[35] Such questions may not allow, on Aristotle's view, any definite answer since much will depend on the particular goals and projects of the particular agent. For more discussion see White 1992, 99–107.

which may suggest the same. They may not individually prove conclusive, but I suggest that the combination offers a plausible case.

First, there is, at least *prima facie*, reason for detecting such concerns even within the very brief *Kryriai Doxai* 19–21 we have already seen. Both *KΔ* 20 and 21 refer to a 'complete life' (βίος παντελής) and 21 qualifies this by referring to the 'whole of a complete life' (τὸν ὅλον βίον παντελῆ). Further, *KΔ* 20 also refers to the 'best life' (ἄριστος βίος), which sounds less ambiguously like the stronger claim that once one thinks about pleasure correctly one can live a good life and—most importantly—depart from it without thinking anything is missing or left incomplete. Certainly, Epicurus uses the language of completeness just as it is found, for example, in Aristotle.[36]

Second, the author of the treatise usually named *On Choices* (*PHerc.* 1251), possibly Philodemus, notes that the uncertainty of when one is going to die leads some to wish to extend their lifetime indefinitely, while others are led to want to depart life immediately (*De Elect.* XVI Indelli and Tsouna-McKirahan). Both reactions are intended to be irrational pieces of behaviour. Death cannot simply be put off indefinitely and the mere uncertainty of death is no reason to cut short one's life. So we are encouraged to think that the uncertainty of the time of death itself is not a cause for concern. Just how this removal of anxiety is to be produced is not entirely clear from the surviving text, but we shall see below a possible Epicurean answer. More interesting for the present discussion is that it does at least show that the Epicureans saw the uncertainty over when we will die as a potential source of disturbance. It is a very short step from recognizing this to recognizing the fear of premature death and it is therefore a plausible claim that they were aware of this too.

Further evidence that the Epicureans considered issues like that provoked by Solon's dictum comes from one of the *Vatican Sayings*:

εἰς τὰ παρῳχηκότα ἀγαθὰ ἀχάριστος φωνὴ ἡ λέγουσα· τέλος ὅρα μακροῦ βίου.

The saying 'look to the end (*telos*)' of a long life is ungrateful to past goods.

Sent. Vat. 75

---

[36] Striker 1988, 327 n. 2, notes these occurrences but rejects them as irrelevant: 'On the most plausible interpretation, he means by this a completely

'Look to the *telos*' is a deliberate reference to Solon's dictum.[37] Unlike Aristotle, the Epicurean author of this saying seems to be criticizing outright the Solonic view rather than accepting that it must contain at least some truth. The thought is, as usual, compressed but the criticism seems to be that Solon is arguing that we cannot be sure of the goodness of a life since the future is unsure and chance may wreak terrible havoc on the person in question. The Epicurean is concerned that this overvalues the future, or the end of a life, since it seems to allow that however good a life has been and however long that goodness has lasted, the future is what will determine the final value of the life as a whole. Surely, this argument runs, there are occasions when a life so far is of such a sort that there is no longer any need to consider its end since it already is of such quality that no matter what happens in the future its goodness is assured. There are lives of such a sort that their value is immune to fortune. As it stands, this criticism of Solon does not depend on a specifically Epicurean analysis of the value of a life but is rather a general criticism of the Solonic privileging of what is to come over the past. But an Epicurean analysis is eminently compatible with the alternative view implied by this critic, and the Epicureans elsewhere promote a view of the good life which is clearly one immune to the extremes of fortune.[38]

The most significant Epicurean discussions of the completeness of a life, however, are to be found not in any context which is explicitly concerned simply with the fear of death. As we have seen already in the case of Aristotle, the notion of a complete life is intimately connected with the particular conception which the philosopher in question offers of the good life. How Epicurus himself conceived of a complete life, therefore, is best revealed by looking closely at his conception of a good life most generally.

pleasant life. Obviously, the inference from complete pleasure to complete life, if intended, would be fallacious.' Cf. Diano 1974, 122–3.

[37] Bailey 1926 ad loc. comments that this is the end of an iambic line, and notes that it is attributed to Solon by Σ to Dio Chrys. 72.13. Cf. *NE* 1100ᵃ11: κατὰ Σόλωνα δὲ χρεὼν τέγος ὁρᾶν ('According to Solon, it is necessary to "look to the end" ').

[38] See *ΚΔ* 14, 39; Cic. *Fin.* 1.62–3, *Tusc.* 3.47; Plut. *Non Posse* 1088c.

Epicurus famously offered an idiosyncratic form of hedonism which not only identified pleasure as the only good but also, and controversially, identified the highest pleasure with the absence of pain. For Epicurus, therefore, there is no intermediate state between pleasure and pain as there is, for example, in the hedonist theory of the contemporary Cyrenaics.[39] He further specifies that this highest state of pleasure, the absence of pain, is not increased by duration but is merely 'varied'.[40] This is Torquatus' description of the Epicurean position:

itaque non placuit Epicuro medium esse quiddam inter dolorem et voluptatem; illud enim ipsum quod quibusdam medium videretur, cum omni dolore careret, non modo voluptatem esse verum etiam summam voluptatem. quisquis enim sentit quemadmodum sit affectus, eum necesse est aut in voluptate esse aut in dolore. omnis autem privatione doloris putat Epicurus terminari summam voluptatem, ut postea variari voluptas distinguique possit augeri amplificari non possit.

And so Epicurus decided that there is no intermediate state between pain and pleasure. For what appeared to some to be intermediate, the absence of pain, is in fact not merely pleasure but indeed the greatest pleasure. For whoever feels the state he is in necessarily is in either pleasure or pain. But Epicurus thinks that the highest pleasure peaks with the removal of all pain, so that afterwards pleasure can be varied and altered but not increased.

Cic. *Fin.* 1.38

Cicero turns to offer his criticisms of this unusual doctrine at 2.87–8. Cicero finds a simple contradiction between the claim that the chief good is pleasure and the notion that this good is not increased by duration. Surely, Cicero claims, Epicurus will want to say that pain is increased by duration. But why should pain increase by duration and not pleasure? No doubt Epicurus may have replied that just as pleasure is not made more pleasant by duration then so too pain is not made more painful by duration. And if the criterion of value is the degree of pleasure or pain perceived then in that sense duration is irrelevant. Even so, Cicero's angry rebuttal of the Epicurean thesis that 'not even a long duration can add anything to a good life and no less pleasure

---

[39] See Eus. *PE* 14.18.32 and the discussion in Tsouna 1998, 151–2, who is inclined to think that the author of this section is Aristocles. Chiesara 2001, p. xxx, disagrees. For a Platonic argument for the existence of an intermediate state see *Rep.* 583c–6c.   [40] *KΔ* 3, 18.

is experienced in a short time than in an everlasting time'[41] may serve to confirm that Epicurus thought that this doctrine would be of help in answering the question of premature death. At least, Cicero introduces this doctrine as a possible Epicurean answer to the question of the completeness of a good life. In the immediately preceding chapters, Cicero has turned to the requirement of any acceptable recipe for the happy life that it should guarantee that a good life will be constant and retained. Pleasure, however, seems to Cicero a quite inappropriate goal for such stability. Will the Epicurean wise man oscillate between living a good life and not, according to whether he is feeling pleasure at the time or not? In Cicero's eyes this will rule out pleasure as a candidate for the goal of life, the *telos*.[42]

neque enim in aliqua parte sed in perpetuitate temporis vita beata dici solet, nec appellatur omnino vita nisi confecta atque absoluta, nec potest quisquam alias beatus esse, alias miser; qui enim existimabit posse se miserum esse, beatus non erit. nam cum suscepta semel est beata vita, tam permanet quam ipsa illa effectrix beatae vitae sapientia, neque exspectat ultimum tempus aetatis, quod Croeso scribit Herodotus praeceptum a Solone.

A life is usually called good not in some part but over its whole course. Indeed it is not called a life at all unless it is completed and finished. No one can be happy at one time and not at another, for whoever thinks that he can be miserable will not be happy. For once a good life is achieved it lasts for as long as wisdom, which is the cause of the good life. It does not wait for the end of life, which is what Herodotus writes was Solon's advice to Croesus.

Cic. *Fin.* 2.87

---

[41] 2.87: *at enim, quemadmodum tute dicebas, Epicurus negat ne diuturnitatem quidem temporis ad beate vivendum aliquid affere, nec minorem voluptatem percipi in brevitate temporis quam si illa sit sempiterna.* ('But, as you yourself were saying, Epicurus denies that the duration of time adds the slightest thing to a good life and says that no less pleasure is perceived in a brief time than if the pleasure were to last forever.') The second part of this is the thesis familiar from *KΔ* 19. The first part is the stronger thesis that a good life is not improved by being extended even finitely. Compare Cic. *Fin.* 1.63, where Torquatus had first offered a version of *KΔ* 19: *neque maiorem voluptatem ex infinito tempore aetatis percipi posse quam ex hoc percipiatur quod videamus esse finitum* ('[He says that] no greater pleasure can be perceived in an infinite length of time than is perceived in this period which we see to be finite').

[42] Cf. Rosenbaum 1990, 27–34.

The reference to Solon's maxim suggests that Cicero's comments are addressed to the same sorts of concerns as exercised Aristotle in *NE* 1.10–11.[43] Cicero too evidently wishes to dissent from the extreme Solonic formulation and allow that someone may be happy when alive; this is allowed since for Cicero here wisdom is the guarantor of a good life and is presumably sufficiently stable to ensure the required constancy in a good life. Nevertheless, Cicero requires any successful account of a good life to show that it can be consistent with the intuition that a good life must be a 'complete life'. Pleasure certainly does not seem to him to be a plausible candidate.

Whatever the merits or failings of Cicero's interpretation of Epicurean hedonism,[44] the course of his discussion with the Epicureans here, in particular his introduction of Solon's dictum into the discussion, can offer support to my claim that their peculiar understanding of the nature of pleasure was deployed in discussions of the complete life. At least, at *Fin.* 2.87 Cicero allows his Epicurean opponents to raise the claim of *KΔ* 19 in answer to Cicero's own concerns about pleasure's chances of functioning satisfactorily as a measure of a good life—a point he allows them to raise only to reject it summarily. It is true that there is little direct evidence from the Epicureans themselves that this is the precise context in which they would have relied on the claims of *KΔ* 19, but given the prima facie reasons outlined above for thinking of this and the surrounding *KΔ* in this context, it is a possibility which deserves to be pursued. It is best pursued, however, not by limiting ourselves to the thesis of *KΔ* 19 alone.

For the Epicureans, once all pain has been removed there follows the highest state of pleasure (*KΔ* 18, Epic. *Ep. Men.* 128). *KΔ* 20 claims that reason can recognize the 'limit of pleasure' which is most plausibly read as a reference to this notion that pleasure cannot be increased beyond the removal of all pain. Further, *KΔ* 20 says that by realizing this limit, we will be able to

---

[43] At Cic. *Fin.* 3.76 (cf. 3.46) the characterization of the Stoic wise man similarly stresses that he can be truly said to be happy before the end of his life. This is followed by the observation that had Croesus truly been happy than he would not have been made unhappy by ending his life on a pyre. Solon, though not named by Cicero (instead we have: *ille unus e septem sapientibus*, 'That one of the seven [sc. sages]'), famously warned Croesus not to count himself happy too soon. See Hdt. 1.29–33 for the story.   [44] See Stokes 1995.

make life complete and no longer in need of an infinite time. $K\Delta$ 19 offers the supporting thought that the amount of pleasure enjoyed is not increased if it is enjoyed over an infinite rather than a finite time, and $K\Delta$ 21 supplies the thought that the ability to remove pain and lack is the mark of someone who knows the 'limits of life' and who can make a life perfect and complete. Two interpretations are compatible with this evidence, both of which construct an Epicurean conception of a complete life. The first, more modest, interpretation holds that the Epicureans therefore considered that beyond a certain finite duration of pleasure the value of a life was not increased. Once this finite period of experiencing the highest pleasure has passed, therefore, life can be considered complete since its value will increase no more. The second, more radical, interpretation would infer that the message of $K\Delta$ 19 and 20 is that as soon as the highest state of pleasure is achieved, its value is not increased at all by duration. Certainly, the state of feeling no pain, the feeling of true katastematic pleasure, is not more pleasant the longer it lasts. This conclusion, coupled with the Epicureans' notion that pleasure is the one and only criterion of value, would produce the conclusion that a person's life will not increase in value—it will become no more pleasant—once this highest state is achieved. This is the best a life can be. It is true, therefore, to say that the life has now become complete, in the sense that it cannot be improved. The more radical interpretation, therefore, makes a very close connection between the 'limit of pleasure' in $K\Delta$ 18 and the 'limits of life' in $K\Delta$ 21. In effect, the two are near synonyms; a life is complete as soon as the limit of pleasure is achieved and recognized.

   Both interpretations allow that the Epicureans are rejecting mere prolongation as a way of improving a life, but the first recognizes a need for a certain amount of prolongation of a life of true katastematic pleasure before a life can be complete. Both accounts will give an Epicurean answer to the completeness of a life. On the first, more modest, interpretation, once the necessary amount of time in the highest state of pleasure has passed then it is true to say that nothing more is added simply by living on and on. From that point in time on, therefore, if death should come then it will not detract from the completeness of a life. Similarly, the second interpretation allows that once a life is complete in Epicurean hedonistic terms then its value cannot be diminished if it is curtailed. However, it differs crucially from the first interpretation in thinking that no prolongation whatsoever is needed once the highest state of pleasure is reached. As soon as that state is achieved, a life is complete. Some supporting evidence could be marshalled on behalf of each of these views. A supporter of the more modest interpretation can point to the Epicureans' own careful recommendations for prudential planning and the maximization of pleasure over time at *Ep. Men.* 129–30, and claim that this points to a conception of an agent who ideally attempts to prolong a life of maximum pleasure. Some duration, therefore, would appear to be envisaged for a complete life. On the other hand, the supporter of the more radical view can emphasize the Epicurean insistence that the highest state of pleasure is attained *as soon as* all pain is removed.[45] There is no explicit mention in the *Letter to Menoeceus* and the *Kyriai Doxai* of some further period of time being necessary in order for a life which has attained this highest state of pleasure to be truly called complete.

Cicero's discussion in *De Finibus* 2.87–8 can offer support to both camps. He certainly repeats the Epicurean assertion that as much pleasure can be enjoyed in a finite as in an infinite amount of time (2.87). However, he also at least implicitly attributes the stronger position to Epicurus: no amount of time increases the value of a good life once the highest good is achieved. In 2.88 Cicero contrasts what he takes to be the implausible and inconsistent Epicurean view with the more promising thought that the highest good is virtue. On this latter view, at least, it is possible to deny that duration increases the value of a good life.

cum enim summum bonum in voluptate ponat, negat infinito tempore aetatis voluptatem fieri maiorem quam finito atque modico. qui bonum omne in virtute ponit, is potest dicere perfici beatam vitam perfectione virtutis; negat enim summo bono afferre incrementum diem. qui autem voluptate vitam effici beatam putabit, qui sibi is conveniet, si negabit voluptatem crescere longinquitate?

For although he places the highest good in pleasure, he denies that pleasure becomes greater in an infinte time than in a finite and modest one. The person who places everything good in virtue, *he* can say that

---

[45] ἅπαξ in *KΔ* 18 and *Ep. Men.* 128.

a good life is made complete with the completeness of virtue, for he denies that a day brings any increase to the highest good. But the one who thinks that a life is made complete by pleasure, how can he be consistent with himself if he denies that pleasure increases by duration?

Cic. Fin. 2.88

This begins with another rehearsal of the claim of *KΔ* 19. But the view to be contrasted with the Epicureans' does not make the weaker claim that an everlasting life of virtue is no better than a finitely long virtuous life. Rather, this view argues for the stronger view that a life of virtue is not increased in value by a single day. Cicero then passes to a criticism of the Epicurean view. They cannot consistently hold that pleasure is the good but deny the importance of duration. It could certainly be argued that this comparison implicitly attributes the stronger temporal thesis to the Epicureans. These virtue theorists can consistently hold that a life which has attained the highest good is not improved by any amount of prolongation, however small, whereas the Epicureans cannot. There is certainly a movement in the passage from a comparison of finitely and infinitely long lives of the highest good to a comparison of longer and shorter such lives. It might still be questioned, however, how much of what Cicero offers is a position endorsed by the Epicureans themselves and how much is a Ciceronian extrapolation—for dialectical and polemical purposes—from views the Epicureans were prepared to expound.

Whichever of these two competing interpretations best captures the Epicureans' view of the relationship between a perfect hedonist life and its duration, Epicurus must also think that this highest state of pleasure is in fact something which a wise Epicurean will be able to maintain, contrary to Cicero's doubts. Mental anxieties caused by false beliefs will presumably not recur once the relevant false beliefs have been eradicated and true beliefs have taken their place. Physical pain can be avoided for the most part, if not removed entirely, by ensuring that one retains only natural and necessary desires which can be fulfilled easily since they are very general (e.g. a desire to drink when thirsty, not a desire for a particular drink). Such desires will rarely prove to be unsatisfiable as a result of external circumstances. In addition, Epicurus could recommend his techniques of recollecting past pleasures or anticipating future pleasures as a means of reducing present pain.[46] An Epicurean life, it turns out from this analysis of the highest pleasure, is complete once that highest pleasure is attained and will remain complete throughout the remainder of the wise Epicurean's life.[47]

More progress towards further characterizing the Epicurean view, and coming to make a decision between the 'modest' and 'radical' interpretations of a complete Epicurean life, can be made by considering what evidence there is of the Epicurean view of different stages of a life. One conception of the completeness of a life, remember, held that a complete life should contain the relevant different stages—youth, maturity, old-age—for each of which there are relevant cares and activities.[48] The Epicureans seem to have thought that there were no morally relevant differences between the various stages. What is appropriate for a human, no matter how old, is to live a life free from pain. Youth. maturity, and old-age are entirely alike in that regard.

οὐ νέος μακαριστὸς ἀλλὰ γέρων βεβιωκὼς καλῶς· ὁ γὰρ νέος ἀκμῇ πολὺς ὑπὸ τῆς τύχης ἑτεροφρονῶν πλάζεται· ὁ δὲ γέρων καθάπερ ἐν λιμένι τῷ γήρᾳ καθώρμικεν, τὰ πρότερον δυσελπιστούμενα τῶν ἀγαθῶν ἀσφαλεῖ κατακλείσας χάριτι.

We should consider most blessed not the youth but the old man who has lived well. For a young man in his prime is distracted and caused to wander by chance. But the old man has docked in old age as if in a port and has secured the goods formerly despaired of with a sure joy.

Sent. Vat. 17

This returns to the subject introduced by Solon's dictum. Here. the old man is to be considered blessed because he has secured what is good and can maintain and retain it. The young man. with much of his life before him, is so much more subject not only to the vagaries of fortune but also to other distractions and instabilities, of his own character as well as of external circumstances. For that reason it is prudent not to call a young

---

[46] This would help to answer the worries of Gosling and Taylor 1984, 359: 'In actual practice it will surely still be true that a wise man will always be concerned with increasing the proportion of pleasure in his life and reducing the amount of (unavoidable) pain. It is only in fanciful utopian conditions that he will not be concerned with duration.'

[47] Cf. for a similar interpretation Mitsis 1988a, 320–2; Rosenbaum 1990, 36–8; Lesses 2002. [48] See above, pp. 115–20.

man blessed. However, this saying notably refrains from saying that a young man cannot be blessed since his life is not complete. Rather, the restrictions on calling him blessed stem from the fact that the young man in question has not yet secured what is good.[49] It still seems possible—if unlikely—for a young person to achieve such a goal, and there are famous examples of prodigiously talented young Epicureans who were lauded for their early achievements.[50] It appears likely that the Epicureans similarly argued that old age and physical infirmity are no impediment to the attainment and enjoyment of a good life. Diogenes of Oinoanda included in his enormous Epicurean inscription, erected during what he himself refers to as the 'sunset of his life',[51] a treatment of the subject of old age. Although it survives only in very fragmentary form, it seems to have included in a similar vein to *Sent. Vat.* 17 a rebuttal of the claim that the elderly are not as able as the young to enjoy life.[52] In short, as the famous opening to the *Letter to Menoeceus* (122) makes clear, for the Epicureans philosophy is of value no matter what one's age and its aim

---

[49] Compare Democritus DK 68 B295: ὁ γέρων νέος ἐγένετο, ὁ δὲ νέος ἄδηλον εἰ ἐς γῆρας ἀφίξεται· τὸ τέλειον οὖν ἀγαθὸν τοῦ μέλλοντος ἔτι καὶ ἀδήλου κρέσσον ('The old man was young, but it is uncertain whether the young man will be old. So the complete good is better than that which is to come and is uncertain').

[50] There is the example of the eighteen-year-old Pythocles, who is mentioned by Plutarch *Non Posse* 1124C and in Philodemus *De Morte* XII.30 ff., which is discussed further below, and of Philista in Carneiscus' work (*Philista* XVII). We have no idea of Philista's age when she died. Nevertheless, her example could serve Carneiscus' polemic against the Peripatetic, Praxiphanes, in two ways. First, it allows him to contrast the Aristotelian insistence on a complete life with the Epicurean claims about the availability of maximum pleasure and goodness in a short time. Second, it allows him to contrast Peripatetic and Epicurean views on the contribution of external goods to happiness and therefore the dependence of each person on others. See Capasso 1988, 78–82.

[51] Diog. Oin. 3.II.7–8: [ἐν δυ]σμαῖς γὰρ ἤδη | [τοῦ β]ίου ('for as I am in the sunset of life...'). Cf. D.L. 10.22, Epicurus' letter to Idomeneus, which begins, following the MSS: τὴν μακαρίαν ἄγοντες καὶ ἅμα τελευτῶντες ἡμέραν τοῦ βίου... ('enjoying and completing the happiest day of life...'). This too would include a metaphorical reference to the 'day of one's life'. Many editors (Hicks, Marcovich) follow Davis in emending τελευτῶντες to τελευταίαν on the basis of Cicero's Latin version at *Fin.* 2.96: *cum ageremus vitae beatum et eundem supremum diem* 'enjoying this happy and final day of my life...'). τελευτῶντες is retained by Bailey and defended by Laks 1976, 91.

[52] Smith 1993 list the fragments of the treatise *On Old Age* as frr. 137–79. Compare the discussion of old age and the fear of death in Musonius Rufus fr. 17 91.21–93.2 Hense.

and method is the same throughout one's life. Anyone who says that he is either too young or too old to study philosophy is like someone who says he is either too young or too old for happiness.[53]

Lucretius on complete lives

Lucretius addresses the question of when a life can truly be said to be complete by offering two examples of people who complain that their deaths will be untimely or their lives somehow marred by their imminent death. To such complaints, Lucretius composes a response which he places in the mouth of a personification of Nature. The first complaint is quite general, since the addressee of the response is 'any one of us' (3.932). Nature's response should therefore be generally applicable.[54]

> 'quid tibi tanto operest, mortalis, quod nimis aegris
> luctibus indulges? quid mortem congemis ac fles?
> nam si grata fuit tibi vita ante acta priorque
> et non omnia pertusum congesta quasi in vas
> commoda perfluxere atque ingrata interiere;
> cur non ut plenus vitae conviva recedis
> aequo animoque capis securam, stulte, quietem?
> sin ea quae fructus cumque es periere profusa
> vitaque in offensost, cur amplius addere quaeris,
> rursum quod pereat male et ingratum occidat omne,
> non potius vitae finem facis atque laboris?
> nam tibi praeterea quod machiner inveniamque,
> quod placeat, nil est; eadem sunt omnia semper.
> si tibi non annis corpus iam marcet et artus
> confecti languent, eadem tamen omnia restant,
> omnia si perges vivendo vincere saecla,
> atque etiam potius, si numquam sis moriturus'.

'What is of such concern to you, mortal, that you indulge overly in miserable laments? Why do you bewail your death and cry so? For if you have enjoyed the life you have led up to now and you have not allowed all those benefits to flow away and be lost without enjoyment,

---

[53] Cf. *Ep. Men.* 126.
[54] For antecedents of this kind of *prosopopoiia* in Cynic literature see Wallach 1976, 61–77.

as if poured into a broken pot, then why do you not leave like a diner fed full of life and find a secure rest with an untroubled mind? But if whatever you have enjoyed has been poured away and lost and life causes you pain, why do you want to add more of something which will again be lost in misery and entirely perish without enjoyment? Why not rather put an end to your life and misery? For there is nothing else I can find or contrive to please you: all things are forever the same. If your body is not already weak with age and your limbs exhausted and limp, then still all the same things remain, even if you carry on and manage to live out all the ages; still more if you should never die at all.'

DRN 3.933–49

The addressee complains that he is going to die and that this will detract from the quality and value of his life. In response, Nature offers a simple dilemma. Either this person's life has in fact been pleasant, in which case he should not be concerned to depart from it since he is satisfied, like a well-fed diner,[55] or his life has thus far been miserable, in which case he should also not be afraid to depart from life since there is no chance of his ever finding anything to enjoy. It would be better for this person to hasten his own end. In neither case, therefore, is there sufficient justification for the desire to prolong life which lies behind the complaint that death is an evil.

As it stands, the dilemma is not very compelling. First, there is no full justification offered here for the claim that if one's life so far has truly been enjoyed then there is no reason to prolong it. After all, if a life is being enjoyed there seems to be all the more reason not to want to leave it—a longer life would surely be a better life. Second, the response to the second life seems incredibly harsh. Why is it not possible for the person whose life so far has contained nothing of any worth to reform and find something late in life to value and enjoy? Lucretius is evidently offering two extreme cases. The first life, for it to be a life which has been enjoyed but would not be made any more choiceworthy were it to be prolonged, must already be a complete life. The second life, for it to be a life which is so miserable that there is no chance of it ever being improved, must be an irredeemably misguided life. The general contrast, therefore, is between a life

---

[55] For a similar analogy see Cic. *Tusc.* 5.118: *aut bibat aut abeat* ('Let him drink or depart').

of constant filling and pouring away and a life of satiety. The former is not worth living and the latter is already complete and therefore does not need to be prolonged.

In order to understand fully the passage and its relevance to questions of a complete life, it is important to recognize that Lucretius makes Nature speak in hedonist terms and that the passage as a whole relies heavily on Epicurean ethical and psychological theory. The goods of life and those which are enjoyed and the mistakes made by the misguided person in the second arm of the dilemma ensure that he finds no pleasure in anything.[56] A further clue that Nature is speaking here in predominantly hedonist terms is the striking metaphor of someone attempting in vain to fill a cracked vessel. Lucretius has already in this book used the metaphor of the body acting as the vessel (*vas*) of the soul.[57] Here the metaphor is more like what is found in Socrates' refutation of Callicles' hedonist thesis in Plato's *Gorgias* 493a–494a. There. Socrates attempts to persuade Callicles of the value of a satisfied and orderly life—which he associates with the picture of a man who has filled his jars and can relax—over an undisciplined and disorderly life—which he associates with the picture of a man who toils constantly to fill and refill a number of cracked and dirty jars.[58] Here in Lucretius' poem, Nature associates true satisfaction with satiety and insists that anything poured into the leaky vessel in fact flows away and is not enjoyed. Indeed, later in this same book Lucretius will interpret the myth of the Danaids, who were sentenced to perform just this task for all eternity in Hades, as a representation of those people who are unable to satisfy themselves (3.1003–10).[59]

---

[56] *grata* 935, *ingrata* 937, *quae fructus* 940, *quod placeat* 945.

[57] Cf. for the body as the *vas* of the soul: 3.440, 555, 793. Compare *Ep. Hdt.* 64, 66. See also Görler 1997. Philodemus *De Morte* XXXIX.1–6 and Sen. *Cons. ad Marc.* 9.3 use the fragility of glass or pottery vessels to illustrate the fragility of a human's hold on life. Cf. Gigante 1983b, 222–4.

[58] Socrates adds the thought that those trying to fill these leaky jars are trying to do so using sieves, 493b7–c2. These sieves are then said to represent the souls of those who have this misguided view of what matters, since they are unable to retain anything. For more on the myth see Keuls 1974.

[59] Note the first person verb *explemur* at 1007: it is *we* who ought to be fulfilled.

Lying behind Nature's dilemma is the Epicurean recognition of two species of pleasure. The first, what they called 'kinetic' pleasure, is the pleasure which accompanies the process of removing a pain (for example, the pleasure of drinking to relieve a thirst). The second, what they called 'katastematic' pleasure, is the pleasure of not being in pain or need (for example, the pleasure of not being thirsty). In addition to recognizing the existence of this second kind of pleasure, which was itself a controversial stance, the Epicureans asserted that it was in fact the highest form of pleasure. Once all pain has been removed the pleasure cannot be increased, merely 'varied'. If this general position is accepted, then it becomes clear why the full and satisfied diner can be described in such positive terms. This is a representation of katastematic pleasure, a state in which all desires are fulfilled and anxieties removed.[60] In that case, it would be correct to think that this person's life is complete and he can indeed depart from life without anxiety.

In contrast, the person who wishes only to feel the pleasures of removing desires and pains is condemned to a never-ending cycle of pleasure and pain and a never-ending task just like that of the Danaids. Since, thinking that there is value only in the process of satisfaction, as soon as a desire is fulfilled he is constantly forced to contrive a new desire and lack which he can try to fulfil. From an Epicurean perspective which recognizes also the pleasure of the state of satisfaction, Nature is quite correct in pointing out that prolonging a life of this sort will not make it any better or bring it any closer to true fulfilment; it will merely extend the misery of the never-ending cycle. For there is a limited number of resources at hand. Nature herself cannot constantly provide ever new sources of enjoyment. From a non-Epicurean perspective which does not recognize the existence of such pleasures of satiety, an equally depressing conclusion emerges. If pleasures can be

---

[60] Two elements of the description in 939 encourage viewing it as a picture of tranquil *ataraxia*: the equanimity of the diner, and his achieving *secura quies* ('sure tranquillity'). This latter, of course, refers first to the rest and *anaisthesia* of death (cf. 3.211, 920). But it is hard not to see also a reference to the absence of pain and calm of the ideal Epicurean state, the presence of which is the reason why this person can depart from life happily. Death and *ataraxia* are alike in being absences of pain. Cf. 3.18: *divum sedes quietae* and, for *aequus animus*: 1.41–2 and 6.78: *animi tranquilla pax*. See also Segal 1990, 70–1, 82.

merely accumulated then it will always be true no matter how long a person lives that a longer time would have given more opportunities for pleasure. It will always be true that death curtails the value of a life.[61] Hence Nature concludes at the end of the passage just cited that the man whose life has not so far been enjoyable will not be benefited by living any longer, not even by living forever. The only rational thing to do in this case is either to end it all or, an alternative not explored by Nature here, to set about sufficient psychological improvements that the true pleasure of satiety can be enjoyed.[62]

That process of psychological improvement is, unsurprisingly, to be carried out by careful study and acceptance of Epicurean doctrine. In the opening lines of book 6, Lucretius describes how Epicurus recognized the psychological failings of those about him and set about curing this malaise. Lucretius reuses the image of the cracked vessel, which now is not only cracked but also tainted. It both allows its contents to flow away and also taints and corrupts them as it does so.[63] Epicurus purges people's minds (6.24) and sets a limit (*finis*) on desire and fear and shows the final goal (*summum bonum*) to which all people should strive (6.25–6). The clear message is that in order to live a complete life and die with equanimity, it is crucial to understand the value of satiety and fulfilment and rid ourselves of the constant search for more and more sources of novel enjoyment.[64]

[61] See the discussion of Feldman's additive hedonism above, n. 10. Some Cyrenaics seem to have concluded from their version of hedonism, which did not recognize such a thing as katastematic pleasure, either that happiness (*eudaimonia*) was impossible to attain or that, all things considered, it would be better to cut life short by committing suicide. See D.L. 2.93–6 and Cic. *Tusc.* 1.83 with Matson 1998.

[62] 943: *vitae finem facis atque laboris* continues the fertile ambiguities of 939. In one sense suicide will indeed put a limit on life and toil. But there is another way to 'round-off' and complete a life and indeed to put an end to toil, which is the attainment of the Epicurean ideal state of *ataraxia* and *aponia*. Reinhardt 2002, 298–9, argues that *finem vitae facere* here must mean 'to accept the end of one's life' and therefore thinks that Nature is addressing someone faced with imminent death. It seems to me, however, that this can be a recommendation of suicide in the extreme case of an irredeemably misguided person: compare *Ep. Men.* 126–7.   [63] As in Pl. *Gorg.* 493e7–8.

[64] Cf. Cic. *Tusc.* 5.96: the soul of the wise man not only is able to anticipate and enjoy future pleasures but also will not allow past pleasures to 'flow away' (*praeterfluere*). See also Sen. *De. Brev. Vitae* 10.5 and Williams ad loc.

A very similar general response is offered to the second objector, who is described as an older man:

'aufer abhinc lacrimas, baratre, et compesce querellas.
omnia perfunctus vitai praemia marces;
sed quia semper aves quod abest, praesentia temnis,
inperfecta tibi elapsast ingrataque vita,
et nec opinanti mors ad caput adstitit ante
quam satur ac plenus possis discedere rerum.
nunc aliena tua tamen aetate omnia mitte
aequo animoque, agedum, †magnis† concede: necessest'.

'Take your tears away from here, wretch,[65] and quell your complaints. Having enjoyed all life's prizes, now you decay. But because what you want is always at a distance you shun what is at hand, your life has slipped away incomplete and unenjoyed, and death stands by your head unexpected, before you can leave things satisfied and full. Now set aside everything unbecoming for your age and with a level head, give way to your sons. You must. It is necessary.'[66]

DRN 3.955–62

This old man has in fact had the chance to live a full and satisfied life but has been prone always to look away from what is at hand and towards the next object of desire.[67] As a result, he has been unable ever to be satisfied and full (960: *satur ac plenus* recalls the satisfied diner of 938) and now, with death at hand, it is too late for him to effect the required changes of attitude which would allow him to lead a full life and die happily and without regret. Since this is an older addressee, Nature can also use further considerations to criticize his conduct. The old must give way to the new, she insists, and continue the process of recycling and renovation which gives life to each generation in turn. Life is given to each of us only on leasehold (964–71).[68]

---

[65] See Smith 2000 for a discussion of the text here.
[66] The text of 962 is debatable. See Bailey and Kenney ad loc.
[67] For Democritean antecedents of this idea see DK B199, 200, 201 and Warren 2002c, 37–8. See also Wallach 1975, 68–74.
[68] Lucretius introduced this theme of the necessary recycling of elements at 2.75–9. See O'Keefe 2003, for a discussion of 3.963–71. One might compare modern discussions of the social and economic costs of increased longevity and the claim that certain people—principally the elderly and the sick— may have therefore a 'duty to die'. This view is strongly criticized by Overall 2003, 52–94.

Lucretius returns to the theme of the unsatisfiable desire to prolong a life in the closing section of the book. Here Lucretius shows us the question of the length of life from two perspectives. First, he shows from the perspective of someone 'inside' a life, living a life and trying to make the best of it, that novelty and prolongation are not relevant to the overall worth and fulfilment of that life (1076–84). Then he moves to a perspective outside a life, from the point of view of the universe, and asks us to view the period of our lives from without, against the backdrop of the whole of time (1087–94). On neither account is it worth struggling to prolong life and therefore the desire for life *per se* (*cupido vitai*) is to be avoided. Once this has been removed, a major obstacle in the way of viewing death correctly disappears. Most important for the construction of a satisfactory Epicurean response to the concerns people feel about their own life perhaps ending prematurely will be the first, 'internal', perspective:

> denique tanto opere in dubiis trepidare periclis
> quae mala nos subigit vitai tanta cupido?
> certe equidem finis vitae mortalibus adstat
> nec devitari letum pote, quin obeamus.
> praeterea versamur ibidem atque insumus usque
> nec nova vivendo procuditur ulla voluptas;
> sed dum abest quod avemus, id exsuperare videtur
> cetera; post aliud, cum contigit illud, avemus
> et sitis aequa tenet vitai semper hiantis.

Again, what is this overwhelming and damaging lust for life which forces us to tremble so much in uncertain dangers? Certainly, there is an end of life for mortals and death cannot be avoided. We must die. Moreover we spend time always among the same things and no new pleasure is produced merely by living longer. But while what we long for is absent it seems to dominate everything else. Then once it is at hand, we long for something else and always the same thirst for life holds us gaping open-mouthed.

DRN 3.1076–84

Many of the themes and metaphors of this passage are familiar by now. But here Lucretius reveals the close connection between the desire for life (*cupido vitai* 1077) and a 'thirst' for life (1084)— a thirst which, given our foolish desire always for something new and something as yet unattained, can never be sated. The language of thirst recalls the leaking jars and endless toil of the

Danaids seen earlier.[69] This constant deferral of the object of desire is the major reason for wishing to continue to live. Once again, Lucretius emphasizes just how misguided this desire is since it simply can never be fulfilled. Pleasure, of course, is what we ought to be pursuing, but the Epicureans are insistent that we should have the correct conception of pleasure. On the misguided view outlined here what is absent seems (*videtur* 1082) more important, but this is a misleading appearance based on an incorrect assessment of the relative values of what is at hand and what is yet to be attained.[70] Further, no matter how long one lives no new pleasure can be extracted from life simply by waiting around for a while longer. Just as Nature reminded one of her addressees that there simply is nothing new she can find to offer him, so here Lucretius insists that there is no novelty to be found in the world.

Most important is Lucretius' emphatic assertion of the limit (*finis*) of a human life. First and foremost in this context he must mean a temporal limit. Everything mortal will die and this end is inevitable. But there is another sense in which Lucretius insists that a human life has a sure limit. We should recall Epicurus' own assertion, particularly in *KΔ* 20, that the key to living a complete life is the proper recognition of the limit (πέρας) of pleasure— precisely what the misguided constantly striving and thirsty fools fail to do.[71] If only they would recognize this limit then they would also see that the fact that a human life has a temporal limit is no impediment to living a complete life. In fact, one cannot live a complete human life unless and until one recognizes and accepts that pleasure is limited in the appropriate sense.

---

[69] Cf. Segal 1990, 71–3. Insatiable thirst is also one of the symptoms of the Athenian plague (*insedabiliter sitis arida*, 6.1176). For disease and plague as Epicurean metaphors of false opinion see also Diog. Oin. 3.IV.3–V.8 and Warren 2000a. Galloway 1986, 59: 'The plague-sufferers' burning thirst (*insedabiliter sitis arida*) echoes and climaxes the mourners' insatiable weeping (*insatiabiliter*) at the dead man's pyre (3.907) and the *sitis arida* of the banqueters at 3.917, whose drinking cups are as inadequate as the *multus imbris*, the "flood of water", was for the plague sufferers.'

[70] For more discussion of Epicurean theories of the comparative assessment of future pleasures see Warren 2001d.

[71] Cf. 5.1433: *finis et omnino quoad crescat vera voluptas* ('the limit and the extent to which true pleasure may grow'); 6.25: *et finem statuit* [*Epicurus*] *cuppedinis atque timoris* ('He set down a limit of desire and fear'). At 3.1021 there is no *finis* to the punishments in Hades which Lucretius interprets as the pains of a guilty conscience.

Philodemus on death and the complete life

The most sustained Epicurean discussion of premature death and the complete life is to be found in Philodemus' *De Morte*. It is worth considering this text in some detail, and also quoting some extensive passages, since not only is it generally not referred to in much of the recent discussion of Epicurean views of death, but it also draws together in a more or less continuous stretch of text many of the themes we have already seen in other Epicurean sources.[72] In the surviving parts of the treatise, Philodemus addresses in turn a number of objections which may be brought against the general Epicurean attitude to death, one of which is that an untimely or premature (ἄωρος) death can be an evil (columns XII–XX).[73] Even before this section of the work, however, Philodemus can be seen to have laid some foundations for his eventual dismissal of such concerns. Early in the surviving text, in what seems to be a discussion of the objection that death is necessarily painful, he refers to the now familiar Epicurean thesis that the limits of pleasure can be reached in a finite time.[74]

ἐπιχέωμ[εθα... |. εἰ]ρημένοις Διὸς σώτηρ[ος διότι | τὴν ἡ]δονὴν ὁπόσος χρόνος τῶι ἄ|[παντι] παρασζευάζειν πέφυκεν ὅτ[αν | τις αὐ]τῆς καταλάβη[ι] τοὺς ὅρους τό | [θ' ἅμ]α τὸ σάρκινον εὐθὺς ἀπολᾳ|[βεῖν τ]ὸ μέγεθος τῆς ἡδονῆς ὅπε[ρ | καὶ ὁ] ἄπειρος χρόνος περιποίη[σεν | ἴσον...]

But let us pour a libation (or: anoint ourselves[75])... of Zeus Soter, for what has been said, because any length of time naturally produces pleasure for all—provided one recognizes pleasure's limits—and because of the fact that at the same time the flesh immediately receives

---

[72] It is to be hoped that the availability of David Armstrong's forthcoming edition of the text will make it better known and offer new resources for the study of Epicurean treatments of death.

[73] See Garland 1985, 77–88, for a discussion of ancient Greek attitudes to 'untimely' deaths and cf. Plut. *Cons. ad Apoll.* 110E–112B, 113C–114C.

[74] Armstrong, forthcoming, wishes to see this part of the treatise as addressed to as wide an audience as possible, relying as little as possible on technical Epicurean doctrine. This thesis about the nature of pleasure must be an exception to this rule, or a counterexample to Armstrong's interpretation.

[75] ἐπιχέω in the middle voice usually means 'to pour over oneself, anoint oneself, or pour oneself a drink' (LSJ s.v. B). For the sense 'to pour a libation to' see Gigante 1983a, 131.

the amount of pleasure equal to what an unlimited length of time provides...

Philodemus, *De morte* III.32–IIIa.1 Gigante

This reprises much of the advice of *KΔ* 19–21, particularly the idea that correct understanding is required to assess correctly the limits of pleasure.[76] Philodemus does not restrict himself here, however, to the weaker thesis that a finite and an infinite time contain equal amounts of pleasure. Rather, he allows himself—perhaps for rhetorical effect, but certainly in line with a case he could make more extensively by relying on the Epicurean notion of katastematic pleasure—to offer the much stronger claim that the flesh can immediately (εὐθύς) receive the exact same amount of pleasure as is offered by the limitless bounds of time. This stronger claim is certainly not in direct conflict with any Epicurean theory, and we have already seen that this consequence can be inferred from what we do know of Epicurean hedonism. Here, however. Philodemus places this claim significantly in his discussion of the nature and value of death. We therefore have good reason for thinking that this particular facet of Epicurean hedonism was thought by the Epicureans themselves to lead to certain conclusions about the completeness of a good life and, crucially, the relation of questions of duration to such complete lives.

Later, Philodemus turns to address the question of untimely death directly.

διότι τὴν ἄωρον τελε[υτὴν ὡς κακόν]‖ τινες ἐκκλ[ίνου]σιν ἐλπ[ίζοντες πολ]‖ λῶν ἀγαθῶ[ν ἔ]ν τῶι πλεί[ονι χρόνωι | κ]τῆσιν ἕξειν, [ἃ χ]ωρὶς τῆς γνησ[ίας σο]‖φίας οὐδ' ἐν ὕπ[νω]ι δύναται [κτήσασ]‖θαι, δι' ἣν αἰτία[ν] αὐτὴν νεότ[ης ὑπὸ | τῶ]ν πλείστων [ἀ]νθρώπων ἐ[κακίζε]‖το, πλεῖστον χ[ρό]νον ἐπίθεσιν [ἀγαθῶν][77] | ποιουμένων ἀπὸ λόγου πως... χρόνωι [γὰ]ρ μετροῦντ[ες τἀγα] |θ [ἀ] οὐδὲν μέ[γα π]εριποιησόμε[νοι φαί|νοντ]αι, τῆς δ[ιαν]οίας ὑπὲρ τῶν...

...because some people shun untimely death as an evil, in the hope that in a longer period of time they will come to acquire many goods which cannot be obtained even in a dream without genuine wisdom. For this same reason youth is thought badly of by most men, since they consider a longer life to be an increase of goods, in a way by their own argument.... Because they measure the goods by time they are

---

[76] For further discussion see Gigante 1983a, 131–6.
[77] ἀγαθῶν supplevi. Kuiper, followed by Armstrong, has σοφίας.

revealed as never going to attain anything of worth, on account of their thought...

Philodemus, *De morte* XII.2–15 Kuiper

Again, parallels for much of what is said here can be found elsewhere. We have seen repeatedly already the contrast between a rational understanding of the limits of pleasure and the common misunderstanding that a greater period of time will allow a greater accumulation of goods and therefore a better life. This cumulative conception of pleasure, also criticized by Lucretius, is here offered by Philodemus as the prime reason why people consider death in youth to be pitiable. The young deceased has been robbed of the usual amount of time people have to accumulate and increase the goodness of their lives. The second half of this section is a little less clear, partly because of an uncertainty about the meaning of the word λόγος at XII.10. It seems most likely that Philodemus is claiming that there is something internally inconsistent in these people's view of the accumulation of pleasure. The text becomes more fragmentary from this point on until it breaks off completely for a couple of lines. One possible reconstruction of what follows would be the thought that if these people agree that what matters is accumulating pleasures and accumulating time in which to enjoy pleasures they will never in fact be able to enjoy anything at all. This is the same thought that Lucretius offered against the pleonectic characters and was dramatized with the image of the Danaids forever attempting to fill leaking pots with cracked water jars. What matters to the people Philodemus is criticizing is the accumulation of good things. But, Philodemus now wants to point out, such a position is self-defeating if by that accumulation is meant a constant search for new and future goods to pursue and attain. Once anything has been attained, after all, it is time to move on and search for something new. Never will these restless people be able to enjoy anything they do acquire due to their constant search for more and more.[78] But their professed aim was to enjoy the best life

---

[78] There is a long history of such criticisms of pleonectic conceptions of goodness. In addition to Socrates' *reductio* of Callicles' position in the *Gorgias* see also Democritus DK B235 and especially B202 and 224. Cf. Warren 2002c, 53–5. For another Epicurean expression of the link see Porph. *De Abst.* 1.53–4 and also the discussion in Schmid 1977, 137 ff.

possible, a life with the greatest amount of goods. This aim has been shown to be made unattainable precisely because of their incorrect notion of this 'greatest amount of goods'.

It is true, Philodemus can say, that on this conception of the goodness of a life an early death will appear to be pitiable. But this is a woefully misguided conception of the goodness of a life, full of internal inconsistencies. It can therefore be rejected as a justification for concluding that an early death is pitiable.

[οὐδὲ μνησθεὶς ὅσων ἀγαθ]ῶν ἔπα|θεν ἐ]ζηκὼ[ς κ]ατὰ σ[οφίαν, λυ]πρός, ἀλ|λ᾽ [ὁ γ]έρων οὐθὲν εὔ[ρὼν φυσι]κῶς ἀγα|θό[ν, π]ε[ι]σ[θεὶς] ἀπολή[ψε]σ[θαι μ]ετὰ τοῦ | μ[έλλο]ντος ἁπάσα[ς τὰς εὐχ]άς. πού γὰρ | ἐλεῆσαι νέον ἐστιν [ὁρῶντι τ]οσοῦτο | ἀναλογιζόμενον [ἐξ] ὧν Πυθοκλ[ῆς, οἷ]|α κελεύει Μητρόδω[ρος], περιπε[ποί]|ηται, γε[γο]νὼς οὐχί[ί π]ω ὀκτὼ καί δέ|κα [ἐτῶν], ἀλλ᾽ οὐχὶ τὸ[ν τῶν ἀφρόνων] | βίο[ν] ζήσας, ἀνυπονόητος [δ᾽ ὢν μή]|τοι πένηται παντὸς εἴδους; ἐ[ξὸν δὲ]| ἐμ ποσῶι χρόνωι τὸ μέγιστον αὐ[τῶν] καὶ περιποιήσασθαι κα[ὶ] ἀπολαῦσαι κ[α]|θαπερ ὑπέδειξ[α], ὁ[ρέξ]ε[τα]ι νέος τις ὁ [μὴ] | μα[ιν]όμενος ἔτ[ι] το[ύ]το<υ> καὶ τῆς ἀπε[ι]|ρίας, οὐχ ὅ[τι] τῆς τοῦ γέροντος προσ[ποι]|ήσεται ζω[ῆ]ς; ἔτι δὲ μειράκιον ἄφθ[ο]|να περι[ποίησ]εται τού[τ]ων ὥστε γε|γανωμένος ἀπέρχεσθαι κἂν ῥηθῆν[αι] | πλέ[ο]ν βεβιωκέναι τῶν ἀναπολαύσ|[τ]ων [ὅσα διέ]ζων ἔτη. σιωπῶ γὰρ ὅ||[τι] πολλάκι πολλοῖς τ[ῶ]ν ἀφρόνω[ν] τὸ | [ν]έ]ου[ς τελ]ε[υ]τῆσαι λυσ[ιτελέ]στερον | [φα]ίν[εται καὶ μ]ὴ κατὰ τὴν ἡλικίαν | [ε]ὐθ[ηνοῦσι] τραφῆν[αι οἴ]κοις . . .

[The young man who cannot remember how many good] things he experienced because he has lived wisely does not deserve pity, but rather the old man who has found so far nothing naturally good, but still has convinced himself that he will attain all his dreams sometime in the future. For how is it possible to pity a young man when one sees how much can be inferred from what Pythocles achieved by doing what Metrodorus advised? Not yet eighteen, he did not live a fool's life, and was nevertheless unconcerned about losing all his looks. But, it being possible both to achieve and enjoy the greatest [goods] in some certain period of time, as I have demonstrated, will any young man who is not insane desire any longer even endless time, or even try to win the life of an old man? While still a young man he will come to possess a plentiful supply of goods and as a result will pass away joyfully and even be said to have lived more of a life than those who do not enjoy all the years they live. For I will not mention the fact that in many instances dying young would seem more profitable for many of the foolish, even when they are raised as children in thriving households . . .

Philodemus, *De Morte* XII.26–XIII.17 Kuiper/Sedley[79]

[79] Sedley 1976, 44, provides new readings of XII.30–XIII.3.

Now Philodemus turns to consider a contrast between the young and the old in order to offer counterexamples to the objector's thesis that it is pitiable to die young. He begins by reversing the comparison seen in *Sent. Vat.* 17. Now, rather than a content and safe old man contrasted with a young and unstable one, we see a young man already benefited by philosophy—presumably Epicurean philosophy—contrasted with an old man who has had no such beneficial exposure to the truth. Instead this poor old man is still fooling himself with the thought that if only he can live on a little more he might achieve something and attain something good. In this case, it is the old man who, paradoxically, is most susceptible to being prevented by death from attaining a happy and complete life. It may in fact be true to say that were he to die even in such old age without ever having achieved that natural goal of life which the young man is already enjoying, his life may have been curtailed prematurely. It may also be possible to argue that if this old man is so misguided that he is unable to come to see the truth of the Epicurean view of what matters in life then he is benefited by an earlier rather than a late death. It will at least spare him an extended period of misery.[80] (And Philodemus does offer at the end of this section the sneering thought that many of the foolish—non-Epicureans or, perhaps, those who could never become Epicureans—would be benefited by dying as soon as possible. Their lives are necessarily miserable, so what reason could they possibly have for prolonging the agony?) In either case, it is the young man whose life is complete and the old man whose death will be pitiable. What matters, therefore, in assessing the goodness of a life is clearly not at all how long that life is but rather whether the person in question has attained the natural goal of life, the absence of pain. That is best done through an engagement with Epicurean philosophy.

---

[80] See also XIX.33–XX.1: ὁ δ' ἄ[φρ]ων οὔτ' ἀξιόλ[ογον] ἐπιλή|ψετ' ἀγαθόν, ἂν καὶ [τ]ὸν Τ[ι]θωνοῦ δ[ια]|γένητ[αι] χρόνον, ο[ὔτ'] ἀλλο[τρι]ώτ[ε]||ρον αὑ[τὸ]ν ἐ[νθένδ' ὅ]ταν γ[ένη]ται [τὴν] | ταχίστην ἀ[ὑτίκ' ἢ βρα]δύτερον ἀ[πιέ]ναι | κἀ[ν μὴ συ]μβουλεύωμεν ἡμεῖ[ς]. ('But the fool will have no happiness worthy of consideration, not even if he lasts out the years of Tithonus, nor is it more alien to his nature to depart hence, once he is born, by the swiftest road and right now, than to leave life more slowly...even if we would not advise him thus' (trans. Armstrong, modified).)

Pythocles, to whom Philodemus refers here, was a prodigiously talented Epicurean, supposed already by the age of 18 to have achieved great things.[81] Here he is offered as a concrete example of the kind of youthful achievement supposed in the original comparison between the youth and the old man. Such a person demonstrates the truth of the theoretical claim that it is possible to achieve the highest good without the need for an infinite time in which to do it (as would be the consequence of the cumulative conception of the good) and in addition that it is not even necessary to live a complete human life and reach old age for it to be true that one has lived a complete life. A right-thinking young man like Pythocles can see that there is nothing to be said for a long life *per se* and that all that matters in the evaluation of a life is whether it contains the highest good. If then, someone like Pythocles were to die at the age of 18, the possibility Philodemus envisages here, then he would depart glowing with joy (γεγανωμένος) and be said 'to have lived' more than those who live longer but without enjoyment however long or short his life is. Philodemus introduces two conceptions of what it is to live a life, one merely descriptive ('surviving', 'persisting') and one more normative. Even the young deceased, provided he has achieved what is good, can rightly be said to have 'lived a life' in this normative sense despite his not having survived for very long, perhaps not even as long as most other people do.[82] But, as we now know, simply living on and on is not what matters.

Now Philodemus offers something of a concession.[83] Importantly, there seems to be a sense in which some amount of duration must play a part in even the Epicurean conception of a complete life.

---

[81] Cf. Plut. *Adv. Col.* 1124c where it is objected that Epicurus indulged in excessive flattery of the young man: προπέτειαν δὲ καὶ λαμυρίαν ἐμποιεῖ νέοις ὁ περὶ Πυθοκλέους οὔπω γεγονότος ὀκτωκαίδεκα ἔτη γράφων οὐκ εἶναι φύσιν ἐν ὅλῃ τῇ Ἑλλάδι ἀμείνω καὶ τερατικῶς αὐτὸν εὖ ἀπαγγέλλειν, καὶ πάσχειν αὐτὸς τὸ τῶν γυναικῶν, εὐχόμενος ἀνεμέσητα πάντα εἶναι καὶ ἀνεπίφθονα τῆς ὑπερβολῆς τοῦ νεανίσκου. ('He makes the young flighty and impudent by writing about Pythocles (who was not yet eighteen years old) that there was no nature better in the whole of Greece, that he speaks prodigiously well, and that he—Epicurus—was made like the women to pray that the young man's superiority should bring him no hatred or envy.')

[82] Cf. Lucr. *DRN* 3.957–60, above, p. 140.

[83] See also Armstrong 2004, 37.

τὸ δὲ ζητεῖν π[αρὰ ταύτη]ν | [τὴν αἰ]τίαν ὡς [π]λεῖστον [χ]ρό[ν]ον ζῆν |
[εὔλο]γον καί τι[νας] νέους τελευ|τῶντας διὰ τοῦτο δυστυ[χ]εῖ νομ[ί]|ζειν. τὸ
μὲν γάρ, ἵνα συντελέσηταί τ[ις] | τὰς συνγ[ε]νικὰς καὶ φυσικὰ[ς] ἐπιθυμία[ς] |
καὶ πᾶσαν ἀπολάβη<ι> τὴν ο[ἰ]κειοτάτην | [ἦ] ἐνδέ[χ]εται διαγωγήν,
ὀρέγεσθαι προσ|[βι]ῶναί τινα χρόνον, ὥστε πληρ[ω]θῆ|ναι τῶν ἀγαθῶν καὶ
πᾶσα[ν] ἐκβαλεῖν ||[τὴ]ν κατὰ τὰς ἐπιθυμίας ὄ[χ]λησιν ἢ|[ρεμ]ίας
μεταλαμβάνοντα, νοῦν ἔχον|[τός ἐ]στιν ἀνθρώπου· τὸ δ' ἵνα τῆς | [ἱστορ]ίας,
πόσα δήποτέ τις [π]ροσ[βιώσε|τ' ἔτη] κα[θ]ά[ερ ἐξὸν ταμε[ῖ]ον τοῦ | [νοῦ
παρ]α[π]λησίως τὸν ἀπέρ[αντον | κόσμ]ον σ[υμπεριέχειν];

But it is reasonable for this reason to try to live for as long as possible
and to think that for this reason some young people die miserably. For
it is the mark of a man of understanding to desire to live for a certain
period of time in order to fulfil the innate and natural desires and grasp
the whole of the most appropriate way of life possible. As a result, being
satisfied with goods and rejecting every disturbance which desires cause,
he comes upon tranquillity. But if one aims at acquiring knowledge,
then how many extra years will one have to live, as though it were
possible to embrace the limitless universe in the storehouse of the mind?

Philodemus, *De Morte* XIII.36–XIV.14 Kuiper

There is one reasonable cause for attempting to live longer, and
that is the attainment and enjoyment of the complete life offered
by Epicureanism.[84] To this extent, it is a matter of some effort
and therefore a matter of some time before anyone can be said to
have a complete life. Philodemus emphasizes here the contrast
between the fulfilment of natural desire, the desire to be free from
pain, and other empty and never-ending desires such as the desire
for acquiring more and more knowledge.[85] Philodemus turns the
same sort of argument he had used against those who saw the good
life as characterized by the constant accumulation of goods against
other thinkers who may have seen themselves as more respectable
and intellectual. At least, rather than offering the accumulation
of goods as the goal of life, they propose a more intellectual

[84] Annas 1993, 346–7: 'Since we manifestly have to take the death arguments
seriously, we have to take seriously the idea that Epicurus is telling us that the
eighteen-year-old who dies is not being deprived of anything that a seventy-year-
old has had. This holds, of course, only if the eighteen-year-old had achieved
happiness, that is, *ataraxia*. Epicurus can perfectly well hold that an ordinary
teenager who dies has been deprived to some extent, since he has been deprived of
the chance to achieve happiness, which perhaps becomes easier after one's youth.'

[85] The conjecture [ἱστορ]ίας XIV.11, meaning something like 'research' or
'enquiry', would convey this well, if this is understood as a kind of never-ending
fact-finding. It would contrast with 'understanding', σοφία.

pursuit. But, Philodemus contends, the constant desire to accumulate bits of knowledge, what we might term 'fact-finding', is just as self-defeating since it too can never be completed. There will always be some further set of things to find out about and a life dedicated to this practice can no more be complete than one devoted to the constant acquisition of novel pleasures.[86] Philodemus then returns to the description of the happy and wise man, emphasizing that he has fully grasped the greatest of goods:

νῦν [δὲ| σ]οφῶι γενομένωι καὶ ποσ[ὸ]ν | χρόνο[ν ἐ]πιζήσαντ[ι] τὸ μέγιστον ἀγα|θὸν ἀπε[ί]ληπται. τῆς δὲ κατὰ τὴν ἰσό|τητα αὐ[το]ῦ καὶ τὴν ὁμοείδειαν πορεί|ας γινομέ[νης] ἕως [ε]ἰς ἄπειρον εἰ δυνα|τὸν εἴη β[αδί]ζειν οἰκεῖόν ἐστιν· ἂν | δὲ παραγ[έν]ηται τῆς μὲν εὐδαιμ[ο]|νίας ἀφαίρ[εσι]ς, οὐ γίνεται τῆς γεγονυίας, κώλυσι[ς] δὲ τῆς ἔτι μετουσίας αὐτῆς. | ἀλλ' οὐδ[ε τοῦ μηκ]έτ' εἶναι ταύτην ἐ|παίσθ[ησις ἔσ]αι.

But as things are, the greatest good is acquired by a man who has become wise and then in addition lived for a certain period of time. His way of life has become stable and consistent and it is quite appropriate for him to proceed on his way forever, should that be possible. But if there is a loss of his happiness, this does not affect the happiness that has already come about, but rather is merely a prevention of his participating in it any further. But nor will there be any awareness of it no longer being present.

                    Philodemus, *De Morte* XIX.1–11 Kuiper

The overall message here is clear enough, and much as we would expect given the preceding discussion. But two points are worthy of note. First, Philodemus appears to offer a further concession to those who wish to insist on the presence of the highest good for some period of time during a life before that life can qualify for being called complete. He has already agreed that death before attaining the complete natural end may be called premature, but he concedes that even after becoming wise a certain further amount of time is required (καὶ ποσ[ὸ]ν | χρόνο[ν ἐ]πιζήσαντ[ι]), offering support to what I called the 'modest' interpretation of

---

[86] There are a number of ancient philosophers who may have held some such thesis about the accumulation of knowledge being the goal of life. This sort of view is attributed to Anaxagoras at Arist. *EE* 1216ᵃ10–16. Anaxagoras appears to have been named by Philodemus at XVII.28. This may also have been in connection with Anaxagoras' famous equanimity on the occasion of his son's death: Galen *PHP* 4.7.392.

an Epicurean complete life (above p. 130). Philodemus is perhaps appropriately non-committal about the precise length of this additional time spent being wise before the Epicurean can truly be said to have achieved the highest good. Significantly, this is indeed the only sign we have in Philodemus' text of a submission to the pressure of the view that a complete life requires some lasting attainment, exercise, or enjoyment of the highest state. Second, Philodemus claims that once in this state the wise man would be perfectly content to live on forever, were that possible. This is apparently because the wise man will have no sufficient reason to curtail a life except under certain extreme circumstances—and we will see below examples which could illustrate the Epicurean view of what those circumstances might be (p. 205ft.). This claim complements the observation that the fool will never achieve anything worthwhile and can never attain a complete life however long he lives. The irredeemable fool has no reason to prolong his life; the wise man has no reason to curtail his. Further, the wise man's happiness disappears only at death, and even then the happiness he has already enjoyed is untouched by this; there is simply no prospect of future happiness. Hence, there will be no perception of this departure.

Philodemus later in the text deploys an arresting metaphor to illustrate the attitude the wise man will have to his continued life. One of the problems for the Epicurean attitude to the duration of a good life, as we shall see further below (p. 199ft.), is that they must walk a precarious tightrope between the claim that for a wise man death cannot be premature (and therefore there is no reason to be anxious about this possibility) and the claim that a wise man has no sufficient reason to continue to live once he has attained a complete life. Passages such as that we have just seen (XIX.1–11) emphasize not only that the wise man will have no sufficient reason to commit suicide once his life is complete but also that, were he to die at any time, death would not constitute any sort of loss. In that case, it becomes unclear whether continued life has any value at all. It is not to be rejected, but neither—so it seems—is it something we should be anxious about preserving. This complicated attitude is well captured by Philodemus.[87]

---

[87] This passage tends to provoke effusive comment. Cf. Armstrong 2004, 49: 'This is an amazing passage: for Philodemus, the Epicurean man or woman

ὁ δὲ νοῦν ἔχων, ἀπει|ληφὼς ὅ[τι] δύναται πᾶν περιποιῆσαι | [τ]ὸ πρὸς
εὐδαίμονα βίον αὔταρκες, εὐ|θὺς ἤδη τὸ λοιπὸ[ν] ἐντεταφιασμέ|νος περιπατεῖ
κα[ὶ] τὴν μίαν ἡμέραν | ὡς αἰῶνα κερδα[ί]νει.

The one who understands, having grasped that he is capable of
achieving everything sufficient for the good life, immediately and for the
rest of his life walks about already ready for burial, and enjoys the
single day as if it were eternity.

Philodemus, *De Morte* XXXVIII.14-19 Kuiper

The wise man is always ready for death. He walks about 'already
prepared for burial' because, presumably, once he has achieved
eudaimonia to die at any point would be no better or worse than
dying at another. But Philodemus is quick to remind us that this
does not mean that this person finds nothing valuable in life.
Each additional day is enjoyed. Nevertheless, such a person's
attitude towards time and duration differs significantly from that
of those who do not view their mortality correctly. The single day
becomes for him eternity, not in the sense that he lives life 'slowly',
but, perhaps, because he has recognized that a single day offers
him the chance of absolute fulfilment.[88] It is difficult to capture
adequately just what it would be like to live with this attitude.
Indeed, it is perhaps questionable whether such an attitude is
coherent or whether anyone can hold such an attitude sincerely.
Certainly, this kind of day-to-day existence which appears to find
in every moment completeness and fulfilment is quite unlike the
experience of most people whose lives are characterized by goals
whose completion may lie in the nearer or farther future and who

---

achieves, because of his or her exact awareness of death, a daily resurrection
from the dead... It is to go to bed as if wrapped in one's shroud every night
and wake up resurrected every day. It is a secular, and yet equally religious
counterpart to Paul... (2 Cor. 4: 10-11). Schmid 1963, 19-20, refers to the
'Zeitenthobenheit des Weisen'. Gigante 1983b, 173: 'Il saggio camina per le vie
della vita, vestito dell'abito di morte: la morte è la sua consueta compagna del
suo περίπατος, preché egli ha saputo e sa conquistarsi quanto basta all' εὐδαίμων
βίος. Ogni giorno è una conquista, è tutta la vita, è l'eternità, l'unica autentica
eternità; ogni giorno in più è una felicità insperata e il suo morire e il suo è felice
e gradito, ed egli s'accompagna alla morte degli altri, in una successione
induttabile e prenne.' See also Amerio 1952, 571-3.

[88] Jufresa 1996, 290: 'La pratica della filosofia epicurea si instaura in un
"presente continuo" fatto di singoli instanti di pienezza, che hanno in se stessi il
massimo valore.'

tend to view the satisfaction of these goals not only as a project which will last some time, but also as a reason for continuing from day to day. It is not surprising, therefore, that those who consider such an attitude offer different and uncertain evaluations of its practicality and desirability.[89] What is clear, however, from Philodemus' description is that such a person—were she to maintain such an attitude—would not be anxious about premature death. She is, explicitly, ready to die since her life is complete.

Conclusions: a final difficulty

Let us try to draw this discussion together. From what evidence survives, there is little sign that there is any room within the Epicurean ethical framework for the conception that there is necessarily or ideally some kind of narrative shape to a life. Indeed, there is good reason to think that the Epicureans deliberately resisted such a conception and stressed instead that the good life and the means of attaining the good life remain the same no matter what a person's age or stage of life. They would not, therefore, use a conception of a narrative shape of a life to offer a description of the completeness of a life. Instead, Epicureanism offers a more radical picture of an ultimate level of ethical achievement which, once reached, allows little or no further scope for significant personal psychological changes.[90] Once one has arranged

---

[89] Compare Wittgenstein, *Tractatus* 6.4311: 'If by eternity is understood not endless temporal duration but timelessness, then he lives eternally who lives in the present'. Cockburn 1997, 201: '[C]onsider someone who is gripped by horror at the thought of his own death in ten or twenty years' time. Whether we say of him that he is living in the future—living as if he is going to die tomorrow—will depend on what we take to be an appropriate response to the fact that one will die in ten or twenty years' time.' Quinn 2001, 79: 'Consider a person who finds himself with all his ambitions fulfilled and his interests secured. Or, even better, someone who, *much* more than most of us, lives for the present, taking little interest either in what his future will be like or whether it will exist at all. Do we regard death as less of a loss for him than for the rest of us? In some ways, yes. But in some important ways, no. And I would not find it absurd for someone to suggest that in dying such a one loses more than we do.'

[90] Cf. Reinhardt 2002, 291–2, although he there claims that the Epicurean sage 'exploits the fuzziness of the notion of a complete life'. On my view the Epicureans have a very clear notion of a complete life to contrast with other competing notions.

one's desires and beliefs and has internalized Epicurean doctrine to such an extent that one has attained the highest form of pleasure, the absence of physical and mental pain (*aponia* and *ataraxia*), no further development is either needed or desired. (We shall see in the next chapter, p. 2, whether precisely this consequence presents important difficulties for the Epicureans in offering an attractive picture of the good life.)

It also appears to be the case that this ideal state is in principle attainable when one is still very young. It requires merely the requisite intellectual abilities and a certain amount of effort and dedication—which will presumably vary according to natural talent and previous education. Once at this state, however, nothing further seems to be needed in order for a life to be truly called complete. (Here we can contrast Aristotle's model, according to which one needs both to have attained virtue and also the time needed to engage in sufficient virtuous activity.) The Epicurean wise man, as soon as he has reached this ethical goal, is—in Philodemus' evocative phrase—'already ready for burial'. He is prepared for death since his life is complete; there are no important absences to rectify nor any goals left to attain. Thus far, the evidence seems if anything to be in support of a more 'radical' interpretation of the completeness of an Epicurean life (above p. 130). However, Philodemus does suggest that 'some period of time' is needed in this state before a life is complete. It is not clear how much time would be needed nor to what extent Philodemus feels he is required to offer any further specification of the duration he has in mind. In any case, his recognition here that some duration is important, offers support for a more modest interpretation of the completeness of an Epicurean life.

The overall picture is as follows. The Epicureans maintain the plausible claim that an infinitely long lifetime would not be desirable. This is supplemented by a more extreme claim that in one particular case—the case of someone who has attained the ethical goal and the highest pleasure—a life is not made more valuable by adding any length of time. Given that katastematic pleasure, the pleasure that is the absence of pain, is not improved by duration, then not even a life of *ataraxia* will be better the longer it lasts. Some evidence suggests that they still thought that it was necessary to be in this state for some time for a life to be complete while other evidence stresses instead the fact that the highest human good can be achieved as soon as all pain is removed. (True, this is rather counterintuitive, but that is not, I suspect, something which of itself would be very worrying to the Epicureans.) On either view, it turns out that in the Epicureans' view a life does not have to last a certain length of time, nor does it have to exhibit a certain narrative shape, in order to be complete. They reject the 'Narrative Model' of the completeness of a life.

In this most extreme form, the Epicurean claim would mean that as soon as *ataraxia* is reached a life becomes complete, whenever and however this is done. Further, as soon as *ataraxia* is attained it is impossible thereafter to die prematurely, whenever and however one dies, since death from this point on cannot prevent a life being complete. It cannot prevent the person in question from living a complete life. It cannot render a life incomplete, prevent it from exhibiting the correct narrative shape, or anything of the sort. In that case, it will be irrational to fear premature death. The attainment of *ataraxia*, therefore, becomes the necessary and sufficient condition of living a complete life. Such a consequence is perfectly consonant with the overall message of the Epicurean ethical project. It just goes to show how important it is to strive to attain *ataraxia*.

There is, however, a final sting in the tail—a difficulty which we can pose for the Epicurean position as just outlined. If this is indeed the Epicureans' intended answer to their problem of the possibility of premature death, then there arises a further problem.[91] We have seen that the Epicureans agree that:

  a. It is possible to die prematurely if one dies before one has attained *ataraxia*.
  b. Once one has attained *ataraxia* one's life is complete.
  c. It is impossible to die prematurely only once one has attained *ataraxia*.

They also claim that:

  d. *Ataraxia* is a state of the absence of all mental pain.
  e. Fear and anxiety are species of mental pain.
    and therefore:
  f. *Ataraxia* is a state of the absence of all fear and anxiety.

---

[91] The importance of this difficulty was impressed on me by Izzy Holby.

Let us assume that it is reasonable to fear death if death may be premature or if death may make a life incomplete. The Epicureans show at least an implied agreement with this if we accept that their characterization of the complete life is in part designed to show how by accepting an Epicurean ethical framework for one's life one can avoid the anxieties brought about by the thought that one may die with one's life incomplete. (If it is not granted even that they go this far in identifying and attempting to address the fear of premature death then the Epicureans are in even worse trouble so far as their general claim to secure the conclusion that 'death is nothing to us' is concerned.)

The only state in which premature death is impossible is a state of *ataraxia*. *Ataraxia* is a necessary and sufficient condition of the impossibility of premature death (c). However, unless one is not anxious about the prospect of premature death one cannot be in a state of *ataraxia*. Absence of anxiety about premature death is a necessary condition of being in a state of *ataraxia* (f). These two claims can be used to produce a difficulty for the Epicureans since we can ask how the Epicureans can allow the possibility of becoming ataraxic from a state in which one is not ataraxic.[92] To make the problem clearer we might consider the case of someone who feels no fear or anxiety other than that caused by the thought that he might die with his life incomplete. (So he does not fear the state of being dead, nor the fact that he will be dead at some time in the future, nor is he labouring under any other false belief about the gods, and so on.) This person is not yet in *ataraxia* since he is still anxious about this one thing. Indeed, he cannot be in *ataraxia* until he has rid himself of this fear. But the only true way of eradicating this fear is to be in *ataraxia*; only then will he have no grounds for fearing premature death. Note that this person does not suffer from a 'second order' fear—a fear about his own state of fear, or a fear that he might not rid himself of fearing death. Such anxieties would presumably be addressed by the Epicureans by stressing that it is never too late and never too early to begin philosophy, that the arguments needed to cure fear and anxiety are not difficult, that most people

---

[92] Reinhardt 2002, 292, seems to see the Epicurean position but not the difficulty it poses: 'We can see that in order to cope with fear of death in all its varieties, one already has to be an Epicurean sage.'

are capable of living a happy life, and so on. Rather, he has a particular first-order fear, of premature death, to which the Epicurean remedy is the thought that a complete life cannot be prematurely ended.

Premature death is not to be feared if and only if one has attained *ataraxia.* So at any point until *ataraxia* is reached it is reasonable to fear premature death. But if it is reasonable to fear premature death, this is sufficient to make it impossible for anyone not yet in *ataraxia* to attain *ataraxia.*

This seems to me to be a very difficult problem for the Epicureans to overcome. The sources of the problem are quite clear. First, the Epicurean identification of mental anxieties and fears as a kind of pain leads them to conclude that the state of complete pleasure must be a state which admits no residual anxieties. Second, the Epicureans seem to have attempted to answer the potentially devastating criticism that they do not address the fear of premature death by telling us that a complete life, one whose value cannot be diminished if its duration is curtailed, is one which has attained this state of complete pleasure. The further analysis of the fear of premature death as one which is both an obstacle to the attainment of this state and also truly eradicable only once the state has been achieved simply draws these two elements together and fashions out of them the current paradox. We should also notice that the problem is particularly difficult since the near-ataraxic budding Epicurean whose position we are envisaging does not merely believe that it is possible for him to die prematurely. Rather, he is correct in thinking that were he to die before attaining *ataraxia* he would die prematurely. The Epicureans themselves must agree that this is a true belief, in which case there is no prospect of attempting to rid the student of this belief by arguing that it is in fact false—the tactic they have generally employed in the removal of the various species of fearing death canvassed so far.

How can the Epicureans escape? Of course, they could hope that the thought that one might die prematurely simply will not occur to us until such a time as we are already in a state of *ataraxia,* by which point it can immediately be dismissed. Apart from being a hopelessly optimistic view, it is already ruled out by their own extant writings which explicitly raise the concern of when and how a life can be complete. In that case, they can revise their claims to say either that there are states other than *ataraxia* in which it would be true to say that death cannot be premature or that one can attain *ataraxia* while nevertheless retaining this one residual anxiety—that one may die prematurely—which will be eradicated once it is realized that by being in *ataraxia* there are in fact no grounds for such a concern. This second alternative, the denial of (f) above, is not very promising since it merely stipulates that *ataraxia* may, contrary to all expectation, still leave room for some anxieties. And why should this anxiety in particular be allowed into the ataraxic state and not others? This looks like special pleading. If it is allowed to stand then it seems equally reasonable to allow someone with some residual concerns about interventionist gods to be called ataraxic. What of the first alternative, in effect a denial of (c) above? Here, we do not allow that *ataraxia* can accommodate some concerns but rather that the presence of some residual concerns is not in fact sufficient to jeopardize one's life being complete. After all, it was specifically the notion that one's life is complete rather than the notion that one had attained *ataraxia* that performed the relevant task in dismissing the fear of premature death. Of course, it is true that someone who has attained *ataraxia* has attained a complete life (b), but there might be room to allow completeness to lives which fall just short of *ataraxia* by, for example, retaining some concerns about premature death. If so then the problem we have outlined for the Epicureans can be avoided, since it is possible to reach a complete life (and by doing so then be able to banish fears of premature death) without that life necessarily requiring one already to have no such fears.

Neither of these alternatives is very attractive since they each require the Epicureans to qualify or modify one of their most important claims. They certainly would not, I think, be comfortable with allowing someone to be said to be in *ataraxia* even if he is disturbed by the thought that he might die too soon. Nor, it seems to me, is it very likely they would think that someone could be said to have attained a complete life—which, remember, was on their view a life in which one has attained the highest state of pleasure which cannot be increased or improved even by duration—if one is still concerned with the possibility of premature death and therefore not in *ataraxia*. They are therefore left with the following difficulty. While their conception of what it would be like to be an Epicurean sage makes clear just how that kind of person would not be anxious about premature death, it is not at all clear how a non-sage ought to go about attaining that state. The fact that he has not yet lived an Epicurean complete life gives him reason to be concerned about premature death, and that concern is itself a sufficient barrier to his ever attaining the Epicurean *telos* and living a complete life.

5

Living an Epicurean Life

οὐθὲν γάρ ἔοικε θνητῷ ζῴῳ ζῶν ἄνθρωπος ἐν ἀθανάτοις ἀγαθοῖς.

For a man living among immortal goods lives a life quite unlike a mortal creature.

Epic. *Ep. Men.* 135

Having outlined the Epicurean arguments against the various species of the fear of death, I turn now to consider another set of arguments against the Epicurean project. These address not the Epicureans' own arguments, their validity and cogency, but rather seek to demonstrate that even if the Epicurean arguments are sound, they should nevertheless be rejected since the consequences of such a view of the nature and value of death are such that it is impossible to continue to live a recognizably human life in accordance with them. This is a familiar style of criticism from other ancient dialectical contexts—a particular theory is shown to be unacceptable because it is impossible to continue to live a recognizably human life in the manner proposed or required by that theory. Indeed, the Epicureans themselves were happy to use just this sort of argument against certain forms of scepticism.[1] The task for the Epicurean, therefore, is to show how his view of a good life can still be maintained if the arguments against the fear of death are agreed to stand and their consequences pursued in full. What are the costs of adopting an Epicurean conception of the nature and value of death?

I will consider two sets of arguments. First, it will be asked whether the Epicureans can allow that there is any reason for a committed Epicurean to write a will. Although this may seem

---

[1] See Lucr. *DRN* 4.479 ff. for an Epicurean use of the familiar *apraxia* argument. Colotes, it seems, produced a whole work devoted to showing that it is impossible to live according to the views of other philosophers. See Plut. *Adv. Col.* and Warren 2002b.

initially a minor complaint, it is an important question since it was pounced upon by ancient critics and therefore can stand as an example of the style of dialectical discussion to be found in those ancient texts. Further, the same question has also received some modern discussion since it clearly relates to the discussion of the possibility of *post mortem* harm. We have already seen staunch Epicurean opposition to the possibility of such harms and this opposition seems to be incompatible with the attempt to affect *post mortem* events by writing a will or, indeed, with the possession by the Epicurean of any desires or projects which have as their object or goal states of affairs located after the Epicurean's death. Second, I turn to a much more general and potentially more devastating criticism against the Epicureans. If it is agreed that there is nothing at all harmful in death, what value is left in continuing to live? In particular, if the arguments which the Epicureans offer against fearing a premature death are allowed to stand, is there ever sufficient reason for an Epicurean to seek to prolong a good Epicurean life?

EPICURUS' WILL

creditur vulgo testamenta hominum speculum esse morum.

It is commonly believed that wills are a mirror of a man's character.

Pliny the younger, *Ep.* 8.18.1

Ought Epicurus to have written a will? Cicero, one of the Epicureans' most vocal critics, raised this difficulty and made the problem more acute by stressing the threatened inconsistency between the very founder of the school's own actions and theories. Did Epicurus 'live his Epicureanism'? Before passing to the substance of Cicero's complaints, and the general problem of Epicurus' will it is worth pausing to ask whether the will preserved in part by Cicero and in full by Diogenes Laërtius is indeed genuine. The generally accepted answer is affirmative. There is no reason to think that the will preserved by Diogenes is not genuine. It is plausibly Hellenistic in its dialect and is authentic in its legal details.[2]

[2] See Gottschalk 1972, 317–18; Leiwo and Remes 1999, 163. Diogenes includes a number of other wills, by Plato (3.41–3), Aristotle (5.11–16), Theophrastus

There is also good evidence that Epicurus himself went to some lengths to ensure the preservation of his will. The will itself notes that a bequest was deposited in the Metröon of Athens, probably along with other documents relating to the school.[3] In this respect it appears that Epicurus was rather unusual. While it was common practice to leave wills with friends or relatives (often the/a beneficiary) and even state officials (see e.g. Isaeus 1.3), Epicurus is the only private individual known to have used what was mainly intended as the storage place of public documents (*dēmosia grammata*—*psēphismata*, decrees, judgements of law cases, indictments, and so on) for storing private documents. This might well have ensured the preservation of either the original will or some other bequest relevant to the school alongside the various copies probably made for consultation within the Epicurean Garden. We have no indication where Cicero, Diogenes, or their sources found and transcribed the will.

It is perhaps surprising to find an Epicurean document in the centre of Athenian political record-keeping, catalogued according to the year's *archōn*, next to civic laws and decrees— especially given the Epicureans' notorious avoidance of political office or participation. However, it is clear that Epicurus was not unfamiliar with the workings of the Athenian legal system. Most of what follows will examine Epicurus' will in terms of his own philosophy. But it is important to remember that there was

(5.51–7), Strato (5.61–4), and Lyco (5.69–74). Besides the general thought that a person's character might be revealed in his will, Diogenes presumably used wills for the wealth of biographical and especially genealogical information which they contain. For a discussion of Cicero's paraphrasing of the will as found in Diogenes, see Laks 1976, 87. Compare *Fin.* 2.101 with D.L. 10.18. *memoria*, included by Cicero, is often used to justify the restoration εἰς τὴν ἡμῶν τε καὶ Μητροδώρου <μνήμην> κατατεταγμένην in Diogenes. Laks retains the transmitted text; cf. Laks 1976, 91.

[3] See D.L. 10.16, and for a discussion of Epicurus' practice of depositing letters in the public archive of Athens see Clay 1982, who convincingly argues that this practice lies behind the otherwise puzzling Epicurean penchant for listing the eponymous *archōn* of the year in which a particular letter or document was first written. Sickinger 1999, 133–4, argues *contra* Clay that, rather than the will itself, a separate bequest (a *dosis*) was deposited which would become active upon Epicurus' death. For a discussion of the Metröon see Cassius 1868, and Sickinger 1999, 105 ff. and for literary and epigraphic *testimonia* see Wicherley 1957, §§465–519. I thank Stephen Todd for his help on this subject.

another audience to which the will had to be addressed, namely the surrounding Athenian society according to whose laws any inheritance had to be arranged. Recently, it has been pointed out that Epicurus' will contains a particular legal manoeuvre, designed to maintain the philosophical community of the Garden, but displaying close attention to the requirements of Athenian law.[4] That manoeuvre is the following. Epicurus' property is given to Amynomachus and Timocrates on condition that they give the Garden to Hermarchus and the other Epicureans. So long as Hermarchus lives, he can remain in Epicurus' house in Melite, but on his death the house passes to Amynomachus and Timocrates. In this way Epicurus, an Athenian citizen, ensures that Hermarchus and the other non-Athenian Epicureans can remain in the Garden although they cannot legally inherit the property. Two citizens, Amynomachus and Timocrates, are designated Epicurus' heirs, although they are probably not Epicureans themselves.[5] In return for acting as a medium for the transmission of Epicurus' property to the non-citizen members of the Garden they keep the house in Melite after Hermarchus' death.

So these particular portions of the will owe more to surrounding Athenian law than to Epicurean philosophy. However, the problem that will concern the rest of my discussion does not depend on any particular clauses in the will. It discusses rather the Epicurean motivation for writing any will at all. But still it will be worth remembering that Epicurus' will is designed for a double audience, for the Epicureans of the Garden to whom many of the injunctions are addressed and who would be expected to honour the particular practices which Epicurus recommends, and also for the surrounding non-Epicurean Athenians, since the Garden must comply with their particular legal codes in order to function as a philosophical school. This latter provides at least

---

[4] See Leiwo and Remes 1999. Cf. Laks 1976. 80. At D.L. 10.120 it is reported that the Epicureans allow that the wise man 'will go to law' (καὶ δικάσεσθαι). but it is not made clear when and why. There is some epigraphic evidence that the office of Epicurean scholarch was handed down by the last will and testament of the previous holder even in the second century CE. See Dorandi 2000.

[5] Leiwo and Remes 1999, 165. These two are not mentioned in any other Epicurean text. In the will Epicurus constantly stresses his affection for Hermarchus and his family and more generally for all the fellow Epicureans, but makes no reference to any particular connection with these two people.

a good instrumental reason for Epicurus to write a will—it
ensured the Garden's continuation according to Athenian law.[6]

Cicero's criticisms

Cicero's general interest in wills was perhaps like that of most
prominent Roman aristocrats in the later Republic, a time when
great political and economic capital could be won through the
manipulation and opportune publication of such documents.[7]
His interest in Epicurus' will, however, is specifically for the light
which he thought it might shed on Epicurus' real attitude to
death, which would presumably be most evident in his attitude to
his own death, and particularly evident when his death was close
at hand.[8]

Epicurus' will is introduced into Cicero's *De Finibus* as a
digression. In his response to Torquatus' exposition of Epicurean
ethics, Cicero has been discussing the Epicurean attitude to pleasure and pain. He has become especially impatient with Epicurus'
insistence that present physical pain can be counteracted by the
recollection and anticipation of past or future pleasures. This
possibility was most evidently displayed by Epicurus himself
during his final days, when—as we have seen—although afflicted
with a terrible illness which caused excruciating pain, he
nevertheless insisted that he could pass the time until his death
in pleasure. Cicero finds this utterly implausible.

audi, ne longe abeam, moriens quid dicat Epicurus, ut intellegas facta
eius cum dictis discrepare: 'Epicurus Hermarcho S. cum ageremus',
inquit, 'vitae beatum et eundem supremum diem, scribebamus haec. tanti
aderant vesicae et torminum morbi ut nihil ad eorum magnitudinem
posset accedere.' ... 'compensabatur', inquit, 'tamen cum his omnibus

---

[6] In addition to the will, we have evidence of a letter written by Epicurus
during his final days, probably to a certain Mithres, who appears to be a friend.
The letter is cited in Philodemus' *ΠΡΑΓΜΑΤΕΙΑΙ*, *PHerc.* 1418 Col. XXXI.
and apparently contained a number of instructions for the care of Metrodorus'
children after Epicurus' death. For text and commentary see Militello 1997.

[7] See Champlin 1991.

[8] Lucretius *DRN* 3.55–8 also claims that a person's true nature is revealed at
such times of adversity.

animi laetitia quae capiebam memoria rationum inventorumque
nostrorum.'

So I do not digress too much, listen to what Epicurus says as he dies, so
you might understand that his deeds are not consistent with his theories.
He said, 'Epicurus greets Hermarchus.[9] I write these words as I am living
out this my final and blessed day. The disorders of my bladder and guts
are so great that nothing could increase them, but nevertheless they are
all compensated by the joy in my soul which I take in recalling my
arguments and discoveries.'

Fin. 2.96

Cicero goes on to claim that this explanation of Epicurus'
maintenance of *ataraxia* will not do. He contends that Epicurus
is trying to counterbalance bodily pains with the pleasures of
intellectual discoveries, pleasures of the soul, and this, Cicero
thinks, conflicts with the Epicurean assertion that all feelings
of pleasure and pain must be bodily (2.97). Whether or not this
is a fair criticism of Epicurus is not my primary concern here
(although it is worth pointing out that it is not).[10] More
important is the first sign of a general tactic which Cicero will
pursue, namely the opposition of Epicurus' actions to his words
(*ut intellegas facta eius cum dictis discrepare*). The critic of
Epicureanism searches through the 'biography' of Epicurus and
pits it against his theory. The *facta* are to be provided by the
scrutiny of Epicurus' behaviour as revealed in his own letters, his
own will, and the like. This is surely better than using a second-
hand source describing Epicurus' behaviour since then Epicurus
will be convicted by his own words, spoken 'off-duty', when he is
not engaged in explicit theorizing (the *dicta*). Cicero repeatedly
tells us that this is what he is doing.

nihil in hac praeclara epistula scriptum ab Epicuro congruens et
conveniens decretis eius reperetis. ita redarguitur ipse a sese,
convincunturque scripta eius probitate ipsius ac moribus.

You will find nothing written in that celebrated letter [sc. the letter to
Hermarchus/Idomeneus] that fits and is consistent with his doctrines.

---

[9] In Diogenes Laërtius 10.22 this letter is addressed to Idomeneus. See Laks
1976, 90.

[10] For Epicurus, all pleasures are 'bodily' in the sense that pleasure is a *sumptōma*
of atomic arrangements. Pleasures are not all 'bodily' in the sense in which 'bodily'
is contrasted with 'psychic'. The soul is also a complex of atoms.

So he is proved wrong by his own hand, and his writings are refuted by his own virtuous character.

Fin. 2.99

Indeed, Epicurus is shown to be better than his word. His own actions reveal him to be concerned with his posthumous reputation and the well-being of his dependants in a manner not consonant with his own theories. Cicero has already taken much the same line on the Epicurean view of friendship—a topic to which I will return.[11] Here Cicero can pick on particular letters written by Epicurus as he was dying, as well as Epicurus' will, to prove his point. This is why he also insists that he has been scrupulous in translating Epicurus' Greek (*Fin.* 2.99). He wishes to impress upon us that it is Epicurus who has convicted himself of inconsistency, and the best way to do that is to place side by side the supposed contradictory statements.

Cicero makes a number of specific complaints against the content of Epicurus' will. In particular, he pokes fun at the provisions it contains for the celebration of Epicurus' birthday, a practice which was part of the cultic characteristics of the Epicurean Garden. The Epicureans' calendar was punctuated by monthly and annual festivals commemorating past prominent members of the school. Since this has been well discussed by other commentators, I shall focus on the most general of Cicero's complaints. He claims that merely by writing a will, regardless of its specific contents, Epicurus is contravening his own insistence that 'death is nothing to us', as concisely distilled into $K\Delta$ 2.[12] There, the major supporting argument for the contention that death cannot harm or benefit us is that what is good or bad must be perceived as such, and can ultimately be analysed in terms of pleasure and pain. That is to say, unless something is perceived by a subject as pleasant or painful, that something cannot be good or bad for that subject. Since, therefore, at death the

---

[11] See *Fin.* 2.80–81.

[12] See *Fin.* 2.102–3 for Cicero's various complaints against the provisions contained in the will for the celebration of Epicurus' birthday and the various monthly festivals which it institutes. For a collection of sources dealing with this cult and a discussion of the Epicurean justification of this practice, see Clay 1986 and Capasso 1987, 25–38. Thompson 1981, 20, insists on the religious function of many earlier fourth-century wills which ensure the provision of sacrifices and cult for the deceased.

subject is annihilated and can no longer perceive, *post mortem* events can have no value for the subject. As a result, we have no rational basis for the fear of death, which Epicurus thinks is one of the major sources of human misery and is the foundation for many of the irrational or empty desires for fame and fortune with which people are afflicted.

As we have seen, those who wish to object to this line of argument and offer a rational basis for the fear of death can try to argue that death or *post mortem* events can affect a subject by making one or more of a number of claims. First, they can claim that there is in fact a *post mortem* subject which can perceive good or harm (the person's immortal soul or some such thing). Second, they can propose that the deceased, while unable to perceive any *post mortem* events, might nevertheless be said to have *interests* which persist in the world. Those interests can be furthered or frustrated, and the now deceased person (or, if we are not comfortable with the idea of the agent persisting as a subject of harm after death, the *ante mortem* person who the now deceased used to be) may be said to be affected by the status of his or her interests. Perhaps a distinction can be maintained between the fulfilment and the satisfaction of desires. Desires are satisfied only if they are believed by the desirer to have been fulfilled. Desires can be fulfilled or frustrated whether or not the desirer perceives that they are.[13] Third, as we have already seen when discussing the timing of the harm of death, there are those who want to argue that *post mortem* events can cause the previously living person harm. The yet-to-die can be harmed by what will happen once they are dead.[14]

Such an account of the reasons for being concerned about *post mortem* events can offer good grounds for the practice of writing wills. If we accept a model of well-being which allows changes on the basis of *post mortem* events (whenever it is thought these changes occur, *ante* or *post mortem*) the agent will surely take every step possible to ensure that his interests will be fostered and fulfilled. He has a good reason to be concerned about *post*

---

[13] One might allow that desires can be fulfilled or frustrated after death but argue that this is not relevant to the agent's decision-making precisely because there is no possibility of this being discovered by him. See Draper 1999, 389–90; Ewin 2002, 19.   [14] See above p. 46 ff.

mortem events, even though he thinks he will not be able to know how these events turn out.[15] So he will, for example, by the means of a legally binding will, try to ensure that his descendants will be cared for financially. Then he can die secure in the belief that he has done the best he can for his own well-being by insulating it as far as possible against potential *post mortem* harm. It is also clear why we all should respect the wishes enshrined in such wills. The executor of the will might be tied to the deceased in such a way that he would wish to act to promote the deceased's well-being. So he would do all in his power to ensure that the wishes are enacted. Similarly, the executor might see that at some stage he too will be in the position of writing a will and trying to ensure that his own interests are preserved and fostered after his death. In that case he has a stake in maintaining a system in which such wills are respected and enacted.[16]

In Epicureanism, of course, the relevant premises concerning the possibility of *post mortem* effects on well-being are lacking.[17] This is where Cicero's criticism begins to take its hold.

quaero etiam quid sit quod cum dissolutione, id est morte, sensus omnis exstinguatur, et cum reliqui nihil sit omnino quod pertineat ad nos, tam accurate tamque diligenter caveat et sanciat 'ut Amynomachus et Timocrates, heredes sui, . . .'

I also ask why it is that although all perception is destroyed with the annihilation that is death, and although there is nothing left behind which is at all of concern to us, nevertheless he so carefully and diligently sees to it and stipulates 'that Amynomachus and Timocrates, his heirs . . .'

Fin. 2.101

Cicero finds a clear inconsistency between Epicurus' theory and practice, between the grounds for the insistence that death is 'nothing to us' and the extreme care and attention lavished upon the provisions made in his will for measures that will necessarily not be enacted until after his own death. In the terms of Epicurus' own theory, these measures can have no effect on his well-being.

---

[15] Cf. Wiggins 1998, 306–7.

[16] See Feinberg 1984, esp. 94–5, for a defence of this kind of position. Compare Pitcher 1984, Grover 1989, and Benn 1998, who offers reasons why we should not, by some symmetrical principle, be similarly committed to furthering the interests of the unborn.   [17] Cf. Nagel 1979, 4.

Why bother at all to write a will, if one believes that it does not matter to oneself whether or not it is enacted? Indeed, Cicero does not merely find Epicurean theory and practice to be inconsistent. Elsewhere, he takes the practice of writing wills to be one of the major indicators that we generally do believe that our souls are immortal and will survive our deaths. In which case, Epicurus' own actions can be cited as grounds for asserting the contradictory of his thesis.

quid procreatio liberorum, quid propagatio nominis, quid adoptiones filiorum, quid testamentorum diligentia, quid ipsa sepulcrorum monumenta, elogia significant nisi nos futura etiam cogitare?

What do the production of children, the promotion of a reputation, the adoption of sons, the care taken over wills, indeed the very monuments erected for tombs, the epitaphs, signify, if not that we are thinking also of things to come?

Tusc. 1.31

Of course, the fact that we do feel such concerns does not show that we ought to feel such concerns.[18] But Cicero needs only the weaker descriptive point for his charge of inconsistency against Epicurus. Epicurus' behaviour betrays such concerns although his doctrine cannot sustain them.[19] Furthermore, if Epicurus' will is addressed to fellow Epicureans, they too must be understood to deny that the dead have any sort of lingering interests. So if they act in accordance with the will they cannot do so simply because 'that is what Epicurus wanted', in the sense that if they were not to do so, somehow Epicurus would be harmed. But what other reason could they have?

Some recent writers have tried to offer explanations which dissolve the apparent contradiction. If they are successful then they will also provide a rebuttal of Cicero's argument. Here is one recent attempt to justify the enactment of wills

The vast majority of us are greatly comforted now to know that after our deaths the law can be used to contribute to the good of the persons and the causes we care about. If maintaining this fiction of harm and wrong

---

[18] Well noted by Soll 1998, 29. On the desire to 'leave a trace' of oneself after death see Nozick 1981, 582–5; Scarre 2001.

[19] Tsouna 2001b, 170–2, considers this passage in the light of Philod. *De Morte* and argues that Cicero is writing in response to Philodemus' insistence on the irrationality of certain *post mortem* concerns.

to the dead in our legal institutions is the most effective way of securing this comfort... then keeping them is exceedingly well justified.

Callahan 1987, 352[20]

While recognizing that no real benefit or harm can come to the dead, this justification argues that we might nevertheless maintain the 'fiction' that it does in order to secure some generally and socially beneficial result, namely the present comforting thought that certain of our *present* interests will be promoted after our deaths.[21] It is important to recognize that the time at which the proposed benefit from this practice is perceived is *ante mortem*, while we are still alive. At no time should we make the mistake of thinking that we would actually do harm to the dead if we do not enact their wishes. That is merely the most effective means of communicating and institutionalizing the real and truly beneficial results of this practice. In fact, we respect wills because we presently are comforted by the thought that our own interests are to be similarly treated.

But here we might begin to see a further problem. In what sense are we really being comforted by maintaining this fiction? In Callahan's formulation above, he claims that we are 'greatly comforted to know now that after our deaths the law can be used to contribute to the good of the persons and the causes we care about'. This is in a way compatible with the view that the dead themselves have no *post mortem* interests since it describes a present state of mind—comfort felt while still alive.

Epicurean texts, notably the inscription of Diogenes of Oinoanda, certainly insist that *present* pleasure can be caused by (the thought of) future events, even posthumous events.[22] So an

---

[20] Cf. Griffin 1986, 22: 'Of course, a lot of desires of the dead do count morally, but that is because they affect the living. There is a good case for honouring wishes expressed in wills. Inheritance satisfies the desires of the living to provide for their offspring and encourages saving that benefits society generally.'

[21] Cf. Donnelly 1994, 166: 'I agree that it can be a useful fiction for the materialist to continue to speak of posthumous harms or benefits. Hard metaphysical facts aside, the fostering of the belief in posthumous harms or benefits has the practical upshot of encouraging others to continue our projects after our deaths. The failure to do so can cause in some living survivors some non-idle shame (or honor).'

[22] Fr. 33.VIII.1 ff. Smith: καίπερ γὰρ ἡδομένων ἤ|δη τῶν ἀνθρώπων διότι | ἔσται τις αὐτῶν μετ' αὐ|τοὺς ἐπ' ἀγάθῳ μνήμη, | ὅμως τὸ ποιητικὸν τῆς ἡδονῆς αὖθις γείνεται ('for although men feel pleasure because there will be some positive

Epicurean would find nothing objectionable in Callahan's observation that we can take pleasure or comfort in imagining future states of affairs. But Callahan's formulation perhaps betrays what an Epicurean might think is a pernicious and persistent investment in what happens after my death. An Epicurean might reasonably ask why, if terrible things were to happen to people I love after my death, that possibility would be of concern to me even in the present? The possible disaster thus imagined should not cause me any anxiety. If part of the Epicurean argument that death is nothing to us is that we can feel no effect of whatever happens after our deaths, why am I now busying myself writing a will in order to be comforted now that certain events (which cannot affect my well-being) will or will not happen?

Let me explain this further, since there is a good objection to my position which must be met. Note the distinction between the following two claims:

A. A *post mortem* event can harm or benefit one's well-being.
B. The prospect of a *post mortem* event can harm or benefit one's well-being.

The objection I have in mind is the following. The apologist for Epicurean will-making might claim that although A is incompatible with Epicureanism, B is not. B refers to a still living subject, able to perceive pleasure and pain. In short, although what actually happens after my death cannot affect me at all after my death, I might nevertheless now be anxious during my life at the thought of such an event. Similarly, I might now experience pleasure at the thought of some future event, whether or not it will turn out that I will be around when that event occurs, and whether or not the event will occur at all.[23] Whenever the

memory of them after their death, nevertheless what produces the pleasure occurs later'). This fragment comprises a general attack on Cyrenaicism, which differed from Epicureanism in denying the possibility of taking pleasure from past or future events. There is good reason, however, to suspect that this is not intended to be a claim strictly compatible with Epicurean doctrine. It is not clear that an Epicurean should take pleasure in fame or reputation at all, whether the reputation comes before or after death. See D.L. 10.137 and Sedley 2002; cf. Smith 1998, 166.

[23] Cf. Gosling 1969, 9–11, who recognizes that *post mortem* wishes, such as those expressed in wills, also offer a possible counterexample to the thesis that

supposed object of the pleasure takes place (in the past, present, future—even *post mortem* future), so long as the pleasure is perceived in the present then Epicurus' egoistic hedonism remains intact. Compare Callahan's position: we maintain the fiction of A whereas in reality we are comforting ourselves by allaying the sort of fears which might follow from B.

Why do I think that B does not give the Epicureans sufficient justification for writing wills? One argument is that Epicureanism elsewhere explicitly argues that we should not allow ourselves to be affected by the prospect of events which when they occur will not cause us any benefit or harm. We have seen that Epicurus argues that one cannot consistently hold both that 'being dead' is not an evil and that nevertheless the prospect of my future state of being dead is a reasonable cause of fear.[24] To do this would be like knowing that tomorrow's dental appointment will involve no pain (because of the anaesthetic), but nevertheless fearing in prospect that same painless procedure.[25] B seems to provide the corresponding claim that although these events will not be enjoyed when they occur, the Epicurean can nevertheless enjoy them in prospect.

Epicurean justifications for will-writing

There are two major possibilities left for an Epicurean trying to justify will-making. First, he can try to find some sense in which the Epicurean can take present pleasure in contemplating positive *post mortem* events which does not suggest that he can also be adversely affected by negative *post mortem* events. Second, he can try to argue that the pleasures promoted by a will, although not the testator's own, provide sufficient justification

all actions are chosen for the sake of pleasure. 'The difficulty of these [sc. desires] is not tied to the fact of generosity but simply to the possibility of desires such that it is no part of their accomplishment that the subject should know of it or even be alive when it comes about' (10). Cf. Scarre 2001, 209–10.

[24] *Ep. Men.* 125. See above pp. 100–5.
[25] I insist here on the force of 'knowing' that X will not be painful in order to head off any suggestion that some doubt about the truth of the dentist's assurance that 'it will not hurt a bit' might introduce anxiety.

for an Epicurean will-writer. The first tactic tries to identify some personal, perhaps vicarious pleasure. The second asserts some altruistic, pleasure-promoting motivation.

First, let us concentrate on asking how an Epicurean might argue that he receives present pleasure from writing a will. I shall try to explain my objection to the idea that prospective attitudes (anxieties and accompanying comforts) aimed at *post mortem* events offer a sufficient grounding for Epicurean will-making by examining the kinds of desires which are necessarily involved.

We might call desires of the kind which are enshrined in wills '*post mortem* desires'. This is a special class of desires which refer to states of affairs which post-date my death.[26] So two examples of such desires would be:

   i. 'I want my ashes to be scattered over Parker's Piece'.
  ii. 'I want the weather to be fine on 21 July in the year 3000'.

Note that (i) necessarily expresses a *post mortem* desire. It is impossible for my ashes to be scattered before I die. The desire in (ii) is only contingently *post mortem* given that I will not live until the date that the desire will be satisfied. The desires expressed in a will are all necessarily *post mortem*.

---

[26] Compare Luper-Foy 1987 who urges that an Epicurean cannot formulate any desires which might be compromised by his death. Luper-Foy does allow the Epicurean to formulate an 'independent desire', a desire which will or will not be fulfilled regardless of my actions, since I cannot possibly affect it (e.g. 'I want it to be a fine day tomorrow'). My *post mortem* desires are a subset of Luper-Foy's independent desires, distinguished by the fact that there is a particular reason why I cannot do anything directly to ensure that I obtain what I desire. Luper-Foy insists that all such independent desires are motivationally inert, and the response of Rosenbaum 1989a, 89, leaves this important point untouched. Cf. Williams 1973a, 263, who gives an example of what he calls a 'non-I desire' (220—desires not in any way *for* the desirer), designed to show that such desires are not necessarily altruistic: 'Some madman, not believing in life after death, might want a chimpanzee's tea party to be held in the cathedral, just because it would be such a striking event.' The denial of life after death is not meant here to be grounds for diagnosing the man's madness, but a mechanism for ensuring that this is not a tacit I-desire (since he thinks his ghost might be around to witness the event). Williams also notes the difficulties of analysing desires for such things as posthumous fame (one of my *post mortem* desires), since the desire passes the test of being an 'I-desire' (it is *for* the desirer) but necessarily the desirer cannot be contemporaneous with the intentional object of the desire.

What sufficient reason could an Epicurean have for formulating such a desire and then acting on it by writing a will?[27] In the section of the *Letter to Menoeceus* which recommends that we should all inspect our desires, the only kinds of desires allowed to remain are those deemed 'natural and necessary' (*Ep. Men.* 127–8). *KΔ* 29 repeats this classification and the brief explanatory scholion attached to it shows that these desires are those which would necessarily bring pain if they are not satisfied (e.g. a desire for drink, thirst). Note that these are very general desires. Someone may have a specific desire for orange juice, for example, but if this is not satisfied it will not *necessarily* produce pain since some alternative drink would do just as well to satisfy a natural desire not to be thirsty.[28] This necessary pain should the desire remain unfulfilled is what distinguishes 'natural and necessary' desires from 'natural and unnecessary desires', such as the desire for orange juice. What I call *post mortem* desires certainly could not fall into the category of natural and necessary desires and so we ought to presume that Epicurus would not think that they ought to be deliberately cultivated. No pain would be experienced were these *post mortem* desires not to be fulfilled. If, therefore, a case is to be made for including *post mortem* desires at all in the Epicurean good life then they must be stripped of all elements of false opinion—so they must be desires felt in the full and secure understanding of the true nature of death—and offered as examples of natural and unnecessary desires, desires that are somehow unavoidable given our human natures but which do not inevitably lead to pain if unfulfilled. In fact, we shall see that there seems to be some evidence in Philodemus' *De Morte* that he at least thought there to be some kind of natural feelings provoked by the thought of the welfare of loved-ones after one's death.[29] Let us first, however, consider whether Epicurus, had he wished to do so in the face of criticism of his own practice, could have included such desires in the class of those which an Epicurean can retain and, perhaps, cultivate on hedonistic grounds. The proposal

---

[27] Epicurus insists on subjective desire satisfaction—it is not enough for my *post mortem* desires to be satisfied if I do not perceive that satisfaction. Also see Scott 2000, 226 n. 25, who compares Aristotle's positions with 'success theories' in which *ante mortem* projects and desires can be satisfied posthumously.

[28] For further discussion see Annas 1993, 190–200, 336–8.

[29] See below pp. 194–7.

currently under scrutiny is that the Epicurean simply writes a will for the pleasure he experiences at the time of writing as he contemplates possible future situations. In that case, a certain self-interest is outlined to motivate the action, which produces present pleasure.

I do not deny that there could be such pleasures. Someone may well be pleased at the thought of his loved-ones being cared-for after his death. Even so, it seems to me that such an explanation is not sufficient to explain why the Epicurean should write a will. My worry can be most succinctly put as follows. It is one thing to contemplate some future pleasurable event and take joy in it, but an altogether different thing to set about trying to ensure that this event will come about by constructing a legally binding document to be enacted after death, especially if one is committed to the claim that 'death is nothing to us', and Epicurus does seem to have gone to unusual lengths to ensure that his will would be safeguarded. To write a will is to take an active hand in attempting to bring about certain events. and such an action surely implies some commitment to the importance of those things actually occurring. If at the thought of various *post mortem* possibilities an Epicurean is stirred into drafting a will, then it is surely reasonable to suspect that this betrays a lingering thought that he should do whatever he can to ensure that these *post mortem* circumstances obtain, either because he thinks that this will promote some *post mortem* interests or because he wishes to promote others' interests regardless of any vicarious pleasure this may provide.[30]

In short, it seems to me that nothing significant is added to the present pleasure of contemplating certain future possibilities by the writing of a will. (Although it may be the case that the act of writing down one's pleasant future fantasies contributes to the strength of their enjoyment.) Rather, writing a will is most plausibly interpreted as an attempt to take an active hand in

---

[30] Luper-Foy 1987, 245: 'It is worth noting that Epicureans will remain unconcerned about what occurs after their projected dying day if they adopt the hedonist claim that everything which does not actually cause them pain or pleasure is a matter of indifference. Hedonists of this sort are capable of caring about the welfare of their children, but only their welfare at times when the hedonist parents believe that they (the parents) will be alive.'

bringing about those possibilities—and to do so is surely to imply that to some degree the present pleasure depends upon the belief that certain states of affairs will come about after death. The will-maker feels comforted by the thought that his descendants, for example, will be cared for when he is dead. If this possibility is allowed, however, it seems to be impossible for Epicurus to continue to resist the claim that *post mortem* events may also have a harmful effect on present well-being, and this jeopardizes his assertion that 'death is nothing to us'. If beliefs about *post mortem* states of affairs are allowed to produce pleasure then they should also be thought to be able to cause pain. But the Epicureans tried to persuade us not to be concerned about *post mortem* events precisely because they cannot cause pain when they occur and therefore should not cause pain in anticipation.

If the Epicureans are to avoid this difficulty they must resist the idea that writing a will is in any sense an attempt to bring about some *post mortem* state of affairs. In order to evade the charge that the Epicurean will-maker is in fact (and contrary to the advice of *KΔ* 2) allowing *post mortem* events some bearing on his present state of well-being, some other characterization of the point of will-making must be offered which does not make the joy felt at the thought of these events at all dependent on the thought of their coming about in the future. The Epicureans must redescribe the act of will-making. Instead of the setting down of some commands with the purpose of ensuring that certain events come about, they must instead claim that writing a will involves no such purpose. Rather, writing a will should be viewed as a kind of day-dreaming. By this I mean that the contemplation of the states of affairs described in the will is in itself a pleasurable act, and *that is all an Epicurean seeks when writing a will*. It does not matter in the slightest whether the events will in fact take place.

This does not strike me as a plausible redescription. First, I can see no reason why an Epicurean would produce a written document rather than merely sit and think pleasant thoughts. Certainly, the process of producing a will and of seeing that it is stored safely as Epicurus did would add nothing to the bare activity of thinking pleasant thoughts about the future. If anything, going to such trouble would appear to be a disturbance.

A further problem may be raised. The redescription I have offered to the Epicureans must include the claim that it does not matter whether the future events being contemplated will in fact take place. That is to say, it does not matter so far as the pleasure the Epicurean feels at the thought of them is concerned. But is this plausible? The Epicureans themselves, when discussing the pleasures of anticipation, regularly couple them with the pleasures of recollecting past events and treat the two as similar, differing merely in their being directed in opposite temporal directions.³¹ But the pleasure to be won from recollecting a past pleasant event is certainly dependent on that past event having occurred and my having enjoyed it at the time. It makes little sense to say I remember a pleasant holiday in Italy last year if I did not go there. If anticipation is analogous then any pleasure I might receive in thinking of a future event depends on my being confident in the expectation both of that event coming about in the future and also of my enjoying it when it does. Of course, it is not always the case that we can predict the future with great security, and we might therefore allow that it is possible to anticipate a merely probable or likely future event.³² I can look forward to a forthcoming summer holiday with pleasure if it is reasonably likely that I will go and various pleasant things will happen. But even then, it is impossible for an Epicurean to look forward to *post mortem* events on the basis that they probably will occur and be experienced since by definition these events will not be experienced. The analogy with recollected pleasures cannot help. Instead, if such *post mortem* events can be objects of

---

³¹ Cf. e.g. Cic. *Fin.* 1.57: *sed ut iis bonis erigimur quae expectamus, sic laetamur iis quae recordamur* ('But just as we enjoy those goods which we look forward to, so we are pleased by those which we recall').

³² The Epicureans take a moderate view of our ability to count on the future. *Ep. Men.* 127: μνημονευτέον δὲ ὡς τὸ μέλλον <οὔτε πάντως ἡμέτερον> οὔτε πάντως οὐχ ἡμέτερον, ἵνα μήτε πάντως προσμένωμεν ὡς ἐσόμενον μήτε ἀπελπίζωμεν ὡς πάντως οὐκ ἐσόμενον ('We should remember that the future is neither entirely ours nor entirely not ours, so we should not count on it entirely to be somehow, nor despair that it will not be somehow at all'). Cic. *Fin.* 1.62: *[sapiens] neque pendet ex futuris, sed expectat illa, fruitur praesentibus* ('The wise man neither depends on things to come, but he anticipates them while enjoying what is present'). Also note Plut. *Non Posse* 1089D: the Epicureans maintain that one can take heart in the present on the basis of a plausible expectation (πιστὸν ἔλπισμα) of some future event.

present pleasure it must be despite the fact that they will never be experienced. That is why I called this process a kind of day-dreaming.[33]

Furthermore, as I have already noted, the Epicureans themselves construct an obstacle to the acceptance of such never-to-be experienced future states of affairs as reasonable objects of pleasure. They claim as part of their arguments against the fear of death that if a future event will not in fact cause pain when it occurs (since it occurs after the subject's death) then it should cause no pain in prospect (*Ep. Men.* 125). Any pain felt at present is 'empty'. By calling such distress 'empty' the Epicureans do not mean that someone troubled by the mistaken thought of *post mortem* evils is not in fact feeling any pain, but rather that such pain can and should be removed. It is baseless and pernicious since the object of this anticipatory distress is in fact not at all distressing. There can be no *post mortem* pain, so it is absolutely senseless to worry now about it in advance. If anyone does worry, then it should be simple to point out this inconsistency among their beliefs.[34] If this is so then it seems that the Epicureans must also claim that if a future event will cause no pleasure when it occurs (since it occurs after the subject's death), then it causes merely empty pleasure in prospect.[35] Just as one cannot consistently both deny the possibility of *post mortem* harm and also feel present distress at the thought of some *post mortem* event, so one cannot both deny the possibility of *post mortem* benefit and also take pleasure in the present at the thought of some positive *post mortem* event. Since any Epicurean

---

[33] It may be argued that the Epicurean in question can choose to concentrate only on possible pleasurable *post mortem* events and ignore the possible unpleasant events. But the Epicureans themselves, in their discussions of recollection and anticipation, tend to stress that only in recollection is there the secure ability to 'edit out' any harmful past events and to concentrate on the positive. See e.g. Cic. *Fin.* 1.57. This must be based to some extent on the fixity (and therefore sure knowledge) of the past contrasted with the contingency of the future.

[34] See Lucr. *DRN* 3.870–83, above p. 21.

[35] Compare the discussion of true and false pleasures at Pl. *Phileb.* 35e–36b. Frede 1985a interprets Socrates as arguing that pleasures can be false in the sense that the state of affairs which is the object of the pleasure did not occur or is not occurring or—in the case of false anticipatory pleasures—will not occur. In this sense the Epicureans could call the empty distress of *Ep. Men.* 125 false distress.

must deny the possibility of *post mortem* benefit or harm, he must also deny that one can consistently take pleasure in the present at the thought of such benefit or harm. There is one remaining move for the Epicurean to make. He must claim that rather than mistakenly contemplating any *personal* benefit or harm in the *post mortem* future, he is thinking about some benefit or harm felt by others—his descendants, for example—and this is enough to motivate him to write a will. These descendants surely can feel pleasure or pain in his *post mortem* future (provided they outlive him). Now we can turn to the possibility of altruistic motivation for writing a will. In another prominent recent discussion of these issues Ernest Partridge accepts the impossibility of *post mortem* harm, but nevertheless thinks that the making of wills can be justified. He identifies three characteristics necessary to justify writing wills despite the non-existence of *post mortem* interests. These characteristics are:

i. The ability to contemplate times and events beyond one's present temporal and physical location.
ii. The awareness of being bounded by temporal and physical limits.
iii. The capacity for moral abstraction. Partridge describes this in the following way. 'Things, places, conditions, ideas, institutions, and most significantly, persons outside himself and detached from his immediate moment and location must matter to [the agent]; he must care about their well-being as such, and not within some brief constraints of time and condition.'[36]

The first two requirements are easily satisfied by all normally functioning humans.[37] Partridge explains that the third characteristic—what he calls a 'capacity of moral abstraction'—is the ability for someone to contemplate states of affairs beyond their own experience, and even beyond the possibility of their own experience without these states being utterly indifferent to them. This condition alone gives what is necessary for a will-maker

[36] Partridge 1981, 255.
[37] Compare Locke's definition of a 'person' at *An Essay concerning Human Understanding* 2.27.9.

who agrees that he will not be benefited even indirectly by the injunctions in his own will, since it allows the simultaneous acceptance that one cannot personally be affected by the events to which the provisions in a will refer, and that nevertheless one is not utterly indifferent to those events, since they will affect people and institutions for which one now has an appropriate tie of affection and concern, and whose well-being one cares about *as such*.

Cicero denies that Epicureans can retain this capacity of moral abstraction. As he understands Epicureanism, all that matters to each Epicurean is his own pleasure, which might well be affected by others during one's lifetime, but by the Epicureans' own insistence cannot be so affected after death.[38]

From these remarks it should be clear that the problem for the Epicureans is not primarily caused by their hedonism, but by their egoistic hedonism. In other words, it might be held that pleasure is the good, but if it is not further specified that the only good for each agent is his or her own pleasure, it leaves room for a variety of specifications about the range of those whose pleasure and pain is relevant to our decision-making. In an extreme form, the claim is that one should act to promote as much pleasure in the world as possible and reduce pain as much as possible—no matter whose pain or pleasure it is.[39] This is by itself a sufficient reason for writing a will which contains various pleasure-promoting or pain-reducing measures.[40]

We know of a second Epicurean who when close to death undertook to ensure that certain acts of munificence were carried out. Diogenes of Oinoanda, who died sometime in the second century AD in Lycia, made sure that a huge Epicurean inscription

[38] Nagel 1970, 27–30, is critical of theories which require every intentional act to be motivated by an underlying desire. He points out that desires themselves may be motivated by a deeper level of considerations about my welfare or that of others. Still, the problem for the Epicureans can be cast in these terms. Why would they have any of the concerns relevant to the formation of these *post mortem* desires? This is the question of what motivates these desires. Nagel's favoured analysis of altruistic motivation rests on the postulation of something quite similar to Partridge's 'capacity of moral abstraction' (82–4).

[39] Nagel 1970, 85, recognizing that the major opposition to his view comes from egoism, claims that it is difficult for an egoist to resist the slide from the claim that '*my* pain is bad' to the claim that 'pain is bad *per se*, regardless of who experiences it'.

[40] Therefore Epicureanism is an agent-relative theory, while utilitarianism is an agent-neutral theory. For these classifications cf. Brink 1990.

was erected, a work which he began in the full knowledge that he was old and ill and unlikely to see it completed. If we understand Epicureanism as Cicero does, we might also wish to ask why as an Epicurean Diogenes of Oinoanda would construct the inscription at all since he is so close to his own death. What possible personal gain might it provide? I have argued elsewhere that this is part of Diogenes' own self-presentation as the ultimate civic euergetist; he cannot possibly be seeking any personal advancement through his benefaction.[41] But for present purposes, my interest lies in a brief explanation which Diogenes gives for his concern for future generations.

Diogenes explains that it is just (δίκαιον) to come to the aid of future generations (3.IV.13–V.4 Smith). Indeed, it is just to help them, he says, 'for they belong to us too, even if they have not yet been born' (3.V.2–4 Smith).[42] Two possible forms of justification present themselves: one based on personal relationships, and another based on issues of justice. Let us consider the second of these first. Diogenes asserts that these unborn generations are relevantly linked to him to the extent that they are bound with him in a community governed by the requirements of justice.[43] Perhaps Diogenes is not speaking at this point in absolute accordance with the substance of Epicurean doctrine. After all, he is announcing his project to the general public passing through the centre of Oinoanda and they would not, at least not yet, be expected to accept Epicurean theory at this stage of their instruction. This appeal to justice is in that case an explanation understandable in non-Epicurean terms which might be thought to act as a *captatio benevolentiae* and draw in potential converts to read the rest of the message. In that case we should not be looking here for a full-blown Epicurean theoretical justification for Diogenes' *post mortem* generosity.

In Epicurean theory what is just is not merely what is expedient for one's own personal well-being,[44] but what in some

---

[41] Warren 2000a. Diogenes also includes, in emulation of Epicurus, what looks like his own will (see esp. fr. 117 Smith).

[42] κἀκεῖνοι γάρ | εἰσιν ἡμέτεροι καὶ εἰ | μὴ γεγόνασί πω ('For they too belong to us, even if they have not yet been born').

[43] Cf. Long 1986, 307–8 and n. 23.

[44] Cicero repeatedly attempts to claim that despite his protestation that he will always obey law and custom an Epicurean hedonist would not obey any law

particular set of circumstances can promote what is objectively good for all members of the society to which this particular code applies (see *Kyriai Doxai* 33 and 37).[45] If he is speaking in strict Epicurean terms, therefore, Diogenes would be asserting that these unborn generations are part of the group to whom these standards of justice apply, and that it will be of general advantage for him to produce this inscription.

This thought might also explain why the injunctions prescribed in an Epicurean will are carried out by other Epicureans who are also convinced that the deceased cannot be affected by their action or inaction. If, rather than expressions of personal interest and desires, the injunctions in the will are expressions of what is objectively to the advantage of the group, then the remaining group members, who share the values of the deceased, will unquestionably be concerned to promote those same values. The will is enacted because it is to the group's general advantage.[46]

In this way, according to the Epicurean theory, the will is just and must be respected.[47] But still one might ask why Epicurus needed to write a will at all, if all that the will does is express measures to be taken for the general good of the surviving Epicurean community. If all the remaining Epicureans shared these values, would they not have carried out just what Epicurus requested whether or not there was a will telling them to do so? In the section of Hermarchus' work on justice, contained now in the first book of Porphyry's *De Abstinentia*, the Epicurean remarks that in a world full of Epicurean sages there would be no need for written prescriptive laws. Everyone in that case would be able to see and remember what contributes to the utility of the community and would act accordingly (Porph. *De Abst.* 1.8.4).[48] If prescriptive laws are superfluous in such a society, so are wills. Still, it would presumably be wrong for us to think that the Hellenistic Garden was a community of sages. Presumably many

which conflicted with his own utility. See *De Legibus* 1.42–50. Cf. Vander Waerdt 1987.

[45] Cf. Lucr. *DRN* 5.958–9, 1154–5; Mitsis 1988b, 80–1.

[46] Compare Partridge 1981, 259, who argues that wills are enacted as part of a kind of social contract. The living respect the wishes of the deceased in order to safeguard their own ability to write binding wills in the future.

[47] See Alberti 1995, *contra* Goldschmidt 1982.

[48] Cf. Diog. Oin. 56.I.6–12 Smith, Us. 530, and O'Keefe 2001.

of its members were new to Epicureanism or had not yet progressed as far as Epicurus towards sagehood. In that case it is still open for the better informed leaders of the group to point out what really would contribute to the general utility.[49]

But still a troubling question arises when it is remembered that Diogenes' inscription is the gift of a dying man. Why would Diogenes wish to invoke such ties at this time? The brief description of the original motivations for entering into such compacts found in $K\Delta$ 36 refers to mutual expedience guaranteed by the understanding that each person will not be harmed by another. Yet again, it must be underlined that Diogenes cannot in this case be acting with an eye to future reciprocation, or even future guaranteed security. Diogenes' desire to erect such an enormous inscription is precisely introduced as a 'post-mortem desire', and no grounding in self-interest is available for such desires. In other words, the Epicureans' own explanation of the basis of and motivation for just action refuses to invoke precisely the sort of 'capacity for moral abstraction' required in Partridge's theory. Even if either of our dying Epicureans thought that it would promote general utility if certain steps were taken, what would motivate them to promote the taking of those steps, since at the time in question they will be dead, and no longer members of the relevant group?

Let us now explore the alternative line of justification suggested by Diogenes of Oinoanda's brief explanation. Here the discussion shifts from the Epicurean theory of justice to their support of ties of friendship. Already we have seen that Diogenes asserted a personal bond between himself and future generations, and clearly those who will benefit from Epicurus' will are his companions and friends—people who had close personal bonds with the school's founder. Indeed, whereas Diogenes' public inscription addresses the inhabitants of Oinoanda most generally, Epicurus' will is primarily addressed to the members of the Garden and to his own family. If any Epicureans could be said to have been bound by bonds of friendship and justice, it will be these. Furthermore, the vigorous promotion of the goods of friendship is one part of Epicureanism which has been seen to threaten the picture of their ethics as based entirely on the calculation of

[49] Cf. Plut. *Adv. Col.* 1124D.

self-interest. If it can be accepted that an Epicurean could act to promote the interests of a friend independently of any further motivation based on self-interest, then the strict egoist requirement on Epicurean action will have been eroded, and room might be made for *post mortem* desires.

Famously, in his exposition of Epicurean ethics Torquatus provides three competing Epicurean interpretations of the nature and foundations of friendship. Unfortunately, the three Epicurean explanations of friendship offered by Torquatus have generally been thought to sit uneasily with Epicurean hedonism.[50] Cicero implicitly relies on what he perceives to be the incompatibility of the two when he picks on this trait to argue that Epicurus' behaviour was less reprehensible than his ethical theory (*Fin.* 2.80–1). One version without embarrassment makes friendship instrumental in this pursuit of pleasure, but—as we shall see— tries to find room nevertheless for genuine altruistic motivation (*Fin.* 1.66–8). A second, proposed by less bold Epicureans (*Epicurei timidiores*), makes pleasure the original motivation for friendship, but also claims that genuine friendship can blossom subsequently (1.69).[51] A third view makes friendship a bond between wise men of such a sort that they 'love their friends no less than themselves' (*ut ne minus amicos quam se ipsos diligant*: 1.70).

The existence of these three views is intended by Cicero to show that the Epicureans themselves were somewhat unsure what to make of the place of friendship within their ethical view. This uncertainty is in turn intended to be a symptom of an underlying problem for the Epicureans' theory. The three views give a gradually increasing role to genuine altruistic feelings, and therefore increasing emphasis on a 'capacity for moral abstraction'.

Cicero is constructing a dilemma. Epicurus thinks that he must make some room for friendship and altruism within his view of the good life, but if he remained consistent with his hedonism it

---

[50] Mitsis 1988b. 98–128: Annas 1993, 236–44: White 2002, 305–11. O'Connor 1989 proposes that Epicurus' view of friendship does indeed exclude genuine altruism. For a general discussion of the conflict between subjective egoist theories of well-being and morality see Brink 1990 and cf. above n. 38. Brink's own proposed solution to this problem rests on accepting an *objective* theory of well-being or welfare. He calls his own version a 'neo-Aristotelian' account.

[51] At Cic. *Fin.* 2.82 Torquatus attributes this view to 'more recent' (*recentiores*) Epicureans. Tsouna 2001b, 161–4, argues that this is the view of Philodemus.

would turn out that friendship is entirely instrumental. In that case, is an Epicurean friend a true friend at all? On the other hand, the more Epicurus insists that he would not always promote his interests to the detriment of others, the more it looks as if he is abandoning his original assertion that we should measure the value of an action by the amount of pleasure it brings us. (This dilemma is well exemplified by the two assertions contained in *Sent. Vat.* 23.)[52]

The problem is worse for Epicurus in the case of altruistic acts which are designed to take effect after the agent's death. For in those cases there is removed the remotest possibility that an act to promote another's interest might in the future be reciprocated. No possible future pleasure can be gained. To a large extent, then, the chances of resolving the problems of Epicurus' will-making and Diogenes of Oinoanda's civic euergetism stand or fall with the more general question of whether any altruistic motivations at all can be fitted into the Epicurean system. Indeed, these two cases of *post mortem* acts of altruism throw the question into its sharpest focus since in these cases, by the Epicureans' own admission, there is not even the remotest possibility of smuggling in any chance of the agent taking pleasure in the later enactment of his instructions.[53]

The most promising line of argument is to claim that the Epicureans' particular brand of hedonism is not incompatible with genuine altruistic motivation. There is some evidence that the Epicureans did advocate what at least appears to be the sort of behaviour we might class as altruistic. For example, Diogenes Laërtius includes the report that an Epicurean sage will on

---

[52] *Sent. Vat.* 23: πᾶσα φιλία δι' ἑαυτὴν αἱρετή· ἀρχὴν δὲ εἴληφεν ἀπὸ τῆς ὠφελείας ('Every friendship is choiceworthy for itself, but it took its origin in expedience'). αἱρετή Usener; ἀρετὴ ('virtue') MSS. O'Connor 1989, 186, resists seeing a tension between the two clauses in the emended version: all friendships are in themselves good things because they have been founded on utility. Brown 2002 argues that Usener's emended text is philosophically objectionable (friendship cannot be 'choiceworthy in itself') but the MSS reading is philologically difficult. He concludes by speculating that the *Saying* was composed by later Epicureans who did indeed believe that friendship is intrinsically choiceworthy.

[53] Annas 1993, 240, argues that the Epicureans expanded the notion of the pleasure that we all should seek as a natural end such that it includes the pleasure to be had from genuine altruistic concerns. However, she finds little clear and unambiguous presentation of this potentially promising view in Epicurean texts. Cf. White 2002, 306–7.

occasion even perform what may be termed the ultimate act of self-sacrifice: he will die for a friend (D.L. 10.120). However, Diogenes does not spell out under just which circumstances this sacrifice is appropriate, and while it is obviously the case that self-sacrifice is compatible with genuine altruism, it does not require it. Indeed, it is also possible to justify such acts as displaying self-interest. If the alternative to self-sacrifice is the death of a friend (which is the situation envisaged by Diogenes) then perhaps, were that friend to die, the surviving Epicureans' life would be full of misery. Perhaps the Epicurean depended materially on this friend. Perhaps in the absence of this friend the Epicurean will not be able to live a life of *ataraxia*. In such circumstances, since death is not an evil then it is preferable to a continued painful life.[54]

The Epicureans' explanations of the origin and justification of friendship are therefore a better source. Let us leave to one side, however, the third of the models which Torquatus outlines, that of the pact of mutual aid between sages. This model is explicitly said to work only between Epicurean sages since only they are able properly to form such compacts. It is therefore perhaps applicable to the case of Epicurus and Hermarchus, but certainly not to the case of Epicurus and Amynomachus and Timocrates—neither of whom are Epicureans, let alone sages. It is also certainly not the case that any such compact of mutual benevolence might be said to exist between Diogenes of Oinoanda and the present and future citizens of that city.[55]

The first of the three suggestions recognizes that friendship is an instrument for the production of pleasure, but attempts to make room for genuine altruism by noting that the most efficient way to ensure the pleasures which flow from one's friends is genuinely to feel concern for them.

[54] See my remarks about the Epicureans' view of suicide in Warren 2000b, 242 and n. 34 and below, p. 205ft.
[55] Of course, Diogenes does seem to invoke a general concern for all humans: φιλανθρωπία. There are similar signs of the Epicureans' acceptance that there is a general psychological propensity for such affection in Hermarchus *ap.* Porph. *De Abst.* 1.7.1: τάχα μὲν καὶ φυσικῆς τινος τινος οἰκειώσεως ὑπαρχούσης τοῖς ἀνθρώποις πρὸς ἀνθρώπους διὰ τὴν ὁμοιότητα τῆς μορφῆς καὶ τῆς ψυχῆς ('Perhaps there is also some natural affinity between humans because of the similarity of their appearance and soul'). Cf. Philod. *De Pietate* 1103–8 Obbink, and Obbink 1988.

quod quia nullo modo sine amicitia firmam et perpetuam iucunditatem
vitae tenere possumus neque vero ipsam amicitiam tueri nisi aeque amicos
et nosmet ipsos diligamus, idcirco et hoc ipsum efficitur in amicitia et
amicitia cum voluptate connectitur.

So in no way is it possible to secure firm and constant pleasure in life
without friendship, nor is it possible to keep friendship itself unless we
love our friends and ourselves equally. Hence this [i.e. loving friends
and ourselves equally] does occur in the case of friendship and friendship is linked with pleasure.

Cic. *Fin.* 1.67

This explanation therefore invokes a familiar paradoxical twist
to the promotion of self-interest: it is best done by not behaving
in a self-interested manner.[56] While it is undeniable that friendship can produce pleasure, the Epicureans might be open to the
following complaints. First, all that is required for the enjoyment
of the goods provided by friends is that one appear to be—
rather than actually be—a friend oneself. This may, of course,
require the occasional altruistic act, but this is hardly to say that
one should in fact value one's friends' pleasures as much as one's
own. Second, this explanation offers an unstable mix of self-
interest and other-regarding motivation which can be made to
cause problems for the Epicureans. What should an Epicurean
do if faced with an exclusive choice between promoting his own
interest and promoting that of a friend? All that the brief passage
just quoted offers is that we are to love ourselves and our friends
equally. But if we grant that such exclusive choices may have to be

---

[56] This paradox is sometimes fashioned into a refutation of self-interest
theories. See Sidgwick 1907, 136–7, 403; Brink 1990, 342–9. The second of
Torquatus' proposed models goes so far as to claim that eventually friendship
blossoms so as to promote altruistic motivation without any further self-
interested aims. As such it seems to deny the Epicureans' claim that we should
act always with a view to promoting our overall pleasure. Cic. *Fin.* 1.69: *itaque
primos congressus copulationesque et consuetudinum instituendarum voluntates
fieri propter voluptatem, cum autem usus progrediens familiaritatem effecerit, tum
amorem efflorescere tantum ut, etiamsi nulla sit utilitas ex amicitia, tamen ipsi
amici propter se ipsos amentur* ('So they say the first comings-together and sexual
acts and desires to form companionships come about because of pleasure, and
only when constant exercise has produced intimacy does love blossom so that,
even if no benefit should come from friendship, nevertheless friends are
themselves loved for their own sake').

made, what should the Epicurean do? Should he act to promote his friend's pleasure, to his own detriment but in accordance with a genuine other-concern? But this other-concern was introduced precisely as a means to further one's own pleasure. Or should he instead on this occasion act to promote his own interests and to the detriment of his friend? In that case it can be argued that Epicurean friendship is indeed entirely one-way; the friend's interests are not valued in themselves but merely when either they further the Epicurean's own interest or can be fostered at no overall cost to the Epicurean. But this sort of picture does not seem to be genuinely altruistic.

More pressing for the specific role which altruism is supposed to play in my present discussion is the fact that friendship is intended in all three of Torquatus' suggestions to function as a means to generate or guarantee further pleasure for the Epicurean himself. But in cases of *post mortem* munificence there is no Epicurean to be benefited by his grateful friends. This problem can be circumvented to a degree by interpreting a will as a gesture towards one's friends (who are here understood to be the main beneficiaries of any bequest) which is known about and appreciated while the testator is still alive. In this situation, the knowledge that a friend will leave certain items in a will to another may ensure the continued assistance of this future beneficiary during the remaining period of the testator's life. The beneficiary reciprocates in advance, as it were, for the goods which he has been pledged and will receive when the other dies. It may even be the case that the time and trouble taken to write a will is repaid by the pre-emptive gratitude of the future beneficiaries. (The eventual acts of munificence contained in the will are, of course, no loss to the deceased.) This may indeed be the most plausible account an Epicurean could give of the motivation and practice of will-making since it does identify a degree of self-interest which would motivate the formulation and (importantly) publication of promises of *post mortem* future other-regarding acts.[57] However, notice that still on this account the testator himself is indifferent to whether the measures in the will are in

---

[57] See Cic. *Fin.* 1.70: *perspicuum est nihil ad iucunde vivendum reperiri posse quod coniunctione tali sit aptius* ('It is obvious that nothing can be found more fitting for living a pleasant life than this sort of alliance').

fact carried out. The function of the will of ensuring the reciprocation of a friend ceases to be relevant once the testator dies.

Whether this is a plausible explanation of the two acts of Epicurean *post mortem* generosity which I have used to anchor this philosophical discussion is another question. Perhaps Epicurus benefited during his lifetime owing to Amynomachus' and Timocrates' knowledge of the measures he had placed in his will to an extent which justified the time, trouble, and expense of writing and ensuring the preservation of the document. The case of Diogenes of Oinoanda is less promising, however. The proposed beneficiaries of his legacy are for the most part non-Epicurean and not known to him personally. It can certainly not be argued that he received some benefit during his life from the future generations he has decided to aid.

There have emerged two major difficulties for a defender of Epicurean will-making. The first is the difficulty of providing any demonstration of the compatibility of genuine altruism with egoistic hedonism. The Epicureans may be able to circumvent this by various contractual stories or with empirical or psychological observations that humans naturally do form true friendships. Nevertheless, there still seems to me to be a tension between the recommendation that one should act always to promote one's own subjective state and the notion that others' well-being is to be valued *as such*, regardless of any personal stake. The provision of *post mortem* acts of kindness to others throws this difficulty into the sharpest relief. Second, there is the difficulty of providing room for any impulse to *post mortem* generosity or commands within a system which recognizes no possibility of *post mortem* benefit or harm. While this may be thought to leave it entirely possible for an Epicurean to be extremely generous with his bequests—since he himself will have no need to retain any of his wealth—there appears to be little or no room for an Epicurean to motivate himself to such acts of munificence.

There are still possible answers to the question of why Epicurus wrote a will and took such pains to see that it was safely preserved. We might have to think that Epicurus was indeed inconsistent and Cicero was right to press his criticisms. In the face of imminent death and against his philosophical judgement, Epicurus began to worry that the affairs of the Garden after his death might after all be 'something to him'. So he made a will to try to preserve his (involuntary) *post mortem* interests. This depressing conclusion should only be offered in the absence of anything better.

There is an alternative view. We should also remember here what I called the 'double audience' of Epicurus' will. This is a will not only for the members of the Garden, but which must also conform to the form and legal requirements of the surrounding Athenian society. The manner in which Epicurus handles the inheritance of his property makes it clear that he is aware of Athenian legal practice and convention. On this view, Epicurus' decision to make a will was determined not by his philosophical outlook at all, but by the fact that his philosophical school existed within a *polis* which did not share its views. Therefore, we might choose to conclude that Epicurus' will had the purely instrumental concern of ensuring the continuation of the Garden and of carving a legitimate place for this community within Athenian property and inheritance law.[58] The making of a will of some sort was unavoidable, and since the Epicureans recommend living by custom and law—in order to secure a quiet life within a city—these legal practices are adhered to but without the Epicurean being committed to them in the same way as the general populace might be.[59]

Philodemus on the writing of wills

I conclude this discussion with a look at Philodemus' *De Morte*, which contains another Epicurean treatment of the writing of wills. In fact, it contains two passages in which will-writing plays an illustrative or significant role in Philodemus' overall project of alleviating possible residual sources of anxiety over the prospect of dying. The first passage comes at the very end of the extant portion of the treatise. Here Philodemus is offering something of a peroration, comparing the lives of fools with those of people who understand the true nature of death.

εἶθ' ὅταν ἐναρ|γὴς αὐτοῦ [sc. τοῦ θανάτου] γένηται θεωρία[[ι]], παράδο|ξος αὐτοῖς ὑποπίπτει· παρ' ἣν αἰτίαν | [ο]ὐδὲ διαθήκας ὑπομένοντες γράφεσ||[θ]αι

---

[58] For the relationship between the Epicurean Garden and the surrounding non-Epicurean society see Long 1986, esp. 313–16.

[59] Cf. some of the assertions gathered in D.L. 10.118–20.

περικατάληπτοι γίν[ο]νται καὶ δί|[χ'] ἐμφορεῖν ἀναγκάζονται κατ[ὰ] Δη|μόκριτον.

Further, when contemplation of death becomes clear, it assails them as a paradox. For this reason they become entirely consumed, cannot bear to write their own wills, and are forced 'to be in two minds' as Democritus says.

XXXIX.9–15 Gigante

As ever with such passing references, it is unclear just how much of what proceeds is intended to be 'according to Democritus'. A more generous account offers all of the previous sentence as Democritus' view. In that case, the early atomist noticed that some people are so paralysed by the fear of death that paradoxically they do not even manage to write a will. The least generous account restricts the reference to the immediately preceding words: 'to be in two minds' (δί|[χ'] ἐμφορεῖν), and must regard this as a Democritean expression which Philodemus feels captures the kind of paradoxical attitude to which these people are prone.[60] At the very least this is what Philodemus attributes to Democritus, but unfortunately the meaning of this Democritean observation is far from lucid.

It seems to me that the sense of the phrase is best explained by seeing it in the context of the preceding text. These people are assailed by the terrifying vision of death, which Philodemus

---

[60] David Armstong tells me that he prefers this more restricted reference to Democritus. The text is disputed: The two major proposals are: δί|[σσ'] ἐμφορεῖν (Diels) and δί|[χ'] ἐμφορεῖν (Gigante and Indelli 1980 456–8). Gigante 1983b, 227–9, has a good discussion of previous conjectures and interpretations. The former possibility, δί|[σὰ] ἐμφορεῖν, retained in Kuiper's edition of the text and accepted in Taylor's edition of the fragments of Democritus and Leucippus, is generally understood to mean something like 'stuffing themselves with double portions' (Taylor 1999, 155). Kuiper 1925, 136 n. 114, suggests that it refers to a dying or condemned person desperate to pack in to his remaining life as many pleasures as possible, and therefore eating twice as much as normal (cf. Pl. *Phaedo* 116e2–5). However, the sense of 'taking one's fill' would be better reflected by a verb in the middle voice (cf. LSJ s.v. ἐμφορέω). Instead Philodemus uses an active verb, which is most naturally translated as 'to fill (something) twice' or 'to pour in double amounts'. The latter suggestion, δί|[χ'] ἐμφορεῖν, is interpreted as being equivalent to διχοφρονεῖν, 'thinking double thoughts', and is further argued to mean in this context that these will-makers are producing inconsistent provisions in their wills: Gigante and Indelli 1980, 458 n. 35. Gigante defends this again at length in Gigante 1983b, 227–33. He compares Plut. *De Virtute Morali* 447c. Also see LSJ s.v. διχοφορέω.

interprets as betraying a lingering commitment to some sort of *post mortem* survival. This commitment would lead them, if they were rational and consistent, to write a will in some attempt to control the fate of their lingering *post mortem* interests in the world. However—and this is why the vision of death can be called paradoxical—the contemplation of death is simultaneously so disturbing that it paralyses them and prevents them even from carrying out this action. When they come to contemplate writing a will, this involves them confronting their mortality and rather than acting in accordance with their presuppositions they fall back into horrified inactivity. (We might recall here the paradoxical attitude displayed by the 'fools' in the Democritean fragments preserved by Stobaeus, especially B199–201.)

For our present purposes, we should consider how these fools differ from the wise man, whom Philodemus goes on to portray in the subsequent text. This man will breathe his last, even if death is sudden and unexpected, with no sense of a lack of fulfilment. It is not, unfortunately, explained here whether the wise man will indeed write a will at all, but he will certainly not do so, we may presume, out of some concern to foster lingering interests in the world nor from some conception of his life as being as yet unfinished and incomplete. (That still leaves the possibility that the wise man may write a will out of some other motive—and therefore leaves some possibility for the justification of Epicurus' own practice.)

The other, more extensive, treatment of will-writing in Philodemus' work appears during his rebuttal of the notion that it is bad to die childless. First, Philodemus assures his concerned objector that our deceased ancestors are not at all aggrieved that their lineage will be coming to an end (XIII.33–6). Then he goes on to explain that whatever happens to our descendants and our property after our death this should not be of concern to us:

λέγω διότ[ι κα]ταλε[ι]‖φθέντων ἢ μ]η| καταλειφθέν[τ]ων | ἐγγόνων καὶ
συν[τ]ελούντω[ν] ἃ προ|είπαμεν τούτων ἢ [τ]ινων ὅθ[ν]ε<ί>ων | η>| μηδένων
ἀπ[λ]ῶ[s] οὐδὲν ἔσται | πρὸς ἡμᾶς μᾶλλον ἢ κατὰ τοὺς ἔ[πὶ] | Φορωνέως
γεγονο[ότ]α[s]. εἰ μὴ νὴ [Δί|α] κατὰ τοῦτο λυπηρόν ἐστιν ἄπα[ιδο]s |
[κ]ατα[σ]τροφή, [δ]ιότι τοῖς κληρόνομο[ις] | ἔστα[ι] τὰ πονηθέντα, καθάπερ οὐ
χρ[εὼν | π]ολλάκις ἅπασιν καταλείπειν ἢ δέ[νδρα | ἢ θέρ]ος [ἄλλοι]s ἢ τισιν
τέκνοις· χωρὶς | [τοῦ] μηδὲ φαύλους ε[ἶ]ναι μηδ' ἀνα[ξί]ους ἐνίοτε τοὺς
κληρονομήσαν|τ[ας]. ἐα|ν δ' ὦσιν παν[η]ροί, προφυλάξασ|θ[αι] δυνατὸν

194 Living an Epicurean Life

[ἀνδράσ]ι σπουδαίοις καὶ | φί[λ]οις ἀπολε[ίποντα, οὓς ὅ]στις οὐκ ἔχει, δι|ὰ
τ[ο]ῦτ᾽ ἐστιν ο<ἰ>κτρ[ός, ο]ὐχ ὅτι χ[ηρω]σ|ται [οὐ]τοι κακ[οὶ]...
τοῖς δ᾽ αὐ|τὸ το[ῦτο κα]το[δυρομέ]ν[οις], ὅτι κυ|ριεύσ[ουσ]ι τῶν σαν[ίδων] οὓς
οὐ θέλου|σιν, ἔ[ξέσ]ται καὶ τέκ[ν]ων ὑπαρχόν|των [κατα]θρηνε[ῖν, ἐπει]δὴ καὶ
τύχη | [ἡ πάντ]ων δυνά[σ]τις ἀνθρώ]πων ο[ἵ]|ά τ᾽ ἐστὶν ἐκε[ί]νων ἀφελομένη
π[ροσ]|ρίψαι τοῖς τ[υ]χοῦσιν. τὸ τοίνυν κα|ταλείπειν γονεῖς ἢ παῖδα[ς] ἢ
γα[μ]ε|τὴν ἢ τινας ἄλλους τῶν ἔ[πι]τηδε[ί]|ων, ἐν συμφο[ρ]αῖς ἐσομένο[υς] διὰ
[τ]ὴν | καταστροφὴν ἡμῶν ἢ καὶ τ[ῶ]ν ἀν[αγ]|καίων ἐλλείψοντας, ἔχει μ[έ]ν
ἀμέ|λει φυσικώτατον δηγμὸν κα[ὶ δ]α[κ]ρύ|ων προέσεις ἐγείρει τῶι νοῦν
ἔχοντ[ι] | μόνον ἢ μάλιστα·

I say that whether or not descendants are left behind, and whether they
carry out what we told them previously or some foreigners do this or if
no one does it then generally this will be no more to us than is what
happened to those born in Phoroneus' time. Unless, by Zeus, to die
without children is harmful because of this, namely the fact that what
we toiled over will then be owned by one's heirs (as though it were not
generally necessary for all men to leave behind either trees or crops to
people other than one's children). This is separate from the question of
whether the heirs are ignoble or unworthy. If they are ignoble, then this
can be guarded against in advance by leaving things to noble friends.
Someone who has none of these is pitiable simply for that reason, not
because his distant relatives and heirs are bad...
...but as for those who bewail the fact that people they do not want
will be in charge of their property, it is possible for those with surviving
children to bewail this too since chance, the mistress of all men, is also
capable of taking it away and tossing it to anyone at all. To be sure,
though, leaving behind parents or children or a wife or any other dear
ones to be in difficulties or even lacking in necessities because of one's
death, that produces a most natural pang and rouses in the wise man
especially floods of tears.

XXIII.33–XXIV.17, XXIV.31–XXV.10 Kuiper

There are a number of suprising things about this passage,
particularly in its closing lines in which Philodemus admits that
the wise man will indeed feel a 'most natural' pain at the prospect
of leaving loved ones ill cared-for after his death.[61] Here we might
find echoes of Diogenes of Oinoanda's *philanthropia* (3.V.4–8

---

[61] For a discussion of the 'natural pang' referred to here see Armstrong 2004,
39–44, who sees this as a means of pre-empting the anti-Epicurean objection
that their discussion of death is in general unsympathetic to the emotional
effects of thinking about one's death. There are further references to such
reactions at XXV.38 (perhaps), and also XXXV.36.

Smith), but applied in this instance to a restricted group of close companions. In any case, here is an apparently sanctioned circumstance in which one will feel pain at the thought of some *post mortem* state of affairs. These references to such 'natural pangs' are the best evidence we have for the suggestion that the Epicureans might consider *post mortem* desires of the sort contained in wills to be examples of 'natural and unnecessary' desires. Such desires certainly will not lead to pain if they are left unfulfilled (for the familiar reasons why nothing after a person's death can benefit or harm him), but may nevertheless be natural in the sense that they are an inevitable response to certain thoughts or provocations given our human nature. Perhaps Philodemus is offering a mitigation of the Epicurean account to allow what might be thought to be an essential psychological fact of ongoing care for loved ones even after one's own death. Certainly, the references to 'natural pangs' here in *De Morte* recall similar passages about painful or biting feelings in his work *On anger* (*De Ira*, *PHerc.* 182). There, such feelings are involved in what Philodemus calls 'natural anger', to contrast it with the 'empty' (κενή) anger which results from incorrect judgements of value (XXXVII.39–XXXVIII.10).[62] Even a wise man will occasionally feel this natural anger, although it will not last long (XL.1–2, XLI.17–31, XLIII.41–XLIV.22). We might say something similar, therefore, about these 'natural' feelings of concern for *post mortem* states of affairs. Perhaps they are feelings which even the wise man will inevitably and naturally feel, although he has no false opinions about the value to him of *post mortem* states of affairs. Just as a wise man may be 'bitten' and feel natural anger, so he might be 'bitten' and feel natural concern for the welfare of people after his death.

However, there are two reasons to be wary of accepting this Philodeman position as a completely satisfying explanation of why an Epicurean would write a will. First, even if it is accepted as an explanation for why even an Epicurean wise man would feel occasional concern at the thought of what will happen to loved ones after his death, it perhaps does not suffice to explain

---

[62] For the most recent text of *De Ira* see Indelli 1988. References to 'biting' pains occur at: XII.18, XXXVII.19, and XLI.8. For an excellent discussion of this material see Procopé 1998. Cf. Annas 1993, 194–200; Tsouna 2001a.

why an Epicurean would indulge such feelings to the extent needed to compose a detailed will. In the case of anger, although Philodemus is adamant that the wise Epicurean will on occasion feel natural anger, he is equally clear that the wise man will take no pleasure from retaliation as a result of that anger, nor from inflicting punishment on anyone who has caused the slight. Anger and thoughts of revenge should not be indulged or revelled in (XLII.19–39). Just so, even Philodemus might think that there are limits to the extent to which any natural concern for what will come to happen after one's death should be indulged and dwelt upon. Second, there is evidence from the *De Ira* to suggest that Philodemus' stance on this matter was not shared by all Epicureans. He is engaged in a lively debate over the nature and value of anger with a number of opponents, including at least two other Epicureans, Timasagoras and Nicasicrates, who seem to have wanted to deny that anger should play any part in the ideal Epicurean life. Perhaps agreeing with his own Epicurean teacher, Zeno of Sidon, Philodemus' view was at the very least not uncontroversial among the Epicurean community and may even have been a minority opinion. Philodemus' views in the *De Morte*, therefore, if they are based on an analogous claim about what even a wise man might naturally feel, cannot be claimed without reservation to be 'the' Epicurean position on this matter. At the time Philodemus was writing there may not have been any clear and settled view about such 'natural' emotions shared by the whole school. That in turn suggests that it was an issue about which Epicurus and his immediate successors were at best unclear. (Certainly in the discussion of anger Philodemus offers support for his case in the writings of Epicurus, Hermarchus, and Metrodorus, feigning disbelief that his well-read ($\beta \upsilon \beta \lambda \iota \alpha \kappa o \iota$) Epicurean opponents had failed to understand the evidence correctly. There was certainly scope for differing interpretations of the early Epicurean texts.)[63] It is even possible that in part this addition to the Epicurean wise man's sphere of concern was intended by Philodemus to explain Epicurus' own—now 'most

---

[63] See *De Ira* XLV.5–33. Cf. Indelli 1988, 242. Recall also the disagreement over the Epicurean conception of the nature and value of friendship discussed above, p. 185, and Philodemus' polemic against other Epicureans' views in the second book of his *Rhetoric*—on which see Warren 2002c, 169.

natural'—efforts to maintain the Garden after his death.[64] He could certainly have pointed to Epicurus' behaviour as support for his view.[65] Whether or not this notion of a 'natural pang' at contemplating *post mortem* events was something in fact anticipated in Epicurus' own writings, it does offer a promising opening for an Epicurean defence of will-writing. Still, Philodemus would have to be careful to maintain that any such practice is done in the full and clear understanding of the truth about death and also that the writing of a will does not involve an excessive and unhealthy preoccupation and cultivation of these initially natural feelings.

The passage from *De Morte* just cited (XXIII.33–XXIV.17, XXIV.31–XXV.10) opens, however, in a more familiar and expected vein. Philodemus begins with another Symmetry Argument. The thought of dying childless is no reason to think death an evil since the world we leave behind at death will be no more of concern to us then than was the world in the time of Phoroneus, the legendary first king of Argos.[66] He then moves on swiftly to consider an alternative reason why dying childless might be an evil. The childless must leave their property to people outside their direct lineage. The rebuttal is equally concise: in fact, this is always the case, even for those with surviving children (XXIV.8–10). The thought here is a little obscure. One possibility is that he is pointing out that eventually (at least after the first generation) the property will be passed on to others besides one's children. That is hardly a convincing argument, of course, since presumably the objector is concerned not with leaving property to his direct offspring so much as leaving his hard-won assets to his descendants, people directly related to him however many generations hence. Philodemus would have to work harder to secure the claim that one will always eventually leave one's property to people outside one's line, but he might offer two thoughts. First,

---

[64] At XXIV.36 Philodemus uses the word διαδοχή for 'lineage', a word which is also applied to lines of philosophical inheritance and the succession of heads of a particular school. Cf. also Philod. *De Oec.* XXVII.5–8 Jensen, where it is urged that one should save up in order to provide for one's friends after death.

[65] As he does in the case of anger: *De Ira* XXXV.1–5.

[66] Armstrong 2004, 33 and 53 while he argues that Philodemus uses a move he thinks is absent from other Epicurean texts—the claim that the *very distant* past and future are nothing to us—at XXXVI.17–25, also claims that there is no sign of a symmetry argument in Philodemus' *De Morte*.

as the generations pass, the property—whatever is left of it—
may be dispersed between siblings and diluted through patterns
of inheritance distribution. Second, distant generations, even if
our direct descendants, may be felt to claim little personal weight
with us. These are people whom we will never know and even
meet and—to invoke a symmetry principle once again—should
be of as much concern to us as our distant ancestors. (Of course,
it may be that even distant ancestors *are* thought particularly
significant, in which case Philodemus' argument here would not
be very persuasive.)

The progression to the next section suggests a second possibility.
People inevitably leave their property to others since heirs often
squander and lose what they are given. That would make some
sense, at least, of the concession that follows: not all heirs are like
that. And even if it is feared that one's heirs may be profligate
then suitable guardians can be appointed to ensure the preservation of one's generosity. Unfortunately, the text breaks off at
this point. This immediately preceding passage appears to be a
further consideration offered by Philodemus' opponent rather
than a further point in defence of the Epicurean position. After
all, it seems to be offering the possibility of ensuring the correct
and secure modes of inheritance, which would suggest that there
is some value in ensuring the well-being of one's descendants
after death. But this thought is not at all consistent with the
notion at the very beginning of the passage that what our descendants do with their lot is indeed 'nothing to us' (XXIII.37–XXIV.5).
Although the reference to the value of friends is compatible with
Epicureanism (XXIV.15–17), it is not its exclusive property. In
that case, the lacuna in the text must be presumed to have
contained some Philodeman retort to this objection.

When the text resumes we find Philodemus arguing that those
who do have children to whom they can leave their property are
no more secure than those who do not. In that case, those who
die childless are no worse off than those who die with direct heirs,
since chance events may well destroy those heirs' prosperity.
Philodemus has to be careful here, since it may now appear that
not only is dying childless a reasonable source of distress but
dying with surviving children ought also to cause anxiety. If it
is no *worse* to die childless, then perhaps it is *just as bad* to die
with children. The argument here must therefore be *ad hominem*.

The objector begins with the premise that it is in fact not bad to die with surviving heirs and this is never questioned. Philodemus then simply equates what the objector assumes *is* bad with what he accepts is not.

PROLONGING LIFE

Creech, the commentator on Lucretius, noted on his manuscript: 'N.B. Must hang myself when I am finished.' He kept his word, that he might have the pleasure of ending like his author. Had he taken on a commentary on Ovid, he would have lived longer.[67]

Voltaire, *Dictionnaire philosophique*

There now arises a potentially devastating criticism of the Epicurean view. If death can never be a harm and is not to be feared, but life can be miserable—and often contains many harms—then what reason would we have for staying alive? The Epicurean account, on this view, has done more than show that we ought not to fear death; it has shown that it is at least sometimes rational to pursue it.[68]

It is rational to commit suicide if death is not an evil and one knows that one's future will be unhappy or—given the assumption that there is some sort of *post mortem* existence—one knows that this *post mortem* existence will be better than any available life before death.[69] Of course, how one is to come to that conclusion is not immediately clear since it is not immediately clear what happiness, or well-being, or *eudaimonia* consist in. To simplify and focus the question, therefore, let us pose it to the Epicureans, who do have a clear account.

It is rational to commit suicide, not to continue living, if one of the three following conditions is met:

1. Being dead is the best state possible.
2. Being alive is the worst state possible.
3. Being dead is always better than being alive.

---

[67] Taken from Enright 1983, 97.　　　　[68] Ewin 2002, 19–21.

[69] This second possibility is the cause of difficulties for Platonism, for example. See my discussion of the *Phaedo*'s argument over the prohibition of suicide in Warren 2001c.

These are extreme and general propositions. It is also rational to commit suicide if a fourth, less extreme, condition is met:

4. Being dead is better than continuing to live one's present life.

Now, from these conditions it is possible to generate mirror-images which will show when it is rational to continue living.

5. Being alive is the best state possible.
6. Being dead is the worst state possible.
7. Being alive is always better than being dead.
8. Continuing to live one's present life is better than being dead.

Epicurus must be able to defend one of propositions 5–8 while maintaining his thesis that 'death is nothing to us'. Otherwise, he is in danger of being forced to agree that for most people proposition 4 will be true. For most people, of course, life is miserable, from an Epicurean point of view. Although they may not see themselves that they are living a miserable life, nevertheless their daily existence is filled with pain, frustration, and anxiety. They are said by the Epicureans to be suffering from a disease. In that case, is it not true that death—the absence of any sensation—will be better than their present state? If so, should they not be encouraged to end it all? In all these formulations, of course, 'being dead' does not refer to some state in which the person will find themselves. Rather, 'being dead' is simply another way of saying 'not being alive' or 'not existing'. Some critics claim that this alone makes any sort of comparison between the two states of being alive and not being alive difficult if not impossible. The agent deliberating between the two is not choosing between alternative states but between a state and the absence of any state at all. Not being alive has no value, as it were, either positive or negative.[70] The difficulty would therefore amount to something like the following. Let us assume that the correct analysis of what is going on when someone rationally contemplates suicide is a comparison between continuing to live a life of an expected kind and not to live any life at all. In that case, the analysis of what is going on when someone decides *not* to commit suicide is that one chooses one of the

---

[70] See Silverstein 1980, 410–13, and cf. Kamm 1993, 15–16.

alternatives—continuing to live—over the other. This too is an exercise of comparative evaluation.[71] If the Epicureans were to argue that when we do not commit suicide (which must be the case most of the time for most people) we are at least implicitly performing this kind of evaluation, then they seem to have jeopardized one of the central planks in their arguments against death being a potential harm. It can be argued that in allowing this sort of comparison the Epicureans are allowing a relational or comparative evaluative procedure of the sort which they staunchly opposed when it was offered as an analysis of the harm of death. If death cannot be a relational harm, then life should not be able to be a relational benefit.[72]

It certainly appears that the Epicureans do try to offer an account which would allow them to advocate 8 above. If one is able to reach the Epicurean ethical goal and live a good life, a life of pleasure and without pain, then this is better than being dead since although death—like *ataraxia*—is the absence of pain, unlike *ataraxia* death is also the absence of pleasure. Furthermore, the Epicureans are insistent that no one is immediately disqualified by their congenital nature or environment and upbringing from being able to attain the goal of a good life. Some may find the process of ethical improvement longer and harder than others but nearly everyone can attain the goal.[73] There is always, therefore, the prospect of living a life which is preferable to not living at all, even though the majority of lives being led by people are painful.

---

[71] Cf. Brandt 1992, 324–32.

[72] Cf. Quinn 2001, 78 n. 21: 'The basic difference between the sceptic about death and his critics is that he is unimpressed by the fact that most of us seem to find it quite possible to consider the alternatives of staying alive and being dead and to form a decided preference for the former. He finds this preference irrational, not because non-existence isn't available as an object to consider, but because it cannot be assigned any value that could make sense of the preference. His critics, however.... find the apparent fact of the preference sufficient reason to believe that death can be assigned a value (presumably a nonpositive value) that makes sense of the strong preference for life.' The problem for the Epicureans is not, I think, that they cannot assign death a value but that the only value it could be assigned is comparative.

[73] See Lucr. *DRN* 3.319–22 for an optimistic account of the possibilities of becoming wise. But cf. D.L. 10.117: there are some bodily constitutions and nationalities which prevent people from becoming wise.

However, at this point we can offer a further problem for the Epicurean view, this time based upon the Epicureans' characterization of the good life. In their attempt to remove the fear of death entirely it might be objected that they have undermined any reasons someone may have for continuing to live a good life once it has been reached. The problem may be set as a dilemma. Either (i) the Epicureans must agree that living a good life for a longer rather than a shorter time is to be preferred or (ii) they must agree that there is no reason, once one has achieved the ethical goal, for wishing to remain in that state. If (i), then they face once again the threat that death may be *premature*; it may rob even the person living the good life of the preferable position of living a good life for a longer rather than a shorter period of time. And if that is the case, then even the person living a good life may justly feel anxious at the thought that he might live a shorter good life than he wishes. If (ii), then they may have to argue that there is *nothing to choose* between continuing to live a good life once one has attained the ethical goal and being dead. This too looks to be an unwanted position. Given that even the ideal Epicurean may be subject to chance, illness, and so on to some, albeit minimized, degree, why should he not decide that, all things considered, given that he is not being benefited by living a longer rather than a shorter good life, death is the best option?

In short, arguments which try to remove the anxiety of dying prematurely by arguing that one is not benefited by living longer undermine reasons for continuing to live at all.[74] And an Epicurean argument which shows that those living the good life cannot die prematurely will undermine any reasons one might have for wanting to continue to live the good life. I have noted above a powerful argument for the conclusion that any desires sufficient to give an agent reason to continue living can, by their very nature, be frustrated by death and therefore provide good reason to avoid death. Death, on this view, is most certainly

---

[74] Cf. McMahan 2002, 140: 'The general lesson here is that, whenever the future promises to be worth living, and perhaps especially when continuing to live is necessary for the achievement of some important goal, death poses a threat of loss that cannot be fully nullified by any degree of previous achievement or, more generally, previous gain from a life.'

therefore an evil.[75] On pain of producing an argument which would show that death is, after all, something to be feared, the Epicureans cannot rely on desires of this sort to give a perfectly happy Epicurean reason to continue to live.

There is some evidence for the Epicureans' own conception of how the wise man would live his life found in the final columns of the work usually attributed to Philodemus, *On choices and avoidances* (*De Elect.*, *PHerc.* 1251). After outlining a number of ways in which non-Epicureans fall into irrational and erratic behaviour in the face of death (XVI–XX), the author turns to the correct attitude and the behaviour of the wise Epicurean (XXI–XXIII).

ἀνεπίβ[λητον] δ' ἐκφ[ύγω]ν τὴν | τελευτ[ήν, ἐ]ργατ[ικ]ός ἐσ|τι τῶι
σ[υ]μβαινοντι [δό]γματι | κατὰ τὴν ἔννοιαν τῆς τηρή|σεως τῶν ἀγαθῶν· καὶ
διὰ τὸ | μὴ ἀποκόπτειν τὴν πολυχρό|νιον ζωὴν ἐνεργείας ἀεὶ και|νὰς ἐνίσταται
καὶ φιλο[π]οΐας·

...| τ]ῶι μακρῶ[ι χρόνωι τ]οῦ [ζῆ]ν· | [κ]αὶ διαπα[ντ]ῶν ἅπασι το[ῖ]ς |
[β]έλτειόν [τι ἔ]χουσιν ἐπα|νάγειν σπ[ο]υδῆς οὐδὲν ἐλ|[λε]λείπει προσδ[ο]κίαι
τοῦ χρό|[νο]ν ἐπιβιώσεσθαι· καὶ τῆς | ὑγιεία μάλιστα δὴ π[ρ]ονο|εῖ· καὶ
τεθαρρηκὼς πρὸς | ἀρρωστίας κα[ὶ] θάνατον εὐ|τόνως ὑπομένει {ει} τὰ
δυ|νάμενα τούτων ἀπαλ|λάττειν.

Avoiding an unforeseen death, he works hard because of the resulting doctrine concerning the notion of caring for one's goods. And because he does not curtail his long life he always instigates new opportunities for making friends.

...in the long extent of life. And he spares no effort in all those opportunities which can bring something better, in the expectation of living longer. And he takes particular care of his health and having considered illnesses and death he vigorously undergoes measures to ward them off.

XXII.4–11 and XXIII.1–11 Indelli and Tsouna-McKirahan

The reference to the doctrine of a concept of preserving one's goods must be recalling a technical piece of Epicurean ethical theory, perhaps something Philodemus dealt with more extensively in his work *De Oeconomia* (*PHerc.* 1424), which described how an Epicurean would manage his household property.[76]

[75] See the discussion of Williams on the tedium of immortality and his notion of 'categorical desires', above pp. 111–12.

[76] For more discussion see Indelli and Tsouna-McKirahan 1995, 214–21, who take this reference to *De Oec.* as possible evidence for Philodemus' authorship of *De Elect.* and, more generally, Tsouna-McKirahan 1996.

The immediately preceding column XXI explains that an Epicurean will not try to amass money and will distribute his possessions, leaving himself only what is necessary for his life since he is confident enough not to need to keep a surplus of goods. More directly relevant to our present concerns, however, are two further claims. The passage insists, first, that the Epicurean will take at least some care of his health in order not to die simply through carelessness and, second, that the Epicurean will continue even to forge new friendships and embark on new activities once he has come to the correct understanding of death. This sounds like a direct denial of the charge brought by some critics that, on pain of inconsistency and the threat of making death a potential harm, the Epicurean ought not to forge such ties if he is to remain free from the anxieties that death may break them. It is nevertheless possible to argue that an Epicurean friendship may be an altogether different thing from a more common understanding of the same attachment, perhaps allowing that an Epicurean will take up new activities and forge new friendships always on the understanding that they are liable to be cut short by death. In that case the Epicurean's psychological commitment to these friends, for example, would be rather unlike that of most people for whom it does indeed appear that death may curtail a beneficial interpersonal relationship or prevent the attainment of some long-term goal.[77] Some may find that the required psychological state is so unlike what most of us would consider a commitment to a friendship or some goal that it is in fact misleading to call it a commitment at all. After all, the Epicurean presumably enters these arrangements convinced that no harm would be done were they to be curtailed at any time by death. Nevertheless, we can say from this passage that the Epicureans appear to have been aware of the need to offer a picture of a life lived with the correct view of death which was not entirely passive nor free from the possibility of conceiving new interests

---

[77] Cf. Indelli and Tsouna-McKirahan 1995, 223–4: 'The way in which the Epicurean gets involved in his occupations and attachments differs from the ways of other men. For the Epicurean knows all along that his existence is ephemeral and is ready to give up his hopes and plans at any given moment, whereas "the many" develop psychological commitments which presuppose that one will live forever.'

and new ties of affection.[78] Just how they justified this to themselves is not clear from the evidence we have, and there are good reasons to think that it would be a difficult task to offer any strong justification.

The author also insists, towards the end of the passage, that the Epicurean will even undergo possibly painful treatment to ward off and cure illness. This can be justified in terms of the common evaluation of present and future pains: it is better to undergo some uncomfortable treatment now in order to avoid longer-term or greater pain in the future.[79] There is no need in this case to insist that the prime motivation for undergoing treatment is the simple desire to continue to live. Rather, this Epicurean expects to live on and is merely ensuring that while he is alive he enjoys more pleasure and less pain and discomfort.

Suicide and positive reasons for living

The emerging picture of the Epicureans' view on the value of continuing a life is further complicated by the Epicureans' own attitude to suicide. For the most part, they seem to take a generally negative attitude to the practice, in contrast to the Stoics.[80] Indeed, the Epicureans often seem to portray the active pursuit of death as caused, paradoxically, by the very fear of death they promise to remove.

> et saepe usque adeo mortis formidine vitae
> percipit humanos odium lucisque videndae
> ut sibi consciscant maerenti pectore letum
> obliti fontem curarum hunc esse timorem.

And often, through fearing death does such a hatred of life and of seeing the light afflict humans that with grieving heart they fashion a death for themselves, forgetting that this very fear is the source of their concerns.

Lucr. *DRN* 3.79–82

---

[78] We might compare this passage with Philodemus *De Morte* XXXVIII. 14–19 (above p. 152) where the wise man lives 'already prepared for burial' but enjoys each day as it comes.

[79] See also Indelli and Tsouna-McKirahan 1995, 226–7.

[80] For further discussion see Englert 1994, Cooper 1999.

Lucretius does not make clear in this passage just how a fear of death can induce suicidal thoughts, but presumably the thought is that the fear of death so affects some people that they cannot manage to find anything of value or find any pleasure in life. Instead, they are constantly assailed by paralysing fear to such a degree that—paradoxically and irrationally—they see suicide as the only end to their ills.[81]

Of course, the Epicureans do agree that suicide would be the end of these people's cares, but it is certainly not the preferred course of action. If only these poor souls would instead find out from the Epicureans that death is nothing to fear, then they would be able to manage their lives properly and find true pleasure in it. Suicide, therefore, is generally a sign of having seriously misguided opinions about the world. However, there are clearly occasions and circumstances when an Epicurean too would be justified in ending his own life. While extolling the virtue of courage, Torquatus allows that in the face of certain pains suicide might be acceptable:

sic robustus animus ... ad dolores ita paratus est ut meminerit maximos morte finiri, parvos multa habere intervalla requietis, mediocrium nos esse dominos ut si tolerabiles sint feramus, si minus, animo aequo e vita, cum ea non placeat, tamquam e theatro exeamus.

A strong soul is so readied against pains that it remembers that the greatest are curtailed by death, the small ones are punctuated by long intervals of peace, and we are in control of those of a medium strength so that if they can be endured we endure them and if not we may leave life calmly if it does not please us, just as we may leave the theatre.

Cic. *Fin.* I.49

The message here is that someone properly schooled can endure even quite severe pains, but if even this ability is challenged by ongoing and unendurable distress then it is open to us to leave life. Importantly, this is done calmly and rationally (*aequo animo*);[82]

---

[81] Cf. Sen. *Ep. Mor.* 24.22–4, 70.8–9, Democritus B199–201, on which: Warren 2002c, 36–8. Lucretius himself is famously supposed to have committed suicide according to the brief biography included by Jerome in his additions to Eusebius' Chronicle for 94/93 BC. It is generally thought that this is unlikely to be based in any historical fact. See Bailey 1947, vol. I, 8–12; Gain 1969; Rouse and Smith 1982, pp. xviii–xxvi.   [82] Cf. Lucr. *DRN* 3.939.

it is the result of a calculation that the alternative would be a continued life of pain. Provided life has pleasure left in it. we will continue to live. And the Epicurean sage will be sufficiently schooled to continue to find pleasure in life under conditions which others would find unbearable—Epicurus' own example of composure in the face of terminal illness demonstrates this.[83]

Seneca reports the suicide of an Epicurean named Diodorus. On this occasion it is not so clear whether or not he is acting in strict accordance with Epicurean teaching.

Diodorum, Epicureum philosophum, qui intra paucos dies finem vitae suae manu sua imposuit, negant ex decreto Epicuri fecisse, quod sibi gulam praesecuit. alii dementiam videri volunt factum hoc eius, alii temeritatem; ille interim beatus ac plenus bona conscientia reddidit sibi testimonium vita excedens laudavitque aetatis in portu et ad ancoram actae quietem et dixit, quod vos inviti audistis, quasi vobis quoque faciendum sit, 'vixi et quem dederat cursum fortuna peregi' (=Verg. *Aen.* 4.653).

They say that the Epicurean philosopher Diodorus, who just recently ended his own life by his own hand, did not act according to Epicurus' doctrine because he cut his own throat. Some want this deed to be seen as madness, others as rashness. But he, happy and full of good understanding, bore witness to himself as he left life, praised the tranquillity of a life spent in port at anchor,[84] and said something which you did not like to hear, as if you too ought to follow its advice: 'I have lived, and finished the course which fortune dealt me'.

Sen. De Vita Beata 19.1

Again, the accusation of un-Epicurean behaviour seems to be on the basis of Diodorus acting not out of a sound and rational consideration of the situation but out of either madness or temperance. Seneca, however, is keen to emphasize Diodorus' calm at the end, based not only on the appreciation of a tranquil life lived but also on the acceptance that that life had come to the end of its course. What is not clear from this description is just why Diodorus had decided to quit a pleasant life, and this is presumably the reason why some were suspicious of his motives.

---

[83] D.L. 10.15, 22. Compare also the example of Bassus Aufidius, the model of fortitude offered by Seneca in *Ep. Mor.* 30.

[84] Perhaps an allusion to *Sent. Vat.* 17.

If his life really was happy and contented, then there seems no reason to end it. These suspicions are perhaps reinforced by Diodorus' dramatic method of suicide and his chosen epitaph. While his words may sound like a calm acceptance of one's fate, they were originally spoken by Vergil's Dido, certainly not an exemplar of measured and rationally calculated suicide. In that case, the doubts about Diodorus centre not so much on the fact that he committed suicide, but on the question whether he did so properly and for the right Epicurean reasons.

Lucretius offers one notable example of a laudable suicide in the section of *DRN* 3 which lists a gallery of noble dead. Democritus appears in the penultimate position, followed only by Epicurus himself.

> denique Democritum postquam matura vetustas
> admonuit memores motus languescere mentis,
> sponte sua leto caput obvius obtulit ipse.

Again, Democritus, after ripe old age warned him that his mind's memory was failing, of his own accord offered up his life to death.

3.1039–41

There are other versions of Democritus' death, some of which stress not that Democritus died voluntarily but that he was able to postpone his death in order to allow his sister to attend the festival of the Thesmophoria.[85] Here, however, Lucretius emphasizes the story that Democritus committed suicide only once he had realized that his mental faculties were failing. More specifically, the failure of his memory prompted his action. Perhaps this is intended to recall the story of Epicurus' own death in which it is supposed that Epicurus counteracted pain by recalling pleasant past experiences. If Democritus' memory failed, then such practices would have been impossible for him and perhaps he therefore realized that a continued life under such circumstances would be inevitably painful. It is also possible that this is supposed to note that, for Democritus at least, intellectual pursuits are a necessary part of a worthwhile life and memory a necessary condition for being able to engage in such pursuits successfully. In that case also this situation is one in which the

---

[85] D.L. 9.43. There are similar stories of Democritus deliberately blinding himself. See Warren 2002c, 127–8.

alternative to death is a life of misery. In that case, in Lucretius'
eyes, suicide was the right option.[86]

The general picture is that the Epicureans allowed suicide only
under the extreme circumstances of inevitable and insupportable
pains. Such occasions would be very rare indeed, since the
Epicureans also argued—implausibly, perhaps—that a wise man
would be able to counteract almost all distress and continue to
live a pleasant life. Even so, the problem remains. What positive
reason can the Epicureans offer for wanting to continue to live
such a life? Even the wise man, it seems, will have to expend no
small effort in counteracting the pains to which he will be
subjected and we are also told that there is no greater value in
living even a good life for as long as possible. Death, on the other
hand, is easily achieved and promises the cessation of all pain
and discomfort.

The position has reached something of a stalemate since, of
course, the Epicurean living the good life will not, it is expected,
have any positive reason to commit suicide. Here we may find the
answer to the dilemma: the Epicureans do not offer a positive
reason to continue to live the good life since they do not see that
there is any particular reason why such a positive recommendation is needed. The default assumption, as it were, is that one will
continue to live unless and until such a time when life becomes
too painful even for the Epicurean wise man. After all, until such
a time the Epicurean's life is a pleasant and happy one. True, its
value is not being increased by duration, but neither would
anything be gained by curtailing it.

> natus enim debet quicumque est velle manere
> in vita, donec retinebit blanda voluptas.
> qui numquam vero vitae gustavit amorem
> nec fuit in numero, quid obset non esse creatum?

For anyone who has been born ought to want to remain alive for as long
as sweet pleasure retains him. But he who has never even tasted the love
of life, and has not been among the living, what is it to him not to have
been created?

Lucr. *DRN* 5.177–80

---

[86] There are other Epicurean recommendations of suicide in what we might
call dialectical contexts. At *Ep. Men.* 126–7 Epicurus asks an objector who claims
that it would be better never to have been born why he does not therefore

This argument appears during Lucretius' attack on creator gods. World-creation would serve no good either for the gods or for us. The second pair of lines restates the Epicurean view that not being, indeed never having been, is not itself a harm. This has appeared a number of times already in the arguments against fearing death, in the view that death is non-existence and therefore not a harm and also in the Symmetry Argument's premise that the time before we came to be was not a time when we could be harmed or benefited. Now Lucretius offers the bald assertion that non-existence *per se* is no bad thing, casting this in the deliberately paradoxical terms of considering someone non-existent, indeed never-to-exist, and seeing if they suffer as a result. This much is consistent with the opening premise of the Symmetry Argument: prenatal non-existence is not an evil. Permanent non-existence is no evil either. More important for the present discussion are the first two lines, which seem to offer some reason why one ought to want to continue to live. So long as life is pleasant then one will want to live, no doubt with the proviso that all the time one will be aware that should death arrive it will not reduce the value of a life by reducing its duration.

All the same, this is not a particularly satisfying conclusion. The Epicureans appear to offer no significant positive reason for wishing to continue to live, beyond a mere inertia. If life is pleasant there is no reason to curtail it. This amounts to saying that the Epicurean will simply continue to live with no sufficient reason either to kill himself or to want to survive until tomorrow. As a picture of the happy life this is quite unappealing, but it is clear why the Epicureans have allowed themselves to be pushed into this position. So great is their emphasis on removing any sense in which death might be an evil, they have left themselves with precious few resources to explain why continued life is worth pursuing.[87] True, it may be allowed that the person trying to attain the good life has a reason to continue to live, since he has a

immediately kill himself. Similarly, at *DRN* 3.940–3 Nature asks someone who claims never to have found any permanent pleasure in life why he does not simply end it all.

[87] Williams 1976, 207, expresses this in terms of what he calls 'categorical desires': 'Most people have many categorical desires, which do not depend upon the assumption of their own existence, since they serve to prevent that assumption's being questioned, or to answer the question if it is raised'. The presence of

project and a goal which he would benefit from reaching. But this also leaves him prey to the possibility of a premature death—a death before he has attained that goal. For those who are so misguided as to see no good in the Epicurean life and who therefore have absolutely no prospect of ever reaching a good life (even though there may be very few of these) death would in fact be better than the life of unending misery they face. Also, those who have attained the Epicurean good life, if death is truly 'nothing at all' to them, seem equally unable to offer any positive picture of continued life.

One proposed defence of the Epicurean position argues that the Epicurean should feel no such constraints in the sort of desires he may conceive. Indeed, he can conceive just the sort of desires the prospect of whose fulfilment would give a sufficient reason to continue living. The core of this defence is the contention that at no point, even when considering future death, will the Epicurean think that death may frustrate desires, since the Epicurean is sure that his desires—fulfilled or unfulfilled—will die with him.[88] At no point, therefore, is the Epicurean prevented from finding reasons to live out of a determination not to allow himself desires which could be frustrated, since death cannot truly frustrate desires. But there is still a lingering suspicion in my mind at least, that a desire or goal held in such a way—held with the thought that it will not matter if its attainment is prevented by death—is not held with sufficient strength for it to function as a reason to continue to live.

A similar defence may suggest that it is perfectly possible to desire something without thereby being distressed by the thought that the object of desire may never be obtained. In other words, it is possible to desire something without this desire also implying a concern should the object of desire never be obtained. In this way an Epicurean may continue to desire things, and these desires would form reasons for action by setting various goals and

these desires, therefore, is sufficient to answer the question why we should not immediately opt for suicide. Luper-Foy 1987, 238, has a similar account, aimed specifically at the Epicureans: 'Epicureans never regard dying as a misfortune. But I have said that they would *have* to regard it as a misfortune if death thwarted desires whose satisfaction would be fulfilling. Hence Epicureans must not *have* any fulfilling desires that can be frustrated by death!'

[88] Rosenbaum 1989a.

objects of pursuit, but by doing so the Epicurean does not lay himself open to the fear of these goals being unfulfilled or the anxiety caused by feeling that it would be bad should these projects or goals not be attained. The desires are insufficiently strong to bring along with them these accompanying anxieties about the prospects of their fulfilment, yet they are sufficient to provide reasons for action and reasons to continue wanting to live. It is still questionable whether such a compromise position can be sustained. It is clearly conceivable that a person may desire something but with insufficient strength that he should also fear or be anxious at the thought of not obtaining the object of the desire. I may, for example, desire the very latest music system, but not feel any anxiety at the thought that I may never own it. But it is plausible to think that although there may be these 'weaker' desires, it is precisely because they can be held without any significant concern about whether they will be fulfilled or not that they cannot provide sufficient grounds to serve as motivations for action or as reasons for continuing to live. I 'desire' that music system only in the sense that on seeing an advertisement in a magazine I imagine that it would be pleasant to own such a thing. I certainly do not desire it sufficiently to save up to buy one. If I were to desire it with sufficient strength to be motivated to take steps to obtain it, then I would also feel disappointment if I should fail to obtain it, and antecedent anxiety over my chances of obtaining it.

It is difficult to see, therefore, that a desire can be strong enough to motivate an agent to act but be weak enough that the individual should remain entirely indifferent to its fulfilment. Further, the problem for the Epicurean is that in order not to fear death at all, in order not to feel anxious at the thought that he might die and be prevented from obtaining some goal, it appears that there should be no desires held with sufficient strength that they are accompanied by an anxiety about their fulfilment. In that case, it is indeed difficult to see how they could identify a set of desires which the wise man could retain and seek to fulfil while remaining entirely free from any concerns about death.

6

Conclusions

[κατακολουθῶ δέ σοι ταῦτα] | περὶ τοῦ θανάτου λέγον|τι καὶ
πέπεικάς με κα|ταγελᾶν αὐτοῦ.

I agree with what you say about death, and you have
persuaded me to laugh in its face.

Diogenes of Oinoanda, 73.I.1–3 Smith

In the pseudo-Platonic dialogue *Axiochus*. Socrates tells of his
being called to see Axiochus, the father of Clinias. Axiochus has
been unwell and is rather old. He does not have long to live and
the thought of his imminent death is causing him immense
worry. Socrates is asked by Axiochus' friends and family to come
and offer some sort of consolation or philosophical counselling
to help to ward off these anxieties.

At the beginning of the dialogue Axiochus confesses that
although he knows a variety of arguments which purport to
show that death is not something to be feared, he nevertheless
finds himself beset by various anxieties now that death is at hand.
He still feels concerned that when dead he may feel deprived of
the goods of life and lie as a rotting and forgotten corpse (365c).
Socrates' response is to offer a heady mix of arguments, some
clearly like the Epicurean arguments we have surveyed in this
study and others from a more Platonist perspective. He stresses
the fact that death is the absence of sensation and that Axiochus
feels no distress at the thought of the time before his birth (365d–e).
He also argues that since death is the destruction of the person it
cannot constitute a harm: there simply is no one there to be
harmed (369b–c). In addition, he offers a long discussion of the
evils of life, its hardships and miseries (366d–369b), and also
claims that in fact life is merely the imprisonment of the
immortal soul in a physical body. Death is therefore a liberation
of one's true self (365e–366b).

Axiochus admits that these are clever arguments, but he remains critical of their therapeutic powers.

σὺ μὲν ἐκ τῆς ἐπιπολαζούσης τὰ νῦν λεσχηνείας τὰ σοφὰ ταῦτα προῄρηκας· ἐκεῖθεν γάρ ἐστιν ἥδε ἡ φλυαρολογία πρὸς τὰ μειράκια διακεκοσμημένη· ἐμὲ δὲ ἡ στέρησις τῶν ἀγαθῶν τοῦ ζῆν λυπεῖ, κἂν πιθανωτέρους τούτων λόγους ἀπτικροτήσῃς, ὦ Σώκρατες. οὐκ ἐπαΐει γὰρ ὁ νοῦς ἀποπλανώμενος εἰς εὐεπείας λόγων, οὐδὲ ἅπτεται ταῦτα τῆς ὁμοχροίας, ἀλλ' εἰς μὲν πομπὴν καὶ ῥημάτων ἀγλαϊσμὸν ἀνύτει, τῆς δὲ ἀληθείας ἀποδεῖ. τὰ δὲ παθήματα σοφισμάτων οὐκ ἀνέχεται, μόνοις δὲ ἀρκεῖται τοῖς δυναμένοις καθικέσθαι τῆς ψυχῆς.

You have offered these clever thoughts from the rubbish that's fashionable these days. That's where this silly talk fashioned for the young comes from. But the deprivation of the goods of life still pains me, and will do even if you come up instead with some arguments even more persuasive than these, Socrates. You see, my mind doesn't understand but is carried along by the eloquence of the arguments. They don't even touch the surface but do produce a fine parade of words. They just fall short of the truth. My woes are not relieved by clever arguments; only those that can get through to my soul will do.

369d1–e2

Axiochus is not the most perceptive follower of a philosophical argument, and his complaint here combines a number of different criticisms. The arguments he has heard so far seem both to be too clever and beguiling, but also not to be persuasive enough. Yet he claims that even if Socrates were to construct some more persuasive arguments these too would not work. Second, he points to a failure on his own part to follow the arguments carefully and completely but then seems to turn this into a failure on the part of the arguments themselves—they are too beguiling for him to internalize them.

Clearly, the *Axiochus* is indebted in no small part to Epicurean arguments of the sort we have been considering throughout this study. It is perhaps not coincidental that Axiochus begins to feel comforted only when Socrates offers him some more detailed thoughts about the immortality of the soul and some eschatological theory taught to him by one Gobryas, a Persian sage. (In fact, this therapy is almost too good. Axiochus begins to long for death: 372a.)[1] Epicurean-style arguments, we can infer from

---

[1] This is a potential problem for Platonism. See Warren 2001c.

this dramatic reversal in Axiochus' spirits, are merely eloquent diversions for the young. Real therapy is to be found elsewhere. Nevertheless, Axiochus' complaints may be brought against the Epicurean arguments which we have been considering. Just how effective are these arguments against the many different fears of death? Crucially, Axiochus' complaints ask us to consider not just their argumentative power—their validity and form—but also whether they are psychologically effective. Can they manage, in Axiochus' words, to 'get through to the soul' ($\kappa\alpha\theta\iota\kappa\epsilon\sigma\theta\alpha\iota$ $\tau\hat{\eta}s$ $\psi\upsilon\chi\hat{\eta}s$)? Let us conclude, therefore, by considering both these criteria of assessment.

First, we can produce a summary of the structure of the Epicureans' arguments against the fears of death and identify areas of strength and weakness. Epicurus' primary argument against the fear of the state of being dead, which is expressed in various related forms in *KΔ* 2, in the *Letter to Menoeceus* 124–5, and by Lucretius at *DRN* 3.830–1, is powerful and convincing if we grant two crucial assumptions. First, he needs us to agree that for something to be good or bad for some person that something (or perhaps, some effect or consequence of that something) must be perceived by that person. This is a founding principle of Epicurean ethical thought and a central thesis of his hedonism. Second, he must persuade us that death is the destruction if not of the person entirely (which is in fact the strong thesis the Epicureans do assert), then at least of the person's abilities to perceive. Granted these two theses, being dead cannot be bad. If the first thesis is denied, as for example Nagel would wish us to do, then the road is open for the exploration of other kinds of harm—relational or comparative harms—which might allow one to say that even if we allow the second Epicurean thesis, nevertheless being dead can detract from the value of a person's life in comparison with a longer or alternative life. There is a fundamental difference of opinion between Epicurean ethics which insists that there are no unperceived harms and the alternative account which insists that there are. In maintaining his own position, however, the Epicurean is not merely being stubborn in the face of compelling counterexamples. Epicurus has his own arguments for the premise that pleasure is the only good and pain the only bad and that therefore 'every good and evil resides in perception' (*Ep. Men.* 124). He could also offer strong criticisms of his opponent's view and the relational or comparative account of the harm of death it offers. In particular, he can reply that its analysis of benefit and harm is potentially too broad; it is difficult to see how limits could be set on true claims of benefit or harm if all that is required is that a comparison be offered between a life actually lived and a life one *could have* lived. What bounds can be set on the realm of possibilities encompassed or excluded by the crucial '*could have*' in this analysis? Most generally, we can conclude that it is relatively easy to see how, given the acceptance of relational or comparative harms, these might with some further specifications be used to give an account of the harm of death. But this does not provide any reasons for accepting that there are such relational or comparative harms in the first place.

The famous Symmetry Argument as found in Lucretius merely secures the same conclusion as can be derived from the two central Epicurean principles (the premise that all good and evil reside in perception and the premise that death is annihilation) by other means, relying on the common belief that pre-natal non-existence is not a harm and the more controversial claim that it is relevantly like *post mortem* non-existence. In that case, it is not the more interesting argument against the prospective fear of death that some have claimed it to be. Nevertheless, even if it is a further argument against the possibility of *post mortem* harm it still produces difficulties for those who wish to maintain the possibility of such harms. Those who wish to deny the Epicurean thesis that being dead cannot be a harm, however, must find some way to counter this argument too. For the most part, they agree with the Epicureans over the value of pre-natal non-existence and therefore must try to deny the relevant symmetry between this and *post mortem* non-existence. Just how this is to be done, however, is a complex matter and demands some account of personal identity which denies the possibility of some given person being born earlier while allowing the possibility that the same given person, once alive, could die later. Even if this symmetry is conclusively denied the Epicureans can retreat and claim they have in any case secured their central thesis by a simpler route, namely via the earlier and simpler arguments that there are no unperceived harms and that there is no *post mortem* subject available to be harmed. At this stage the debate returns to the question of the possibility of unperceived and—importantly—unperceivable harms.

Many commentators have been happy to grant to the Epicureans some success at showing that being dead is not an evil, but object that this is not in fact the central cause of the 'fear of death'. I hope to have shown in response how the Epicureans deal both with the fear of mortality—the fear that life will end sometime—and the fear that death may end *too soon*. They manage this even without needing to use a form of the Symmetry Argument which deals with retrospective and prospective attitudes towards non-existence. Their major contention here is that a life will not be made better if it merely accumulates goods. Many are inclined to agree with this, but think it addresses merely the first of these fears, the fear of mortality. Certainly, if a life is not improved by mere accumulation of goods, an infinitely long life has more chance of being a good life than a finitely long life. However, if the value of a life is not diminished simply by its being finite, it may nevertheless be diminished by its being too short. In that case, although we may have a reason not to fear the fact that we will die at some time in the future, we may well have reason to be anxious not to die too soon. We may reasonably desire to postpone death for as long as possible, without necessarily wanting never to die. In answer to this last fear of premature death, the Epicureans offer a radical conception of what makes a life complete, based on their controversial and idiosyncratic hedonist theory. This is perhaps the least plausible of the Epicurean arguments, not simply because it relies heavily on other aspects of Epicurean theory (since, of course, so did the argument of $K\Delta$ 2), but because it relies heavily on counterintuitive and highly debatable elements of that Epicurean theory, in particular the claim that pleasure cannot be increased beyond the absence of all pain. Whereas it is easy to share the Epicureans' own premises which generated the argument of $K\Delta$ 2, or at least premises which are relevantly similar and can do the same argumentative job by showing that the soul—or the person—is mortal, in the case of the arguments against premature death the required premises about the nature of pleasure and the complete life are hard to find plausible or attractive. Even so, that is the Epicurean conception of what makes a life complete. It is not the case, therefore, that they had nothing to say about the question of a premature death. What they did have to say, however, may not be particularly attractive given not only its controversial basis but also the extremely revisionary nature of a life which would emerge if we grant the full force of the claim that 'death is nothing to us'.

A more devastating set of criticisms of Epicurean theory can be constructed by following through the consequences of the full endorsement of its desired conclusions. Not only would practices such as the writing of wills seem to lack rational foundation but, more powerfully, it also becomes unclear why an Epicurean who thinks that death would not diminish the value of his life in the slightest should expend any effort continuing to live. A powerful and arresting dilemma looms. Either, it seems, there is a value in prolonging one's life, in which case there appears to be the possibility that death may diminish the value of a life (and therefore it is rational to feel anxious about this) or, if death cannot diminish the value of a life, then there appears to be no strong reason to prolong that life. If life is worth living then it is worth being anxious that it might be cut short. The Epicureans seem prepared to pay for the prize of a life free from fear by offering a picture of an ideal life in which one is not at all concerned about the prolongation of that life. Most would, I think, prefer to think that life is worth continuing to live (for some reasonable amount of time, if not forever), accepting that the price of this is the background anxiety that death may come too soon. In fact, this anxiety that a project or plan may be curtailed could even be seen as part of what it is for the project or plan to be worth pursuing.

This is the picture I wish to offer of the Epicureans' assault on the fear of death. It is a complex assault, combining arguments against the evil of death and arguments for the value of a life in which certain fears of death have been excluded. And it is in parts a particularly powerful assault, especially against the fear of the state of being dead. But is it a persuasive and attractive set of arguments? Ought we to be more impressed than Axiochus?

I have already noted the philosophical and theoretical weaknesses in the Epicureans' arguments. But there are in addition numerous reasons why we might doubt in principle the power of rational argument to cure such ills as the fear of death. Even if the Epicureans' arguments were entirely sound, would they command universal assent? Would they persuade us even then not to fear death? It is possible to think that there are, in addition to rationally justified opinions and beliefs about what is and is not of value, other sources of motivation within us, perhaps not so amenable or perhaps not amenable at all to rational persuasion. Emotions, fears, and desires may be thought to have at least some non-rational elements but nevertheless be motivationally effective. If the fear of death is generated or sustained from these sources then the Epicurean rational therapy, even an ideal rational therapy, will not be so effective. No therapy based solely on reason and argument will stand a chance of total success. Nevertheless, it will still have some power if we agree that there is at least some use in rational argument, something most people would grant provided they think that there is any sense in which ethical argument can affect changes in what people value. To the extent, therefore, that rational argument is allowed an influence or restraining force on our emotions, then, to that extent, even on this conception of our moral psychology the Epicurean arguments will have some force. Even on this view, they cannot be dismissed entirely.

A related, perhaps more modern, psychological theory finds similar reasons to doubt that the fear of death in particular is entirely, if at all, susceptible to rational therapy. Some may think that it is a fear which lurks predominately at the level of the unconscious or subconscious and cannot be immediately addressed by conscious rational thought. If this is indeed true, and I have no intention of trying to settle the issue here, then the Epicureans' preferred method of addressing these fears is once again threatened. (As I have noted already, there are those who interpret Lucretius as a poet who recognized such sources of motivation and distress and see his poetry as a means of addressing these unconscious and irrational fears.)[2]

For their part, the Epicureans remain convinced of the power of rational argument and persuasion to remove the debilitating

---

[2] See, for example, Segal 1990, 5–25, and 11: 'The combination of common-sense argumentation, the "hard" evidence of Epicurean science, and the humane wisdom and authority of an ancient poetic tradition enables him to meet diverse anxieties at many levels and for many different kinds of readers'.

fear of death.[3] This assumption is a consequence of their general intellectualist stance on the emotions, which they tend to analyse as based in value judgements. Value judgements are at least necessary conditions of emotions such as fear, longing, anger, and so on. So the various fears of death are caused by various judgements of the form: 'it is bad that X', where X can be 'I will die', 'I might die earlier than later', and so on. The arguments are designed to remove these opinions and therefore remove the related fears.[4] Someone like Axiochus would appear to be a counterexample to this view. After all, he has heard the relevant Epicurean-style arguments but still fears death. Perhaps, therefore, the fear of death is not so amenable to rational inspection and criticism. There are obvious replies for the Epicurean to make. Perhaps Axiochus has not in fact understood the arguments and needs them to be further explained. Perhaps like the person whom Lucretius describes, who still feels anxiety at the thought of what will happen to his corpse although he claims not to believe that he will survive death, there is some difficulty in fully integrating the correct opinions drawn from the Epicurean arguments with other potentially conflicting opinions he also holds. Epicurus is under no illusion that there may be difficulties in fully understanding and coming to terms with the revisionary view he is offering. He begins the section on the fear of death in the *Letter to Menoeceus* with the recommendation that we are to 'accustom ourselves' (συνέθιζε, *Ep. Men.* 124) to the thought that death is nothing to us. This thought is not something which can simply and immediately be integrated into our beliefs, since it requires a reconsideration of many other attitudes and beliefs about our lives and the value of what we do. As ever, the Epicureans recommend constant attention to these arguments, and the constant recollection of their conclusions through the contemplation of the *Kyriai Doxai* and the words of Epicurus himself. The *Letter to Menoeceus* ends by recommending that the Epicurean reader should practise these thoughts day and night, rehearsing and remembering them. Nevertheless, the overwhelming

---

[3] See e.g. Lucr. *DRN* 3.1068–75 for an insistence on the power of studying *natura rerum* for removing the fear of death.

[4] See *KΔ* 20: reason (διάνοια) drives out the fear of the infinite and makes life complete. Cf. Nussbaum 1994, 104–39.

conviction is that argument and rational persuasion are the appropriate, indeed the only, tools for the important job of healing our opinions and setting us on the path towards the good life. Still, we can be sure that Epicurus would not think that Axiochus is merely too old or too near to death to be properly affected by these arguments. After all, he begins the *Letter to Menoeceus* with the assertion that both the young and the old can come profitably to study philosophy:

οὔτε γὰρ ἄωρος οὐδείς ἐστιν οὔτε πάρωρος πρὸς τὸ κατὰ ψυχὴν ὑγιαῖνον.

No one is either too early or too late for the health of the soul.

Ep. Men. 122

Although it is never too late to begin, Epicurean philosophy is not a 'quick fix'. Axiochus should have studied longer and harder before now. Had he done so, perhaps these arguments would have got through to his soul, lodged there, and been integrated fully into his other beliefs, transforming his view of a good life and his view of death.

REFERENCES

ALBERTI, A. 1990. 'Paura della morte e identità personale nell'epicureismo', in A. Alberti (ed.) *Logica, mente, persona*. Florence: 151–206.

—— 1995. 'The Epicurean Theory of Law and Justice', in A. Laks and M. Schofield (eds.) *Justice and Generosity*. Cambridge: 161–90.

ALGRA, K. A., Koenen, M. H., and Schrijvers, P. H. (eds.) 1997. *Lucretius and his Intellectual Background*. Amsterdam.

AMERIO, R. 1952. 'L'epicureismo e la morte'. *Filosofia* 3: 541–76.

ANNAS, J. 1992. *Hellenistic Philosophy of Mind*. Berkeley.

—— 1993. *The Morality of Happiness*. Oxford.

ARMSTRONG, D. 2004. 'All Things to All Men: Philodemus' Model of Therapy and the Audience of *De morte*', in J. Fitzgerald, G. Holland, and D. Obbink (eds.) *Philodemus and the New Testament world*. Leiden: 15–54.

ARONOFF, P. 1997. 'Lucretius and the Fears of Death'. Ph.D. dissertation, Cornell University.

BAILEY, C. 1927. *Epicurus: The Extant Remains*. Oxford.

—— 1947. *Titi Lucretii Cari de rerum natura libri sex*. 3 vols. Oxford.

BARNES, J. 1983. 'Ancient Skepticism and Causation', in M. F. Burnyeat (ed.) *The Skeptical Tradition*. Berkeley: 149–203.

BELSHAW, C. 1993. 'Asymmetry and Non-existence'. *Phil. Studies* 70: 103–16.

BENN, P. 1998. 'Morality, the Unborn, and the Open Future', in R. Le Poidevin (ed.) 1998: 207–19.

BIGELOW, J., CAMPBELL, J., and PARGETTER, R. 1990. 'Death and Well-being' *Pacific Philosophical Quarterly* 71: 119–40.

BLANK, D. 1998. *Sextus Empiricus: Against the Grammarians*. Oxford.

BOBZIEN, S. 1998. *Determinism and Freedom in Stoic Philosophy*. Oxford.

BOSWELL, J. 1777. 'An Account of my Last Interview with David Hume esq.', in Boswell's Journal. See C. McC. Weis and F. A. Pottle (eds.) *Boswell. In Extremes. 1776–1778*. London: 11–15.

BRANDT, R. B. 1992. 'The Morality and Rationality of Suicide', in his *Morality, Utilitarianism, and Rights*. Cambridge.

BRINK, D. O. 1990. 'Rational Egoism, Self, and Others', in O. Flanagan and A. O. Rorty (eds.) *Identity, Character and Morality: Essays in Moral Psychology*. Cambridge, Mass.: 339–78.

BROWN, E. 2002. 'Epicurus on the Value of Friendship (*Sententia Vaticana* XXIII)'. *CPh* 97: 68–80.

BROWN, P. M. 1997. *Lucretius. De Rerum Natura III (edition, translation, commentary)*. Warminster.

BRUECKNER, A. L. and FISCHER, J. M. 1986. 'Why is Death Bad?'. *Phil. Studies*. 50: 213–21.

—— —— 1993a. 'Death's Badness'. *Pacific Philosophical Quarterly* 74: 37–45.

—— —— 1993b. 'The Asymmetry of Early Birth and Late Death'. *Phil. Studies*. 71: 327–31.

—— —— 1998. 'Being Born Earlier'. *Australasian Journal of Philosophy* 76: 110–14.

BRUNSCHWIG, J. 1986. 'The Cradle Argument in Epicureanism and Stoicism', in M. Schofield and G. Striker (eds.) *The Norms of Nature*. Cambridge: 113–44.

CALLAHAN, J. C. 1987. 'On Harming the Dead'. *Ethics* 97: 341–52.

CAPASSO, M. 1987. *Comunità senza rivolta: quattro saggi sull'epicureismo*. Naples.

—— 1988. *Carneisco: il secondo libro del* Filista *(PHerc. 1027)*. Naples.

CASSIUS, D. 1868. *Das Metroon in Athen als Staatsarchiv*. Berlin.

CHAMPLIN, E. 1991. *Final Judgements: Duty and Emotion in Roman Wills 300 B.C.–A.D. 250*. Berkeley.

CHIESARA, M. L. 2001. *Aristocles of Messene: Testimonies and Fragments*. Oxford.

CLAY, D. 1982. 'Epicurus in the Archives of Athens', in *Studies in Attic Epigraphy, History, and Topography presented to Eugene Vanderpool, Hesperia* suppl. 19: 17–26.

—— 1983. *Lucretius and Epicurus*. Ithaca.

—— 1986. 'The Cults of Epicurus'. *CErc* 16: 12–28.

COCKBURN, D. 1990. *Other Human Beings*. London.

—— 1997. *Other Times: Philosophical Perspectives on Past, Present, and Future*. Cambridge.

—— 1998. 'Tense and Emotion', in R. Le Poidevin (ed.) 1998: 77–91.

COOPER, J. 1999. 'Greek Philosophers on Euthanasia and Suicide', in his *Reason and Emotion: Essays on Ancient Moral Psychology and Ethical Theory*. Princeton: 515–41.

DAINTON, B. 2001. *Time and Space*. Chesham.

DECLEVA CAIZZI, F. 1993. 'Early Hellenistic Images of Philosophical Life', in A. W. Bulloch et al. (eds.) *Images and Ideologies: Self-definition in the Hellenistic World*. Berkeley: 303–29.

DIANO, C. 1974. *Epicuri ethica et epistulae*. Florence.

DONNELLY, J. 1994. 'The Misfortunate Dead: A Problem for Materialism', in his (ed.) *Language, Metaphysics and Death* (2nd edn.). New York: 153–69.

DORANDI, T. 2000. 'Plotina, Adriano e gli Epicurei di Atene', in M. Erler (ed.) 2000: 137–48.

DRAPER, K. 1999. 'Disappointment, Sadness, and Death'. *Phil. Rev.* 108: 387–414.

ENGLERT, W. 1994. 'Stoics and Epicureans on the Nature of Suicide'. *Proceedings of the Boston Area Colloquium in Ancient Philosophy* 10: 67–98.

ENRIGHT, D. J. 1983. *The Oxford Book of Death.* Oxford.

ERLER, M. (ed.) 2000. *Epikureismus in der späten Republik under der Kaiserzeit. Akten der 2. Tagung der Karl-und-Gertrud-Abel-Stiftung vom 30. September–3 Oktober 1998 in Würzburg.* Stuttgart.

——— 2002. 'Epicurus as *deus mortalis*: *homoiosis theoi* and Epicurean Self-cultivation', in D. Frede and A. Laks (eds.) *Traditions of Theology: Studies in Hellenistic Theology, its Background and Aftermath.* Leiden: 159–81.

ERNOUT, A. and ROBIN, L. 1963. *Lucrèce de rerum natura* (2nd edn.). Paris.

EWIN, R. E. 2002. *Reasons and the Fear of Death.* Lanham, Md.

FEINBERG, J. 1984. *Harm to Others: The Moral Limits of the Criminal Law.* i. Oxford.

——— 1992. 'Wrongful Life and the Counterfactual Element in Harming', in his *Freedom and Fulfilment.* Princeton: 3–36.

——— 1993. 'Some Puzzles about the Evil of Death', in J. M. Fischer (ed.) 1993: 305–26.

FEIT, N. 2002. 'The Time of Death's Misfortune'. *Nous* 36: 359–93.

FELDMAN, F. 1990. 'F. M. Kamm and the Mirror of Time'. *Pacific Philosophical Quarterly* 71: 23–7.

——— 1992. *Confrontations with the Reaper. A Philosophical Study of the Nature and Value of Death.* Oxford.

——— 2004. *Pleasure and the Good Life.* Oxford.

FERRARI, F. 2000. 'La falsità delle asserzioni relative al futuro: un argumento epicureo contro la mantica in Plut. *Pyth. orac.* 10', in M. Erler (ed.) 2000: 149–63.

FISCHER, J. M. 1993. 'Introduction: Death, Metaphysics, and Morality', in his (ed.) *The Metaphysics of Death.* Stanford: 3–30.

——— 1994. 'Why Immortality is not so Bad'. *International Journal of Philosophical Studies* 2: 257–70.

——— 1999. 'Death, Badness, and the Impossibility of Experience'. *Journal of Ethics* 1: 341–53.

FREDE, D. 1985a. 'Rumpelstiltskin's Pleasures: True and False Pleasures in Plato's *Philebus*'. *Phronesis* 30: 151–80.

——— 1985b. 'The Sea-Battle Reconsidered: A Defence of the Traditional Interpretation'. *OSAPh* 3: 31–87.

——— 1990. 'Fatalism and Future Truth'. *Proceedings of the Boston Area Colloquium in Ancient Philosophy* 6: 195–227.

FURLEY, D. 1986. 'Nothing to Us?' in M. Schofield and G. Striker (eds.) *The Norms of Nature*. Cambridge: 75–91.

GAIN, D. B. 1969. 'The Life and Death of Lucretius'. *Latomus* 27: 545–53.

GALLOIS, A. 1994. 'Asymmetry in Attitudes and the Nature of Time'. *Phil. Studies* 76: 51–69.

GALLOWAY, A. 1986. 'Lucretius' Materialist Poetics: Epicurus and the "flawed" consolatio of book 3'. *Ramus* 15: 52–73.

GARLAND, R. 1985. *The Greek Way of Death*. London.

GIANNANTONI, G. and GIGANTE, M. (eds.) 1996. *Epicureismo greco e romano*. Naples.

GIGANTE, M. 1983a. 'L'inizio del quarto libro "Della Morte" di Filodemo', in his *Ricerche Filodemee* (2nd edn.). Naples: 115–61.

——— 1983b. 'La chiusa del quarto libro "Della Morte" di Filodemo', in his *Ricerche Filodemee* (2nd edn.). Naples: 163–234.

——— 1986. 'Biografia e dossografia in Diogene Laerzio'. *Elenchos* 7: 7–102.

——— 1999. *Kepos e Peripatos. Contributo all storia dell'aristotelismo antico*. Naples.

——— and INDELLI, G. 1980. 'Democrito nei Papiri Ercolanesi di Filodemo', in F. Romano (ed.) *Democrito e l'atomismo antico*. Catania: 451–66.

GLADMAN, K. R. and MITSIS, P. 1997. 'Lucretius and the Unconscious', in K. A. Algra, M. H. Koenen, and P. H. Schrijvers (eds.) 1997: 215–24.

GLANNON, W. 1994. 'Temporal Asymmetry, Life and Death'. *APQ* 31: 235–44.

GOLDSCHMIDT, V. 1982. 'La théorie épicurienne du droit', in J. Barnes, J. Brunschwig, M. F. Burnyeat, and M. Schofield (eds.) *Science and Speculation*. Cambridge: 304–26.

GOOCH, P. W. 1983. 'Aristotle and the Happy Dead'. *CPh* 78: 112–16.

GÖRLER, W. 1997. 'Storing up Past Pleasures', in K. A. Algra, M. H. Koenen, and P. H. Schrijvers (eds.) 1997: 193–207.

GOSLING, J. C. B. 1969. *Pleasure and Desire: The Case for Hedonism Reviewed*. Oxford.

——— and TAYLOR, C. C. W. 1984. *The Greeks on Pleasure*. Oxford.

GOTTSCHALK, H. 1972. 'Notes on the Wills of the Peripatetic Scholarchs'. *Hermes* 100: 314–42.

GREEN, O. H. 1982. 'Fear of Death'. *Philosophy and Phenomenological Research* 43: 99–105.

GREY, W. 1999. 'Epicurus and the Harm of Death'. *AJP* 77: 358–64.

GRIFFIN, J. 1986. *Well-being: Its Meaning, Measurement and Importance.* Oxford.

GROVER, D. 1989. 'Posthumous Harm'. *Phil. Q* 39: 334–53.

HAJI, I. 1991. 'Pre-vital and Post-vital Times'. *Pacific Philosophical Quarterly* 72: 171–80.

HOLBY, I. 2002. 'Epicurus on Death'. M.Phil. thesis, University of Cambridge Faculty of Philosophy.

HONDERICH, T. 2002. *After the Terror.* Edinburgh.

INDELLI, G. 1988. *Filodemo. L'ira.* Naples.

—— and TSOUNA-MCKIRAHAN, V. 1995. *[Philodemus] [On Choices and Avoidances].* Naples.

IRWIN, T. 1985. 'Permanent Happiness: Aristotle and Solon'. *OSAPh* 3: 89–124.

JUFRESA, M. 1996. 'Il tempo e il sapiente epicureo', in G. Giannantoni and M. Gigante (eds.) 1996: 287–98.

KAMM, F. 1993. *Morality, Mortality,* i: *Death and Whom to save from It.* Oxford.

KAUFMAN, F. 1995. 'An Answer to Lucretius Symmetry Argument against the Fear of Death'. *The Journal of Value Inquiry* 29: 57–64.

—— 1996. 'Death and Deprivation; Or, Why Lucretius' Symmetry Argument Fails'. *Australasian Journal of Philosophy* 74: 305–12.

—— 1999. 'Pre-vital and Post-mortem Non-existence'. *APQ* 36: 1–19.

KENNEY, E. 1971. *Lucretius: de rerum natura III.* Cambridge.

KEULS, E. C. 1974. *The Water Carriers in Hades: A Study in Catharsis through Toil in Classical Antiquity.* Amsterdam.

KRAUT, R. 1989. *Aristotle on the Human Good.* Princeton.

KUIPER, T. 1925. *Philodemus over den Dood.* Amsterdam.

LAKS, A. 1976. 'Édition critique et commentée de la 'vie d'Épicure' dans Diogène Laërce 10.1–34', in J. Bollack and A. Laks (eds.) *Études sur l'épicurisme antique.* Cahiers de Philologie 1, Lille: 121–59.

LAMONT, J. 1998. 'A Solution to the Puzzle of When Death Harms its Victims'. *AJP* 76: 198–212.

LEIWO, M. and REMES, P. 1999. 'Partnership of Citizens and Metics: The Will of Epicurus'. *CQ* 49: 161–6.

LE POIDEVIN, R. (ed.) 1998. *Questions of Time and Tense.* Oxford.

LESSES, G. 2002. 'Happiness, Completeness, and Indifference to Death in Epicurean Ethical Theory'. *Apeiron* 35, special issue, L. J. Jost and R. A. Shiner (eds.) *Eudaimonia and Well-being: Ancient and Modern Conceptions*: 57–68.

LEVENBOOK, B. B. 1984. 'Harming Someone after his Death'. *Ethics* 94: 407–19.

—— 1985. 'Harming the Dead, once Again'. *Ethics* 96: 162–4.

LONG, A. A. 1986. 'Pleasure and Social Utility: The Virtues of being Epicurean', in H. Flashar and O. Gigon (eds.) *Aspects de la philosophie hellénistique*. Entretiens Hardt 32: 283–324.

—— 1997. 'Lucretius on Nature and the Epicurean Self', in K. A. Algra, M. H. Koenen, and P. H. Schrijvers (eds.) 1997: 125–39.

LUPER-FOY, S. 1987. 'Annihilation'. *Phil. Q* 37: 233–52.

MACINTYRE, A. 1984. *After Virtue* (2nd edn.). London.

MCMAHAN, J. 1988. 'Death and the Value of Life'. *Ethics* 99: 32–61.

—— 2002. *The Ethics of Killing: Problems at the Margins of Life*. Oxford.

MARGALIT, A. 2002. *The Ethics of Memory*. Cambridge, Mass.

MATSON, W. I. 1998. 'Hegesias the Death-Persuader; or, the Gloominess of Hedonism'. *Philosophy* 73: 553–7.

MELLOR, D. 1998. *Real Time II*. London.

MELLVILLE, R. 1998. *Lucretius: On the Nature of the Universe. A New Verse Translation*. Oxford.

MILITELLO, C. 1997. *Memorie Epicuree*. Naples.

MITSIS, P. 1988a. 'Epicurus on Death and the Duration of Life'. *Proceedings of the Boston Area Colloquium in Ancient Philosophy* 4: 303–22.

—— 1988b. *Epicurus' Ethical Theory: The Pleasures of Invulnerability*. Ithaca.

—— 1996. 'Epicureans on Death and the Deprivations of Death', in G. Giannantoni and M. Gigante (eds.) *Epicureismo greco e romano*. Naples: 805–12.

—— 2002. 'Happiness and Death in Epicurean Ethics'. *Apeiron* 35, special issue, L. J. Jost and R. A. Shiner (eds.) *Eudaimonia and Well-being: Ancient and Modern Conceptions*: 41–55.

MOORE, A. W. 2001. *The Infinite* (2nd edn.). London.

MUNRO, H. A. J. 1886. *T. Lucreti Cari de rerum natura libri sex* (4th edn.). Cambridge.

MURPHY, J. G. 1976. 'Rationality and the Fear of Death'. *The Monist* 59: 187–203.

NAGEL, T. 1970. *The Possibility of Altruism*. Princeton.

—— 1979. 'Death', in his *Mortal Questions*. Cambridge: 1–10.

—— 1986. *The View from Nowhere*. Oxford.

NOZICK, R. 1981. *Philosophical Explanations*. Cambridge. Mass.

NUSSBAUM, M. 1994. *The Therapy of Desire*. Princeton.

—— 2001. *Upheavals of Thought*. Cambridge.

O'CONNOR, D. K. 1989. 'The Invulnerable Pleasures of Epicurean Friendship'. *GRBS* 30: 165–86.

O'KEEFE, T. 2001. 'Would a Community of Wise Epicureans be Just?' *Anc. Phil.* 21: 133–46.

——2003. 'Lucretius on the Cycle of Life and the Fear of Death'. *Apeiron* 36: 43–65.

OAKLANDER, L. N. 1994. 'On the Experience of Tenseless Time', in L. N. Oaklander and Q. Smith (eds.) *The New Theory of Time*. Chelsea, Mich.: 344–50 (originally published in *Journal of Philosophical Research* 18, 1993: 159–66).

OBBINK, D. 1988. 'Hermarchus *Against Empedocles*'. *CQ* 38: 428–35.

OLSON, E. 1997. *The Human Animal: Personal Identity without Psychology*. Oxford.

OVERALL, C. 2003. *Aging, Death, and Human Longevity: A Philosophical Inquiry*. Berkeley.

PARFIT, D. 1984. *Reasons and Persons*. Oxford.

——1986. 'Comments'. *Ethics* 96: 832–72.

PARTRIDGE, E. 1981. 'Posthumous Interests and Posthumous Respect'. *Ethics* 91: 243–64.

PITCHER, G. 1984. 'The Misfortunes of the Dead'. *APQ* 21: 183–8.

PRIOR, A. N. 1959. 'Thank Goodness that's Over'. *Philosophy* 34: 12–17.

PRIZL, K. 1983. '*Nicomachean Ethics* 1.10–11: Aristotle and Happiness after Death'. *CPh* 78: 101–11.

PROCOPÉ, J. 1998. 'Epicureans on Anger', in J. Sihvola and T. Engberg-Pedersen (eds.) *The Emotions in Hellenistic Philosophy*. Dordrecht: 171–96.

QUINN, W. 2001. 'Abortion: Identity and Loss', in J. Harris (ed.) *Bioethics*. Oxford: 62–89, first printed in *Philosophy and Public Affairs* 13: 24–54.

RAZ, J. 2001. *Value, Respect, and Attachment*. Cambridge.

REINHARDT, T. 2002. 'The Speech of Nature in Lucretius' *De Rerum Natura* 3.931–71'. *CQ* 52: 291–304.

RORTY, A. O. 1983. 'Fearing Death'. *Philosophy* 58: 175–88.

ROSENBAUM, S. E. 1986. 'How to be Dead and not Care: A Defense of Epicurus'. *APQ* 23: 217–25.

——1989a. 'Epicurus and Annihilation'. *PhilQ* 39: 81–90.

——1989b. 'The Symmetry Argument: Lucretius against the Fear of Death'. *Philosophy and Phenomenological Research* 1: 353–73.

——1990. 'Epicurus on Pleasure and the Complete Life'. *The Monist* 73: 21–41.

ROSS, W. D. 1939. *The Foundations of Ethics*. Oxford.

ROUSE, W. H. D. and Smith, M. F. 1982. *Lucretius: de rerum natura* (2nd edn.). Harvard.

RUDEBUSCH, G. 1999. *Socrates, Pleasure, and Value*. Oxford.

RYLE, G. 1954. 'It was to be', in his *Dilemmas*. Cambridge: 15–35.

230   *References*

SANDBACH, F. H. 1985. *Aristotle and the Stoics*. Cambridge Philological Society, supplementary volume 10.

SCARRE, G. 2001. 'On Caring about One's Posthumous Reputation'. *APQ* 38: 209–19.

SCHLESINGER, G. N. 1980. *Aspects of Time*. Indianapolis.

SCHMID, W. 1963. 'Ein Tag und der Aion', in *Wort und Text für Fritz Schalk*. Frankfurt: 14–23.

—— 1977. '*Lucretius ethicus*', in O. Gigon (ed.) *Lucrèce*, Entretiens Hardt 24, Geneva: 125–57.

SCHOPENHAUER, A. 1958. *The World as Will and Representation*, trans. E. F. J. Payne. 2 vols. Toronto.

SCOTT, D. 2000. 'Aristotle on Posthumous Fortune'. *OSAPh* 18: 211–29.

SEDLEY, D. N. 1976. 'Epicurus and the Mathematicians of Cyzicus'. *CErc* 6: 23–54.

—— 1993. 'Chrysippus on Psychophysical Causality', in J. Brunschwig and M. Nussbaum (eds.) *Passions and Perceptions: Studies in Hellenistic Philosophy of Mind*. Cambridge: 313–31.

—— 1996. 'The Inferential Foundations of Epicurean Ethics', in Giannantoni and Gigante (eds.) 1996: 313–39.

—— 1997. ' "Becoming like God" in the *Timaeus* and Aristotle', in T. Calvo and L. Brisson (eds.) *Interpreting the Timaeus–Critias*. Sankt Augustin: 327–39.

—— 1998. *Lucretius and the Transformation of Greek Wisdom*. Cambridge.

—— 2002. 'Diogenes of Oenoanda on Cyrenaic Hedonism'. *PCPS* 48: 159–74.

SEGAL, C. P. 1990. *Lucretius on Death and Anxiety*. Princeton.

SICKINGER, J. P. 1999. *Public Records and Archives in Classical Athens*. Chapel Hill.

SIDER, D. 1997. *The Epigrams of Philodemos*. Oxford.

SIDGWICK, H. 1907. *The Methods of Ethics* (7th edn.). London.

SILVERSTEIN, H. 1980. 'The Evil of Death'. *JPhil* 77: 401–24.

SLOTE, M. 1983. *Goods and Virtues*. Oxford.

SMITH, M. F. 1993. *Diogenes of Oinoanda. The Epicurean Inscription*. Naples.

—— 1998. 'Excavations at Oinoanda 1997: The New Epicurean Texts'. *Anatolian Studies* 48: 125–70.

—— 2000. 'Lucretius 3.955'. *Prometheus* 26: 35–40.

SOLL, I. 1998. 'On the Purported Insignificance of Death', in J. Malpas and R. C. Solomon (eds.) *Death and Philosophy*. London: 22–38.

SOLOMON, R. C. 1976. 'Is there Happiness after Death?'. *Philosophy* 51: 189–93.

SORABJI, R. 1983. *Time, Creation, and the Continuum*. London.

STOKES, M. C. 1995. 'Cicero on Epicurean Pleasures', in J. G. F. Powell (ed.) *Cicero the Philosopher*. Oxford: 145–70.

STRIKER, G. 1988. Commentary on Mitsis [1988]. *Proceedings of the Boston Area Colloquium in Ancient Philosophy* 4: 323–30.

—— 1993. 'Epicurean Hedonism', in J. Brunschwig and M. Nussbaum (eds.) *Passions and Perceptions: Studies in Hellenistic Philosophy of Mind*. Cambridge: 196–208.

SUITS, D. B. 2001. 'Why Death is not Bad for the One who Died'. *APQ* 38: 69–84.

TAYLOR, C. C. W. 1999. *The Atomists: Leucippus and Democritus*. Toronto.

THOMPSON, W. E. 1981. 'Athenian Attitudes towards Wills'. *Prudentia* 13: 13–23.

TOOLEY, M. 1997. *Time, Tense, and Causation*. Oxford.

TSOUNA-MCKIRAHAN, V. 1996. 'Epicurean Attitudes to Management and Finance', in G. Giannantoni and M. Gigante (eds.) *Epicureismo greco e romano*. Naples: 701–14.

TSOUNA, V. 1998. *The Epistemology of the Cyrenaic School*. Cambridge.

—— 2001a. 'Philodemus on the Therapy of Vice'. *OSAPh* 21: 233–58.

—— 2001b. 'Cicéron et Philodème: quelques considérations sur l'éthique', in C. Auvray-Assayas and D. Delattre (eds.) *Cicéron et Philodème: la polémique en philosophie*. Paris: 159–72.

VAN EVRA, J. 1971. 'On Death as a Limit'. *Analysis* 31: 170–6.

VANDER WAERDT, P. A. 1987. 'The Justice of the Epicurean Wise Man'. *CQ* 37: 402–22.

VELLEMAN, J. D. 2000. 'Well-being and Time', in his *The Possibility of Practical Reasoning*. Oxford, (originally published in *Pacific Phil. Q.* 72 (1991), 48–77).

WALLACH, B. P. 1976. *Lucretius and the Diatribe against the Fear of Death*. Leiden.

WARREN, J. 2000a. 'Diogenes *Epikourios*: Keep taking the Tablets'. *JHS* 120: 144–8.

—— 2000b. 'Epicurean Immortality'. *OSAPh* 18: 231–61.

—— 2001a. 'Lucretian *Palingenesis* Recycled'. *CQ* 51: 499–508.

—— 2001b. 'Lucretius, Symmetry Arguments, and fearing Death'. *Phronesis* 46: 466–91.

—— 2001c. 'Socratic Suicide'. *JHS* 121: 91–106.

—— 2001d. 'Epicurus and the Pleasures of the Future'. *OSAPh* 21: 135–79.

—— 2001e. 'Epicurus' dying Wishes'. *PCPS* 47: 23–46.

—— 2002a. 'Democritus, the Epicureans, Death and Dying'. *CQ* 52: 193–206.

WARREN, J. 2002b. 'Socratic Scepticism in Plutarch's *Adversus Colotem*'. *Elenchos* 23: 333–56.

—— 2002c. *Epicurus and Democritean Ethics: An Archaeology of Ataraxia.* Cambridge.

—— forthcoming. 'Diogenes Laërtius, Biographer of Philosophy', in J. König and T. Whitmarsh (eds.) *Ordering Knowledge in the Roman Empire.*

WATERLOW, S. 1982. *Passage and Possibility: A Study of Aristotle's Modal Concepts.* Oxford.

WEST, D. 1969. *The Imagery and Poetry of Lucretius.* Edinburgh.

WHITAKER, C. W. A. 1996. *Aristotle's De Interpretatione: Contradiction and Dialectic.* Oxford.

WHITE, N. 2002. *Individual and Conflict in Greek Ethics.* Oxford.

WHITE, S. A. 1992. *Sovereign Virtue. Aristotle on the Relation between Happiness and Prosperity.* Stanford.

WICHERLEY, R. E. 1957. *The Athenian Agora III: Literary and Epigraphical Testimonia.* Princeton.

WIGGINS, D. 1998. 'The Concern to Survive', in his *Needs, Values, Truth.* Oxford: 303–11.

WILLIAMS, B. 1973a. 'The Makropulos Case: Reflections on the Tedium of Immortality', in his *Problems of the Self.* Cambridge: 82–100.

—— 1973b. 'Egoism and Altruism', in his *Problems of the Self.* Cambridge: 250–65.

—— 1976. 'Persons, Character, and Morality', in A. O. Rorty (ed.) *The Identities of Persons.* Berkeley: 197–216.

—— 1995. 'Resenting One's own Existence', in his *Making Sense of Humanity.* Cambridge: 224–32.

WILLIAMS, G. D. 2003. *Seneca: De Otio, De Brevitate Vitae.* Cambridge.

WOLF, S. 1986. 'Self-interest and Interest in Selves'. *Ethics* 96: 704–20.

YOURGRAU, P. 1993. 'The Dead', in J. M. Fischer (ed.) 1993: 135–56.

INDEX LOCORUM

GENERAL INDEX

For references to works by ancient authors see the *Index locorum.*

CPSIA information can be obtained
at www.ICGtesting.com
Printed in the USA
BVOW06s0223221217
503437BV00019B/679/P